"If it is true that all Christians believe in election, since the Bible affirms it, where is the controversy? Kirkpatrick lays out the two major positions, Reformed and non-Reformed. The former understand election and predestination to be based on divine decree while the latter view God's choice is based on divine knowledge of those who will believe. The tone of this work is irenic, the argument is clear, and the conclusions are ministerially significant. Throughout the work, Kirkpatrick addresses the pastoral implications of these doctrines directly, honestly, compassionately, and charitably."

—Glenn R. Kreider,
Editor in Chief, *Bibliotheca Sacra*,
Professor of Theological Studies, Dallas Theological Seminary

"Discussion and debates about the doctrine of election are often hampered by a lack of clarity of essential concepts and terminology. This '40 questions' approach lends itself to the careful nuancing necessary, and it is here that Kirkpatrick excels. His work shows precision in both theological concept and biblical statement. Well informed, clearly stated, and easily accessible. A welcome contribution to this wonderful study."

— Fred G. Zaspel,
Pastor, Reformed Baptist Church,
Executive Editor, *Books At a Glance*,
Adjunct Professor of Theology, The Southern Baptist Theological Seminary

"I cannot think of another term in Scripture that is the cause of as many seemingly endless arguments as is that of divine 'election.' And each time I think that nothing more can be said or written that would contribute positively to helping us understand what it means, I come across yet another volume that does precisely that. Daniel Kirkpatrick's contribution to the 40 Questions series of books is one of the clearest and most comprehensive treatments of this issue that I've read. There is nary a question, issue, objection or problem that he does not address. His defense of unconditional election is rooted in Scripture and sound reasoning. Although many will not be persuaded of his position, none will charge him with avoiding problem texts or misrepresenting those with whom he disagrees. If you've never examined election and assessed the many alternative perspectives, this is the book for you."

—Sam Storms,
President, Enjoying God Ministries,
Executive Director, Convergence Church Network

40 QUESTIONS ABOUT Divine Election

Daniel Kirkpatrick

Benjamin L. Merkle, Series Editor

40 Questions About Divine Election

Published by Kregel Academic, an imprint of Kregel Publications, 2450 Oak Industrial Dr. NE, Grand Rapids, MI 49505-6020.

This book is a title in the 40 Questions Series edited by Benjamin L. Merkle.

Italics in Scripture quotations indicate author's added emphasis.

The English translation of the Septuagint (LXX) is the author's translation.

The Hebrew font, NewJerusalemU, and the Greek font, GraecaU, are available from www.linguistsoftware.com/lgku.htm, +1-425-775-1130.

ISBN 978-0-8254-4797-6

Cataloging-in-Publication Data is available from the Library of Congress.

Printed in the United States of America

25 26 27 28 29 / 5 4 3 2 1

To Caedmon, Anna, and Tess

Oh, that you may know how deeply loved you are by your perfect heavenly Father and imperfect earthly father. You have been to me another glorious gift of undeserved grace.

Contents

Part 3: Ethical Considerations of Election

Part 4: Practical Considerations of Election

Introduction

The title of this book is *40 Questions About Divine Election*. It is not entitled *40 Answers About Divine Election* (though there are, indeed, answers given to each question). Perhaps more significant than any answers provided herein are the questions themselves. The fascinating doctrine of divine election has been studied, debated, and defended as far back as Old Testament times. It has birthed pressing questions about the nature of God and human beings in addition to whole Christian traditions and points of view. The doctrine has brought unity as well as division within the church because of the implications one's views bring. Thus, the questions raised in this book reflect the underlying thoughts and concerns many people and traditions have had over this doctrine, and understanding what they are asking (and why they are asking it) is just as important as coming to a conclusion on the matter.

It is our sincere hope that this book will reflect accurately and respectfully the various traditions represented here. Every book has limitations, and it is worth noting up front that more effort has been spent on presenting the various perspectives on a given question fairly than on immediately coming to a conclusion and defending it exhaustively. Our questions about divine election matter, not just the answers. Readers should consider carefully the underlying concerns and overarching implications of a question before arriving at their own conclusions, and hopefully what is presented here will inform the issue.

The book is arranged in four major parts (with subsections in parts 2 and 3). The first part considers how the doctrine of election has been understood historically, from its earliest mentions in the Old and New Testaments to modern-day perspectives. As we find how the doctrine has been defined and developed across church history, we will discover that it has birthed two significant schools of thought, which are traditionally called Calvinism and Arminianism. It is here we need to draw a most important distinction.

Coming to a term agreeable to everyone on what to call the schools of thought that align with historic Calvinism and Arminianism has been difficult (if not impossible). Using traditional labels such as "Calvinist" or "Arminian" fails to appreciate the nuances and differences in thinking within these two broad historic traditions. Not everyone who holds to John Calvin's doctrine of election would call themselves Calvinists. Similarly, not everyone who agrees with Jacobus Arminius's doctrine of election identifies as Arminian. There are traditional (or classical) Arminians, Wesleyan Arminians, and Reformed Arminians who embrace the term of Arminianism, while other traditions that hold similar beliefs about election reject the label. We have to call these two contrasting perspectives something, but no term is perfect. We have chosen to employ the term *Reformed* to refer to the view of election articulated by the Protestant Reformers, such as Martin Luther and John Calvin (see Question 4), and *non-Reformed* to refer to the view of election held to by Jacobus Arminius (see Question 5). It is fully appreciated that Arminians are by-products of the Reformed tradition (coming from John Calvin's movement as opposed to, say, Luther's), just as it is appreciated that there are Arminians like J. Matthew Pinson, author of *40 Questions About Arminianism*, who identify as Reformed Arminians. The use of *Reformed* and *non-Reformed* is an imperfect attempt to include traditions and perspectives that do not embrace traditional labels, and intention has been made to distinguish any nuances in each tradition as appropriate.

The second part of this book explores the doctrine of election biblically and theologically, beginning with a subsection on the workings of election. There we explore foundational issues such as the will of God and the will of people, the individual and corporate nature of election, the historic debate of the conditionality or unconditionality of election, reprobation, and more. The second subsection examines how divine election intersects with other major Christian doctrines such as the Trinity, the atonement, and the church.

The third part of this book is also divided into two subsections, with the first exploring the ethical implications of one's view of the divine will and the second regarding the ethical implications of the human will. We will explore questions such as whether God loves everyone and wants everyone to be saved if he only elects some people to salvation, as well as whether the non-elect are responsible for their sin and disbelief if unconditional election is true.

Finally, in the last part of this book, we will explore practical considerations the doctrine of election has in areas such as Christian life, prayer, evangelism and missions, and pastoral ministry. Our sincere hope is that readers will find divine election to be of utmost practical importance as they seek to love and serve their gracious Lord.

Special thanks are in order to the people who made this book possible. I am particularly thankful for Dr. Benjamin Merkle, the series editor, who embraced the idea of this book for the 40 Questions series. It is an honor to author a book in this respectable series alongside many distinguished scholars. Thanks are also in order for the excellent staff at Kregel Academic who brought this work to publication. A special word of thanks is due to Dr. Matthew Pinson, who was gracious to enter into an email exchange to provide some much-appreciated clarity on the unique viewpoints of Reformed Arminianism.

I am particularly indebted to Dr. John Depoe, headmaster of Kingdom Preparatory Academy in Lubbock, Texas, who is not only a distinguished philosopher and insightful theologian but also a dear friend. The idea for this book came through conversations with John, and he has been gracious in discussing the ideas of this book and reviewing certain sections. Any mistakes or inaccuracies are my own, but I acknowledge his helpful contributions in the writing of this book.

Finally, I wish to thank my beloved wife, Michelle, for her love, friendship, partnership in ministry, and support while writing this book. Why God has sovereignly, graciously chosen for her to be my bride I cannot say, but I am grateful he has. I am also thankful for my precious three children: Caedmon, Anna, and Tess. As my home office (where much of this writing took place) is in the family playroom, they non-begrudgingly gave me time and space to write this book. Thanks for turning the TV down so Dad could write. I love you.

PART 1

Historical Overview of Election

QUESTION 1

What Is Divine Election?

Defining divine election is no simple task. Ask someone the meaning of it, and you are sure to hear something like, "It's the belief that God eternally predestines certain people to heaven or hell," or, "God chooses to save people who choose Jesus as Savior." Some people will define it with mentions of Calvinism and Arminianism, others with talk of reprobation, and perhaps others will raise concerns about the meaningfulness of evangelism. The difficulty is largely because divine election has been understood, defined, debated, and nuanced in many ways throughout church history.

While the historical development of the doctrine is fascinating in its own right, we should be ever mindful that divine election is first and foremost a biblical doctrine rooted deeply within the Old and New Testaments. Though various theological traditions hold to specific beliefs about this doctrine, election itself does not belong to them but to God. It is Scripture that teaches us that God elects and how he goes about it. As such, we will begin our study by exploring the Scriptures in an attempt to develop a biblical definition of election, then we will explore how this definition unifies Christians while leaving room for differences of opinion.

Surveying the Scriptures

The Hebrew term most commonly associated with election is *bāḥar*, a verb that simply means "to choose."[1] The primary Greek verb for election is *eklegomai*, and its basic meaning is "to choose (for oneself), to select someone/

1. Francis Brown, S. R. Driver, and Charles A. Briggs, *A Hebrew and English Lexicon of the Old Testament* (Oxford, U.K.: Clarendon Press, n.d.), s.v. בחר. See also Ludwig Koehler and Walter Baumgartner, *The Hebrew and Aramaic Lexicon of the Old Testament*, ed. M. E. J. Richardson (Leiden: Brill, 1995), s.v. בחר.

something for oneself."[2] The corresponding noun is *eklektos*, a term meaning "pertaining to being selected, chosen."[3]

Divine election, therefore, refers broadly to what God chooses or selects to do. The Scriptures are full of God making choices and selections to fulfill his perfect will. We see God electing people for various roles and positions, like Adam and Eve as the first parents in Genesis 1–2, Abraham as the father of nations from whom the Messiah would come (Gen. 12–13; 15; 17; 22), Moses as the leader of the exodus, and Jesus as the Savior of the world. We also see God sovereignly choosing tasks to be carried out by specific people, such as the duties of the Levites when they came before God's holy presence and offered sacrifices for atonement, or the disciples who were tasked with following and serving Jesus.

Furthermore, we see God sovereignly choosing the agency of salvation, meaning that God alone determines how he will save people. In the Old Testament, God entered into a covenant relationship with Abraham and his descendants, through whom all the nations would be blessed (Gen. 12:3). They were marked by the sign of circumcision (Gen. 17:11) and entered into this covenant by faith (Gen. 15:6; Rom. 4:16–17; Gal. 3:8–9). By God's sovereign choice, there were not many pathways toward a relationship with God, and humanity did not determine the processes by which they could become saved. Rather, in the Old Testament the Lord unilaterally determined the method, sign, and limits of salvation. The same is true in the New Testament. Jesus affirmed he is the way, truth, and life, and that no one comes to the Father except through him (John 14:6).[4] God has sovereignly chosen the gospel of Jesus to be the only means of salvation for the world, and disciples are to make it known through proclamation.

As we can see, God elects to do many things so that his will is accomplished, and most of the choices mentioned above are not problematic for Christians. What is problematic, however, is God's choice for those human beings to be saved. When we consider God's choice of saving sinners, we immediately have to consider things such as human freedom and responsibility, the fate of the unsaved, and the sovereignty of God. Reconciling these issues is no small task, for we are ultimately trying to reconcile divine sovereignty with human will. Therefore, it is no wonder why church history has been so

---

2. Walter Bauer, *A Greek–English Lexicon of the New Testament and Other Early Christian Literature*, eds. William F. Arndt, F. Wilber Gingrich, and Frederick W. Danker, 3rd ed. (Chicago: University of Chicago Press, 2000), s.v. ἐκλέγομαι.
3. Bauer, ἐκλεκτός.
4. For more treatment on this, see Bruce Demarest, *The Cross and Salvation: The Doctrine of Salvation*, Foundations of Evangelical Theology (Wheaton, IL: Crossway, 2006), 118–35; and Daniel Kirkpatrick, *Monergism or Synergism: Is Salvation Cooperative or the Work of God Alone?* (Eugene, OR: Pickwick, 2018), 56–68.

divided on the issue. Despite such division, there are a few points of common agreement that build up to an agreeable definition for most people.

Election and Common Agreement

When referring to salvation, we define *divine election* as "God's gracious choice to save certain sinners through the person and work of Jesus Christ." This definition is almost universally accepted by evangelical Christians today because it is broad enough to include a variety of perspectives while conforming to the clear teaching of Scripture.

Jesus mentioned election both directly and indirectly. In Matthew 24:22–31 and parallels, we read how Christ will ransom the elect in the last days from false messiahs and terrible persecutions. He also spoke in John 10:14–28 of the elect as his sheep for whom he died, and that as God's elect they have eternal life and no one can snatch them out of his hand. Additionally, in John 13:18 Jesus referenced those disciples whom he had chosen while also knowing that Judas would betray him.

Paul spoke often about election to salvation. In Ephesians 1:4–5 he told the church in Ephesus that they were chosen in Christ, before the foundation of the world, to be holy and blameless before him. In Romans 9:11–13 the apostle talked about God's purpose of election continuing through Jacob. The church of Thessalonica was called the beloved and chosen of God in 1 Thessalonians 1:4–5.

Other New Testament writers referred to the "elect" and "election," and those terms can be used in various ways. The elect can be a synonymous term with the church or chosen people of God (Titus 1:1; 1 Peter 1:1; 2 John 1, 13). Jesus Christ himself, moreover, was called the elect (or chosen) in Luke 23:35 and 1 Peter 2:4, 6. As such, election can refer to many things. However, as it pertains to the doctrine of salvation, election primarily refers to God's choice to save certain sinners through his Son, which is the sense on which we will focus our study.

Unity Amongst Traditions

Again, most evangelicals agree that election is a biblical doctrine and refers (in the doctrine of salvation) to God choosing to save certain sinners through the person and work of Jesus Christ. The doctrine is believed and embraced by Reformed and non-Reformed traditions[5] as well as many more groups and denominations who seek to believe the whole counsel of God. It

5. Arminius and the Arminian tradition are Reformed in the broad sense, coming out of the Reformed (as opposed to Lutheran) movement. Additionally, see J. Matthew Pinson, *40 Questions About Arminianism* (Grand Rapids: Kregel Academic, 2022), 55–61, and 63–68, where many commonalities between Arminians and Reformed are shown. Throughout this book, we will use the term "Reformed" in a way typical in modern nomenclature to refer to non-Arminian traditions that lean toward Calvinism even if they do not accept

is not a belief limited to any particular group, and we would do well to understand not only each tradition's distinctions but also how they agree.

Take, for example, the Calvinist and Arminian traditions. They are unified in their agreement that God elected people groups (namely Israel and Christians) to be his treasured possession. Together, they agree that God sovereignly elects people for tasks and positions (such as Old Testament prophets or modern-day pastors). These traditions are also agreed that God elects and determines the pathway and limitations of salvation. These agreements should be acknowledged while myths and mischaracterizations are dismissed. For example, Roger Olson rightly calls it a myth that Arminians do not believe in election and predestination.[6] Arminian scholar William Klein readily affirms that God chooses people individually and corporately to carry out God's will.[7] Recognizing that election is much broader than election to eternal glory, Arminian scholar Jack Cottrell also affirms that God, in his sovereignty, elects persons to fulfill appointed tasks, including the election of Jesus, the election of Israel, the election of the church, and the election of persons to salvation.[8]

Similarly, Reformed theologians and traditions readily embrace the aforementioned categories of election. Bruce Demarest affirms God's election to service, of people, and to salvation in Christ.[9] Louis Berkhof begins his discourse on election with notice that election has multiple senses (including election of people, election for service, and election to salvation).[10] James Oliver Buswell urged his readers to carefully note the usages of *election*, which include election to function, eternal life, and personal holiness.[11] Of these types of election, there is great consensus.

Another fascinating area of agreement between many Reformed and Wesleyan-Arminian parties is the treatment of election within the eternal decrees of God. Jacobus Arminius's treatment on divine election falls within his section on predestination, a belief he calls the "precise and absolute decree of God . . . by which God decreed to save and damn certain particular persons."[12]

---

all tenets of that perspective. We do not mean to suggest that Arminians (or at least some Arminians) are not Reformed in a broader sense. See the introduction of this book.

6. Roger Olson, *Arminian Theology: Myths and Realities* (Downers Grove, IL: IVP Academic, 2006), 179–99.
7. William W. Klein, *The New Chosen People: A Corporate View of Election* (Eugene, OR: Wipf & Stock, 2001), 26–35.
8. Jack W. Cottrell, "Conditional Election," in *Grace Unlimited*, ed. Clark H. Pinnock (Minneapolis: Bethany Fellowship, 1975), 70–73.
9. Demarest, *The Cross and Salvation*, 118–35.
10. Louis Berkhof, *Systematic Theology*, 4th ed. (Grand Rapids: Eerdmans, 1941), 114.
11. James Oliver Buswell, *A Systematic Theology of the Christian Religion* (Grand Rapids: Zondervan, 1962), 2:148–52.
12. *The Works of James Arminius*, trans. James Nichols and W. R. Bagnall, 3 vols. (Spring Valley, CA: Lamp Post, 2009), 1:185. See also Kirkpatrick, *Monergism or Synergism*, 63–65.

John Wesley, following Arminius's thought, also held to divine election in salvation as an eternal decree of God.[13] This claim is not unlike the belief John Calvin, who also viewed divine election as an eternal divine decree.[14] Granted, these traditions understand and apply election in the divine decrees differently, but we can appreciate that both of these traditions find election to be a divine decree.

Election and Differing Perspectives

Despite much common agreement, this doctrine has led to lasting debate and division. Michael Bird aptly answers why:

> In general, all theologians agree that God "elects" people to salvation. . . . The point of contention is the *basis* for this election. Does it lie in God's foreknowledge of persons who would freely choose for themselves to believe in him, or does it pertain to God's free and inscrutable decision to save some but not others? That is the debate.[15]

Although Christians agree that persons are elect, they disagree on the basis for such election (as because of faith or because of the unilateral decision of God). To be elected to service is not in doubt, but rather the extent of election to service (whether Christ's service was for all or only some people). Most Christian traditions fully affirm divine election of saving agency (as in Christ by faith); however, they disagree whether divine electing activity of specific persons is foreordained from eternity past by immutable decree.

What is more, Christians throughout church history have considered where their positions on divine election logically lead. Are certain sinners enduring eternal torment in hell because of their sin and disbelief, or because God did not elect them? If God loves everyone, why would he limit his saving activity to just a few people of his choosing? Are some people elect and others not because of something God finds inside each person? These are just some of the questions people raise when exploring divine election, and this book intends to explore them from biblical, historical, and ethical perspectives.

Summary

Divine election in salvation is a difficult and contentious doctrine because there is so much difference of thought. Is election based upon what God

---

13. John Wesley, *Calvinism Calmly Considered: Sovereignty, Predestination and Free Grace* (Salem, OH: Schmul, 2001), 23.
14. John Calvin, *Institutes of the Christian Religion*, 3:21.
15. Michael F. Bird, *Evangelical Theology: A Biblical and Systematic Introduction*, 2nd ed. (Grand Rapids: Zondervan Academic, 2020), 565 (italics original).

foresees (his knowledge) or what he desires (his will)? Are people elect because of what they do or simply because of what God does? Are people in hell because of their sin and disbelief or because God did not want them? These differences are significant and will occupy much of our attention in this book. However, these differences need not suggest a lack of common agreement. On the contrary, most Christians agree that God has elected some people for salvation and service as well as electing a pathway for people to be saved. Returning, then, to the initial query of "What is divine election?," we may broadly state that it is God's sovereign choice. When speaking to the specific matter of election unto salvation (the focus of this book), we mean God's gracious choice to save certain sinners in Jesus Christ, and of that definition Christians share much common agreement.

REFLECTION QUESTIONS

1. What types of electing activity does God do?
2. What was the basis for God's choices (in its many forms) in the Old and New Testaments, in your view?
3. What areas of common agreement do you see among the vast Christian viewpoints?
4. How significant is it that Reformed and Arminian traditions understand divine election within the eternal decrees of God?
5. How is defining divine election in salvation, as done here, both helpful and limited?

QUESTION 2

How Did the Early Church Understand Election?

In the previous question, we provided this basic definition of divine election: God's gracious choice to save certain sinners through the person and work of Jesus Christ. However, who is God, who is Jesus Christ, and what is the nature of their personhood and saving work? These questions became of central importance to the period known as the *early church*, which ranges from the late second century (beginning with the letter of First Clement in ca. A.D. 96) to September 3, 590 (the day Gregory the Great was consecrated as St. Peter's successor of the Catholic Church). Encompassing numerous councils, theologians, and heresies, the early church period helped form essential foundations that framed the doctrinal development of divine election.

The God Who Elects

Early on, with no official creeds or councils in place, the church relied upon the apostles to guide them through emerging heresies. Upon the apostles' natural and unnatural deaths, however, the church had to find ways of addressing new heresies that challenged the apostolic faith. The early church gathered in councils to create creeds and confessions that would define their beliefs on God and salvation.

One of the earliest heresies was *Sabellianism*, named after a third-century Roman presbyter named Sabellius.[1] This belief claims that God is one in person, three in presentations. Known today as *modalism*, this view argues that God manifested himself sometimes as Father, sometimes as Son, and sometimes as Spirit (a divine monad in three separate expressions), with the Son and Spirit being inferior and subordinate to the Father.

1. Much of what we know of Sabellius comes from his critics. It is difficult to be certain that everything attributed to Sabellius is true of him.

Another heresy arose in the third century through an Alexandrian presbyter named Arius. Appealing to the Father's immutability and distinctness, Arius taught that the Son is a created being who was not ontologically equal to or sharing the same substance with the Father. The same argument was later applied to the Holy Spirit. Only the Father is divine in this view, and though the Son and Spirit have similar (*homoiousios*) natures as the Father, they do not have the same (*homoousios*) nature.[2]

Other heresies developed during and after this time. *Subordinationism* is the belief that the Son and Spirit are divine but not equal in divinity. *Tritheism* affirms the divinity of the three persons at the expense of their unity of essence, while *partialism* believes that each person makes up a third of the Godhead (and thus not each truly, fully divine). Furthermore, the relationship between the two natures (human and divine) of Christ became a matter of importance. Some heretics claimed Jesus had only one nature (*Eutychians*), others that he did not have a human mind or spirit (*Apollinarians*), and others that the two natures were separate (*Nestorians*).

During the fourth century, the Cappadocian Fathers (Gregory of Nyssa, Gregory of Nazianzus, and Basil of Caesarea) distinguished between *ousia* and *hypostasis*. Building upon the theology of the Cappadocians, the First Councils of Nicaea (325) and Constantinople (381) both affirmed that the Son is *homoousios* (of the same divine substance) as the Father yet distinct in *hypostasis* (person). Still, there is only one God. Their view was predicated upon Athanasius in the third century, who wrote strongly against the Arians; yet, as Nicaea was not universally accepted, Athanasius continued to write against heretics in the East who denied Christ's divinity until Arianism was dealt a fatal blow at Constantinople.

Ambrose of Milan (339–397) championed Nicene orthodoxy both in the West and East, leading to a catholic (i.e., "universal") understanding of the divinity of Christ. Moreover, the Council of Chalcedon (451) settled the controversies on the person of Christ. Its conclusion was that Christ was *truly* man (contra Apollinaris) who was indivisible and inseparable in one person (contra Nestorius), yet having two natures that are neither confused nor changed yet remain distinct (contra Eutyches).

By defining their beliefs about the Trinity and personhood of Christ, the church had a basis to frame divine election and salvation. Consider the Nicene-Constantinopolitan Creed of 381. Built upon a robust Trinitarian theology, they included this phrase: "Who for us men and for our salvation came down from Heaven." The same phrase, "for us and for our salvation," is found in the 451 Creed of Chalcedon. The Athanasian Creed articulates a full Trinitarian theology that refutes the claims of the heresies above, but the early

---

2. For an excellent overview, see Rowan Williams, *Arius: Heresy and Tradition*, rev. ed. (Grand Rapids: Eerdmans, 2002), 95–116.

church took such pains to define the nature of the Godhead because, "He therefore that will be saved, must thus think of the Trinity."[3] A proper theology of the Godhead and Christ meant that they could then develop a theology of salvation and, specifically, election. That is to say, the church fathers before Augustine did not articulate a mature, clear doctrine of election.[4] Although the reasons for such an absence are debated, it is clear that the historic councils that upheld high Trinitarian and Christological theology, matched with Augustine's doctrine of original sin (discussed below), provided the necessary framework for the doctrine to be developed.

Human Nature

The early church needed to articulate not only their beliefs about the God of salvation but also of the people who needed salvation. Two of the earliest heresies the church faced were *Gnosticism* and *Stoicism*. Amongst other things, these schools of thought affirmed pagan notions of fatalism, where human destiny was controlled and determined by impersonal forces. Wishing to disassociate themselves from these heresies, early Christians like Justin Martyr (ca. 100–165) and Origen (ca. 185–254) adamantly rejected eternal predestination to salvation in favor of a human-divine synergism. Foreknowledge, in their view, precedes foreordination so that humanity can be free. Origen claimed that God foreknows (and subsequently elects) people whose inclinations are toward piety.[5] Justin, on the other hand, believed God elects people he foresees will freely respond to the gospel.[6] Both views hold to a type of synergism in which God conditionally elects based upon the actions of a person. Underlying these affirmations is the belief that humanity had to be free from external control or fate. However, was humanity free from internal control that determined their eternal trajectory?

During this time, the works of a British monk named Pelagius (354–420) came to prominence. Taking a step further than his contemporaries, Pelagius believed not only that election was based upon God's foreknowledge of the worthy, but that human beings were unaffected by original sin. This belief came to be known as *Pelagianism*, a view where humans do not inherit a depraved nature. Rather, they have the capacity to obey God's law without

---

3. Philip Schaff, ed., *The Creeds of Christendom*, 6th ed., 3 vols. (Grand Rapids: Baker, 1998), 2:68.
4. Philip Schaff, *History of the Christian Church*, 3 vols. (Grand Rapids: Eerdmans, 1987), 3:852.
5. See *Origen: An Exhortation to Martyrdom, Prayer, and Selected Works*, trans. Rowan A. Greer (New York: Paulist, 1979), 91–92.
6. See Justin Martyr, *First Apology*, 43, and *Second Apology*, 7, in *Ancient Christian Writers*, trans. Leslie William Barnard (New York: Paulist, 1997), 52–53, 78–79. It is significant to note that Justin did not believe in original sin and corruption, thinking that someone had the power to choose good or evil.

preceding and intervening grace.[7] Human nature is thus uncorrupted, guiltless, and capable of utmost piety. The Massilians adapted this view. Known eventually as *Semi-Pelagians*, they claimed that salvation begins with a person's free and unencumbered assertion of faith (unaffected by original sin), though final salvation and growth require divine grace. Election, then, was more of a person choosing God than God choosing a person.

The greatest theologian of the early church, the father of Western Christianity, Augustine of Hippo (354–430) argued against Pelagians and Semi-Pelagians. While his premature views aligned with synergists like Justin who claimed God elects people who will freely believe in Christ for salvation, Augustine would later (ca. 397) conclude that corrupted human natures prevented people from freely believing in Christ unto salvation.[8] All people sinned in Adam, claimed Augustine, meaning all people are guilty and corrupt before God. In such a condition, humanity freely, willingly, and yet inevitably does nothing but sin. Free will remains intact (as does responsibility), but that free will can only do what it *can* do, not what it *should* do (which is to believe the gospel).

Thus, if humans are ever to be saved, it must be owed to operating (monergistic) grace from God rather than cooperating (synergistic) grace. This grace must precede any goodness from a person (thus making it undeserved, unconditioned favor). For some twenty years, Augustine fiercely fought the Pelagians and Semi-Pelagians until the Council of Carthage (418) condemned Pelagianism as heresy. The Council of Orange later condemned Semi-Pelagianism in 529. Interestingly, though Augustine's view on original sin and human nature became the official position of the church, his views on election were not universally accepted.

Election During and After Augustine

Augustine's doctrine of election is well articulated in his *Anti-Pelagian Writings* as well as in his *Enchiridion*. Election to salvation was predestined from all eternity and determined according to God's good pleasure. Relatedly,

7. *The Letters of Pelagius*, ed. Robert Van de Weyer (Worcestershire, U.K.: Arthur James, 1995), 5.
8. This change may largely be attributed to the influence of Ambrose, who articulated inherited corruption in humanity through Adam's fall before Augustine did. Important in Augustine's thought is that eternal life comes by being born again through baptismal regeneration (see Question 32); Augustine, "On Forgiveness of Sins, and Baptism," in *Anti-Pelagian Writings*, Nicene and Post-Nicene Fathers, ed. Philip Schaff 14 vols. (Peabody, MA.: Hendrickson, 2012), 1.23, 23–24. This baptismal regeneration itself is grace. It does not mean, though, that God's operative grace renders the human will superfluous. Augustine rejected the notion that people are saved without use of their reason or will. Still, this expression of the will was not of someone's own doing, and why God enables one person over another to believe is beyond humankind's ability to know. See "On Forgiveness of Sins, and Baptism," 2.6, 46.

the non-elect (who cannot change their status) are reprobate of God and punished according to their sins.[9] Having built the case of humanity's fallenness, Augustine argued that election is of grace, not merit, and if it is of God, then he will see the elect's salvation through into eternity.[10] The non-elect, however, were predestined to be punished for their sins. As for what Augustine viewed as the purposes of election, his view was twofold. On the one hand, the purpose of election is holiness. God chose the elect not because they were holy but in order to make them holy (Eph. 1:4).[11] On the other hand, the purpose of election is to replace the number of fallen angels. That is to say, Augustine believed the number of the elect was fixed and corresponded exactly to the number that God lost in the rebellion of the angels.[12]

Influenced by Augustine's work against Pelagianism, the Council of Orange made six propositions. First, humans inherit sin and death because of Adam's transgression. Second, human free will is distorted and weak, making us unable to believe in God or love him without preceding divine grace. Third, Old Testament saints owed their merits to grace and not to natural goodness. Fourth, baptism enables all Christians to do their duties for salvation provided they make the proper effort. Fifth, predestination to evil was emphatically rejected. Finally, any good action is predicated upon God's grace (including seeking baptism and all other spiritual duties).[13] While these decrees from this council do not directly correlate with election, they correlate indirectly and had significant implications on the development of the doctrine (even if both Carthage and Orange were seemingly forgotten by the time of the Scholastic period). If God is to elect people to salvation, it cannot be owed to innate goodness. Additionally, it cannot be owed to human effort. God must take all initiative in the salvation process, and any good outcome is owed entirely to grace. Without a high Trinitarian and christological theology, matched with a biblical theology of human sinfulness, divine election would be meaningless.

Summary

The early church period was consumed by heresies that primarily concerned the nature of God and human beings more so than election. Some heretics denied the oneness of God's nature while others denied the plurality of persons. Some heretics denied the human nature of Christ while others the divine. Great effort was made to reach conciliar agreement on the nature of God (and for good reason). Simply put, the early church knew that if God were not one in essence, three in persons, or if Christ were not truly human

9. Augustine, "On Rebuke of Grace," in *Anti-Pelagian Writings*, 39, 42, 487–89.
10. Augustine, "On Rebuke of Grace," 13–15, 476–77.
11. Augustine, "On the Predestination of the Saints," in *Anti-Pelagian Writings*, 35, 515.
12. Augustine, "Enchiridion," in *Confessions and Enchiridion*, ed. and trans. Albert C. Outler (Philadelphia: Westminster, 1955), 9.28–30, 355–57.
13. J. N. D. Kelly, *Early Christian Doctrines*, rev. ed. (New York: HarperCollins, 1978), 371–72.

as well as truly divine, there would be no salvation. In each of the earliest decrees of major councils, the continually repeated phrase that accompanies such high theology and Christology is "for us and for our salvation." There would be no election if God were not three and one, nor Christ human and divine. For there to be elected people, there must be an electing God who is able to save.

The same thing can be said regarding human nature. Augustine emphatically emphasized the corruption of human nature for the purpose of showing God's election by grace. Rightly framing the human condition was particularly evidenced at the Council of Orange, which dispelled Pelagianism for a time. If we deny our inherited corruption, we deny God's mercy and assume we can save ourselves (which cannot be) per canons 7, 14, and 19. Thus, the early church (particularly during and after Augustine) formed and framed the election debate around the triune God, the person of Christ, and the fallenness of humanity. They showed that God is the only one able to save, and humans are the ones in need of saving. From this foundation, the church began to explore how divine election relates to the human will, a matter of great importance during medieval Christianity.

REFLECTION QUESTIONS

1. What problems arise when someone denies the Trinity?

2. Why is it essential for Jesus to be truly human and divine?

3. What capacity does the human will have to obey God in its natural state?

4. How are the church's beliefs about salvation affected when the nature of the Trinity or humanity is wrongly defined?

5. How did Augustine help develop the doctrine of election?

QUESTION 3

How Did Medieval Theologians Understand Election?

The year was A.D. 476 when Odoacer, a barbarian Gothic king, invaded Placentia, deposed the young emperor Romulus Augustulus, and put an end to the western part of the Roman Empire. As Western civilization continually faced invasions, turmoil, anarchy, and disease until around 1000, it became difficult to create and preserve intellectual thought. This period, marked by hardship and intellectual stagnation, came to be known as the medieval era or Middle Ages (though the term Dark Ages is just as appropriate), and it lasted until the birth of the Renaissance in the fourteenth century.

What little learning there was at the time came from the monasteries in the form of theology. The rule of Charlemagne helped bring stability to the West and a period of prosperity to the church. Additionally, Christian witness flourished at the turn of the millennium, and many barbarian invaders were converted to Christianity. Monasticism and piety were prominent in the eleventh century as the church in Rome began to flourish. During these ebbs and flows, many theological works were developed that shed light on how the medieval church understood divine election.[1]

As one would expect, there was not one single view of election for the church at this time. The Greeks in the East ignored the strong predestination views of Augustine. The Latin church of the West held Augustine in high regard but did not widely accept his beliefs about election because they largely believed that God's grace precedes and enables human cooperation unto salvation (which came to be known as Semi-Augustinianism). Still, the matter of election was not largely debated until the Gottschalk controversy.

1. See Tony Lane, *A Concise History of Christian Thought*, rev. ed. (Grand Rapids: Baker Academic, 2006), 88.

Gottschalk and Double Predestination

Gottschalk of Orbais (d. 869) was involuntarily sent as a child to a monastery in Hesse, Germany, to become a monk, though he was later transferred to Orbais, France. Despite his dislike of such subjugation by his parents, it was in the monastery that he encountered and embraced the works of Augustine and others who shaped his strong views on predestination. Gottschalk's perspective would best be defined as *double predestination*, the belief that God in his divine sovereignty elects some people to everlasting life while also reprobating others to eternal death. To believe that salvation is based upon God's foreknowledge of the choices of depraved sinners and not the eternal counsel of God was Semi-Pelagian, according to Gottschalk, and expressly anti-Augustinian. On October 1, 848, he appeared before the Synod at Mainz to express his belief that God from eternity past elects some people to eternal life by free grace while justly reprobating others to eternal death. Both election and reprobation, according to Gottschalk, were immutable decrees independent of human choices.[2]

Gottschalk was condemned as a heretic in 853 at the Synod of Quiercy, where he was deposed of his priesthood, beaten nearly to death, and imprisoned in a monastery where maltreatment led to his early demise. While political issues surrounding ordination played a role, Gottschalk's condemnation was grounded in the assumption that he made God the author of evil (a view he expressly denied).[3] In the years that followed, the division between election and free will grew, with archbishops, bishops, and synods lining up on both sides of the issue. The National Synod of France in 860 sided against Gottschalk's views, making Semi-Augustinianism prevalent; however, there was no official decree sanctioned by pope or council on the matter of divine election.

Late in the medieval period, however, came the works of the greatest thirteenth-century Scholastic, Thomas Aquinas (1225–1274). Aquinas had a fascination with cause and effect, and he was also a faithful student of the early church fathers. Coming to accept Augustine's positions on sin, grace, and predestination, Aquinas held both to God's sovereign, eternal election and to reprobation. The following quote is indicative of his view:

> I answer that, God does reprobate some. For it was said above that predestination is a part of providence. To providence, however, it belongs to permit certain defects in those

2. "On Predestination," in *Gottschalk and a Medieval Predestination Controversy: Texts Translated from the Latin*, eds. Victor Genke and Francis X. Gumerlock (Milwaukee: Marquette University Press, 2010), 120.
3. See Philip Schaff, *History of the Christian Church*, 8 vols. (Grand Rapids: Eerdmans, 1987), 4:531.

> things which are subject to providence. . . . Thus, as men are ordained to eternal life through the providence of God, it likewise is part of that providence to permit some to fall away from that end; this is called reprobation.[4]

Notice the role of causation in Aquinas's view. God does elect and ordain persons to eternal life. This election is not the doing of the human who is under sin. Rather, it is owed to the purposes of God. But when God reprobates, he does so permissibly. As Aquinas went on to say, "Reprobation includes the will to permit a person to fall into sin, and to impose the punishment of damnation on account of that sin."[5] It is this permissive language that separates Aquinas from Gottschalk. Two noteworthy conclusions may be made here. First, God in both election and reprobation is the efficient cause. His eternal decree prevails, and human merit is never the cause of election. Second, reprobation is caused by human demerit and may be thought of passively and permissibly (the view of Aquinas) rather than actively (the view of Gottschalk).

Baptism and Election

These views on predestination and election were not the norm during the medieval period. As already stated, Augustine's predestination views were widely rejected, and the general attitude of the church was that such views led to lawless living and irresponsibility. While there was agreement (at least early on) with the Council of Orange, which affirmed God's initiating and prevenient grace in salvation, more emphasis was given to how a person, enabled by grace, can cooperate with God to be elected and saved.

By the medieval period, grace was understood as inseparable from the sacraments. The prevenient grace necessary to remove original sin was provided in infant baptism, a universal practice in the West. With God taking the initiative through his overcoming grace during baptism, a person (from infancy) is able to cooperate with that grace via the sacraments in order to become saved. Naturally, this led to the doctrine of infused righteousness, which would become a major factor during the Protestant Reformation. Nevertheless, what is significant here is that election, during this time, was linked to the sacraments and membership in the Catholic Church. If election concerns the chosen people of God, and the church is the people of God, then naturally the elect are the members of the church (in Rome). There they receive the means of grace via the sacraments to grow in this grace. As there were no other Christian churches besides the Roman Catholic Church, to belong to Christ is to belong to the Catholic Church, the chosen people of God.

---

4. Thomas Aquinas, *Summa Theologica*, trans. Fathers of the English Dominican Province (Notre Dame, IN: Christian Classics, 1948), vol. 1, First Part 23.3, 127.
5. Aquinas, *Summa Theologica*, vol. 1, First Part 23.3, 127.

This understanding reinforced the belief, first articulated in the third century by Cyprian, that there is no salvation outside the church (Lat. *extra ecclesiam nulla salus*). Only people belonging to the Roman Catholic Church have access to the sacraments, and the sacraments are the means of grace. People who die outside of grace are cut off from the church (and thus are not elect).[6] One's election was conditioned upon dying in favor with the church. People who do not die in favor with the church must suffer eternal torment in hell. This view made the threat of excommunication formidable. Thus, election during this period was largely viewed corporately and conditionally.

The Purpose of Election

While these views are interesting constructs, they relate to a broader issue of utmost concern: Why would God choose to elect anyone for salvation?[7] The medieval theologians gave some fascinating answers, which tie closely to their views on the atonement (a connection of extreme importance).

Anselm (ca. 1033) believed—like Augustine before him—that the purpose of election was to restore the number of fallen angels lost from heaven. Anselm discussed this purpose in chapters 18 and 19 of his famous work, *Cur Deus homo* (*Why God Became Man*). He argued that humanity cannot be saved without atonement for sin, which is the reason God became man.[8] The number of saved persons corresponds exactly to the number lost by the fall of angels. Even still, if pressed further, the reason the Father sent the Son to atone for sin and restore the number lost by the fall of angels was to restore God's wounded honor (a view that has come to be known as the *satisfaction theory* of the atonement). Sin brings infinite dishonor to God, so it cannot merely be forgiven; it must be satisfied. God could have destroyed humanity as a consequence of bringing dishonor upon him, but then God would not have had anyone to replace the fallen angels. Thus, God became man to restore the honor that sin marred, electing persons through the atonement of Christ to replace fallen angels.

Contrary to this position, Peter Abelard (1079–1142) claimed that nothing objective had to be overcome for sinners to be restored back to God. There was no payment needed for sin or wounded honor needing satisfaction. Rather, Christ died to show love to humanity in its purest form. Known today as the *moral influence* theory, this view of the atonement claims the elect are people saved by divine love, and they thereby express that love to others. The purpose of election, then, is to show God's love to sinners by suffering with

---

6. See Francis A. Sullivan, *Salvation Outside the Church? Tracing the History of the Catholic Response* (New York: Paulist, 1992), 58–62.
7. For more on the purpose of election, see Question 16.
8. Anselm, "Why God Became Man," in *The Major Works*, eds. Brian Davies and G. R. Evans, Oxford World's Classics (New York: Oxford University Press, 2008), 291–303.

them. His views met opposition by Bernard of Clairvaux (1090–1153) and were deconstructed altogether by William of Ockham (ca. 1280–1349). A strict empiricist, William believed all knowledge could be observed through the senses. Though better known for elevating reason above faith, his views on God's grace and free will nevertheless had great influence on the late medieval era. By his day, the condemnation of Semi-Pelagianism at Orange some seven hundred years prior was seemingly forgotten, and its resurrection was imminent due to William. He believed that unbelievers who do their best can merit God's grace through unassisted merits whereby they could become elected to salvation.[9]

Via Moderna and the Revival of Semi-Pelagianism

William of Ockham, like other adherents to the *via moderna* (Lat.; "modern way," referring to the fourteenth- and fifteenth-century European ideology of nominalism), championed a theological belief that revived Semi-Pelagianism.[10] In this view, God's covenant with humanity entails obligations on both sides. The expectation God places upon himself is to extend saving grace to people who fulfill his expectations to the best of their ability. The obligation placed upon people is to do their best with what lies within them. Gabriel Biel, a person who influenced Martin Luther, taught that doing one's best meant resisting evil and doing good.[11]

The similarities between the *via moderna* and Semi-Pelagianism are evident. Humanity has intrinsic goodness and is capable of living a life pleasing to God. Sinners must take the first steps toward God through unassisted free will. As long as the person is doing his or her best, God must reward such merit with salvation.[12] This thinking became prominent in the church because it was taught within the great Western universities where priests were trained.

It also became the backdrop for the Protestant Reformation that would shortly follow. Doing one's best included participation in the sacraments, through which a person would be infused with Christ's righteousness, which merits eternal life. As it specifically relates to divine election, God elects people who meet their end of covenant expectations by doing their best in participation with the sacraments.

---

9. See Gwenfair M. Walters, "The Atonement in Medieval Theology," in *The Glory of the Atonement: Biblical, Theological, and Practical Perspectives*, eds. Charles E. Hill and Frank A. James III (Downers Grove, IL: IVP Academic, 2004), 239–62.
10. See William Ockham, "Physics and Ethics," in *Philosophical Writings: A Selection*, trans. Philotheus Boehner (Indianapolis: Bobbs-Merrill, 1964), 160.
11. See Alister E. McGrath, *Reformation Thought: An Introduction*, 4th ed. (Malden, MA: Wiley & Sons, 2012), 67–69.
12. Heiko A. Oberman, *The Harvest of Medieval Theology: Gabriel Biel and Late Medieval Nominalism* (Grand Rapids: Baker Academic, 1983), 192–96, 206–8.

Summary

Implicit in the historical survey above is the unique nature of divine election, particularly whether election is conditional or unconditional, corporate or individual, and from eternity past or upon conversion. All these issues appeared during the time of Augustine and carried on well into the medieval period. From this survey, we can see that election was viewed corporately and conditionally due to human cooperation with the sacraments. As long as a person did his or her best and died in a state of grace within the church, he or she would be elect. However, how could people know if they were truly doing their best? This question would become a major issue during the next major era, the Protestant Reformation.

REFLECTION QUESTIONS

1. Does the double predestination view of Gottschalk make God the author of evil, in your view?
2. How did the medieval church make election conditional?
3. Why was individual election not as prominent a view during the medieval period?
4. How does the doctrine of election tie into someone's view on the atonement?
5. How was the *via moderna* Semi-Pelagian in nature?

QUESTION 4

How Did the Protestant Reformers and Their Successors Understand Election?

Modern readers of theology can hardly disassociate the doctrine of election from Protestant reformers like Martin Luther and John Calvin. This association is entirely appropriate, as the Reformers made extraordinary contributions to the theological development of the doctrine; however, we should not think that their thoughts were entirely original or the first words on the subject. In many ways, the Reformers' views on election were much the same as Augustine's (and not by coincidence). Election, for both Augustine and the Reformers, was the way to confront a heresy they both faced—Semi-Pelagianism. When we understand the cultural setting of the Reformers, we better understand why they held the views on divine election that they did.

The Spiritual Setting of the Reformers

As discussed in the preceding question, the Roman Catholic Church inseparably tied divine grace to the sacraments. Almost everyone was baptized at infancy and thus became a de facto member of the Roman Catholic Church. Emphasis was simply not placed upon original sin and corruption in that day. Baptism was sufficient prevenient grace to remove original sin, and people believed themselves elect of God by virtue of their membership in the church. Additionally, baptism brought out the inherent good within people, making them able to cooperate with God via the sacraments to increase in grace and merit. Upon their deaths and an unspecified time in purgatory, they would enter heaven as long as they died in a state of grace with the church.

This line of thinking led to a resurrection of Semi-Pelagianism. Gabriel Biel and others who adopted the *via moderna* championed the belief that God does not despise people who do their best. While humans are still sinners, they are capable of taking the initial steps to God by turning away from sin and turning to him in faithfulness (a concept known as *condign merit*).

Without divine assistance and performed entirely by free will, people only had to show utmost allegiance to God to merit the reward of grace and acceptance. Because God graciously tied himself to these covenant expectations, he is equally required to reward the good efforts of people with salvation.[1] The Lutheran Reformation was positioned against this theological backdrop.

The Lutheran Tradition

Biel's writings influenced an attorney-turned-monk by the name of Martin Luther (1483–1546). In an attempt to do his best, Luther joined an Augustinian monastery and left his career in law (much to the displeasure of his father) after the famous lightning-storm incident. Contrary to Biel, who wished to present condign merit as good news, Luther viewed it as condemning. He was in considerable anguish for fear he could not do his best and that God was infinitely displeased with him. If God accepts people who show utmost allegiance, Luther agonized that he never showed enough.

While the development of Luther's thought is too much to outline here,[2] we can say that between 1515 and 1516 Luther, in his appointment as a professor at the University of Wittenberg, began distancing himself from the *via moderna* as he lectured through the book of Romans. Romans 1:17 held meaningful significance for him when he began to see the righteousness of God as what justifies (not condemns) sinners. In his commentary on Romans, Luther stated: "God's righteousness is that by which we become worthy of His great salvation, or through which we are (accounted) righteous before Him."[3] This change of perspective led him to post ninety-five theses for debate that affirmed Augustinian belief and rejected the Semi-Pelagianism prevalent in his day.

While his thoughts would continue to mature throughout his lifetime, from this point on Luther never wavered on salvation *sola gratia* (by grace alone). Sin left humanity in a state of spiritual death; therefore, people cannot do their best. All people can do in their natural condition is disbelieve and disobey. If anyone is to be saved, it must be by grace alone.[4] In his ruthless attack of Desiderius Erasmus's *Diatribe* in 1525, Luther argued in his *The Bondage of the Will* that divine election ensures that salvation is of grace, not merit. Sinners bound to sin may not attain the righteousness of God. It must

1. Alister E. McGrath, *Reformation Thought: An Introduction*, 4th ed. (Malden, MA: Wiley & Sons, 2012), 67–69; Tony Lane, *A Concise History of Christian Thought*, rev. ed. (Grand Rapids: Baker Academic, 2006).
2. For an excellent resource, see Alister E. McGrath, *Luther's Theology of the Cross: Martin Luther's Theological Breakthrough*, 2nd ed. (Malden, MA: Blackwell, 2011).
3. Martin Luther, *Commentary on Romans*, trans. J. Theodore Mueller (Grand Rapids: Kregel, 2003), 40–41.
4. See Carl Trueman, *Grace Alone: Salvation as a Gift of God, What the Reformers Taught . . . and Why It Still Matters*, Five Solas (Grand Rapids: Zondervan Academic, 2017), 117–20.

be freely given by divine choice. Luther thought it reprehensible that salvation could be purchased by human merits or that divine love is earned through obedience rather than grace.[5] Election is unconditional and unilaterally dependent upon the will of God. Luther, then, is thoroughly Augustinian on election in that regard. He responded to Erasmus's Semi-Pelagianism much like Augustine responded to Pelagius, contending strongly that salvation is based solely in God's sovereign choice, not human ability.

As it relates to the negative side of election, Luther acknowledged that God leaves some people to their perilous condition in reprobation, but the divine reasons are unknown to humankind. As such, it is best not to inquire into the mysteries of God but to trust and honor God, who is sovereign.[6] What is important to Luther, however, is that sinners deserve condemnation for their sins and that the gospel must still be preached to all.

Philip Melanchthon (1497–1560), a dear friend of Luther's, carried on the Lutheran movement after Luther died. Unlike Luther, however, Melanchthon was not as forceful with his views on divine election. More mild-mannered, Melanchthon developed a doctrine of predestination and election that tied closely with ecclesiology (the doctrine of the church). He stated that the gospel promises are for all people through the Word and sacraments. Further deviating from Luther, he adopted a synergistic approach whereby the human will could respond to the gospel, leading to conversion,[7] which denied that faith was given only to the elect.[8] The Formula of Concord rejected Melanchthon's views and clearly stated the Lutheran position on election (article 11). This confession affirms that God sovereignly elects before the foundation of the world without consideration of merit, while simultaneously affirming that he reprobates and condemns people who willfully reject the gospel (article 40).

The Reformed Tradition

While the Lutheran Reformation swept Germany, another reformation was taking place in Switzerland through the work of Ulrich Zwingli (1484–1531). Zwingli came to similar positions on Reformation principles as Luther (and roughly at the same time), particularly on matters of justification by faith, the need for moral reform in the church, the use of a Bible in the vernacular, and the primacy of Scripture over tradition. Unlike Melanchthon,

5. See Luther's treatment of Jacob and Esau in *On the Bondage of the Will* in *Luther and Erasmus: Free Will and Salvation*, eds. E. Gordon Rupp and Philip S. Watson (Louisville: Westminster John Knox, 2006), 249–55. See also Cornelis P. Venema, "Predestination and Election," in *Reformation Theology: A Systematic Summary*, ed. Matthew Barrett (Wheaton, IL: Crossway, 2017), 247–50.
6. Luther, *On the Bondage of the Will*, 206–7.
7. *Melanchthon on Christian Doctrine*, trans. Clyde L. Manschreck (New York: Oxford University Press, 1965), 187–91.
8. Venema, "Predestination and Election," 251.

however, who tied election to the doctrine of the church, Zwingli tied election to God's providence.[9] Under providence, God predestines salvation to the elect graciously and efficaciously while passively leaving other sinners in their willful sin. By electing some people to salvation, God displays his mercy. By choosing to pass over others, he displays his justice. What is significant about Zwingli's position, though, is that such condemnation is still attributed to God's providence whereby God rules and directs all things.

Zwingli's views, however, are largely overshadowed by the greatest of the Reformed tradition's theologians, John Calvin (1509–1564). While Calvin (like Zwingli) initially placed his treatment on divine election under God's providence in his *Institutes of the Christian Religion*, the final edition of the work treats the matter within his discourse on salvation and the church. This placement is no small matter. As a Reformer, Calvin was overarchingly concerned about justification by faith and viewed himself expressly Pauline in his theology. Having built an entire theology upon grace and justification through faith alone, he turned his attention to predestination. While election precedes faith in Calvin's view, it is treated later in the *Institutes*. The reason is found in the very first sentence of his discourse on eternal election found in book 3, chapter 21 of the *Institutes*. Calvin stated, "In actual fact, the covenant of life is not preached equally among all men, and among those to whom it is preached, it does not gain the same acceptance either constantly or in equal degree."[10] Calvin anticipated his reader's questions: Why do some people respond to the gospel in faith and others do not? Is it because of something intrinsic to a person (like the Pelagian *via moderna* claimed)? No. For Calvin, predestination explains why some people respond to the gospel while others do not.[11] Thus, before any conclusions on Calvin's theology of election can be made, it must be premised upon salvation being all grace and no human merit.

As we may expect, election is unconditional and from eternity past in Calvin's theology. God has the right to choose as he pleases, keeping salvation all of grace. While this perspective may strike modern readers as unfair favoritism, this was the very point Calvin was writing against. It was not as though there was anything intrinsic within people leading to their salvation. Calvin pointed to the election of the Israelites in book 3, chapter 21 of his *Institutes*. Israel was not chosen because of merit or ability. It was simply the eternal and unchangeable plan of God to elect this people group to the exclusion of others. The same thing goes for individuals chosen for salvation. Salvation is by grace alone because it is God's choice alone. Election does not depend

---

9. Ulrich Zwingli, *On Providence and Other Essays*, ed. William John Hinke (Durham, NC: Labyrinth, 1983), 184–92.
10. John Calvin, *Institutes of the Christian Religion*, ed. John T. McNeil, trans. Ford Lewis Battles, 2 vols. (Louisville: Westminster John Knox, 1960), 3.21.1.
11. See McGrath, *Reformation Thought*, 200; Trueman, *Grace Alone*, 139.

upon the goodness of the sinner, but the goodness of God. While the invitation to be saved should be preached to all people, God invites only the elect to partake of his saving goodness.[12] Thus, the reason why some respond to the gospel and others do not rests ultimately upon what is in God, not a person.

Famous as his *Institutes* are, Calvin also dealt with the doctrine thoroughly in a mounted attack against the free will theology of Albert Pighius in *De aeterna Dei Praedestinatione* (*Concerning the Eternal Predestination of God*). Between this source and the *Institutes*, we may see that Calvin was greatly concerned about rightly understanding God's sovereignty and human ability. Election and predestination ensure that salvation is of grace, not human merit. For Calvin, even faith was not the cause of election, lest faith be a meritorious achievement of the sinner. Building upon Augustine's theology, he stated, "Again, if it be examined and enquired how anyone is worthy (for salvation), there are some who will say: By their human will. But we say: By grace or divine predestination."[13] Notice, for Calvin, grace is almost synonymous with predestination. Predestination ensures that salvation is all of God's grace, not of human achievement. Pighius, who argued for human ability while simultaneously arguing against the slavery of the soul to sin, believed the cause of election was internal (making election conditioned upon both belief and charity).[14] For Calvin, election is what keeps Christians from falling into Pighius's error of Semi-Pelagianism. The cause for one's salvation must be in God, not a person, making election unconditional.

If Calvin is known for something more than his doctrine of election, it is his doctrine of reprobation. While it is true that Calvin called predestination to eternal damnation a "horrible decree,"[15] he viewed it not so much as a terrible thing as much as a terrifying and wonderous decree that invokes awe and wonder.

For Calvin, predestination is double, meaning that God predestines sinners either to eternal life or death. To reiterate, his view of election and reprobation is predicated upon the question of why some people believe the gospel while others reject it. Thus, we should not suppose Calvin believed people's condemnation is undeserved. Sinners are condemned because of their sin and rejection of the gospel. Reprobation is God appointing people to remain in their sin. To be clear, the non-elect were created for dishonor in Calvin's view, and God from eternity past appointed them for such destruction. Throughout the non-elect's life, God may deprive such people the capacity of hearing the

---

12. Calvin, *Institutes of the Christian Religion*, 3.22.
13. Calvin, *Concerning the Eternal Predestination of God*, trans. J. K. S. Reid (Louisville: Westminster John Knox, 1997), 64. For Calvin, election must be prior to any human merit, even faith.
14. Calvin, *Concerning the Eternal Predestination of God*, 113–20.
15. Calvin, *Institutes of the Christian Religion*, 3.23.7.

gospel or otherwise blinding them to the gloriousness of Christ.[16] Even so, God is not the author of evil, nor are people excused from their sin. Their condemnation is deserved, even if they were not provided with an alternative.

Summary

Though the Councils of Carthage and Orange condemned Pelagianism and Semi-Pelagianism in the fifth and sixth centuries, the church seemed to show no awareness of these proceedings. Semi-Pelagianism was alive and well throughout the church and the ministerial training grounds of universities. The Reformers found themselves in a theological context much like Augustine's and relied heavily upon him for their views on election. If they were to remain consistent with their view that salvation is by faith alone, they must also hold to salvation by grace alone. If salvation is by grace alone, then it must be in Christ's sovereign will alone, which for the Reformers was the safest place for it to be.

REFLECTION QUESTIONS

1. How were the contexts of Augustine and the Reformers similar?

2. Does knowing the contexts of the Reformers better inform our understanding of unconditional election?

3. How did the Reformers' doctrine of election address Semi-Pelagianism in the *via moderna*?

4. How do we reconcile the Reformers' beliefs that election is unconditional from eternity past but that the gospel must be preached to everyone everywhere?

5. How did the Reformers understand election and reprobation in light of providence?

---

16. Calvin, *Institutes of the Christian Religion*, 3.24.12–13.

QUESTION 5

How Did Jacobus Arminius and the Remonstrants Understand Election?

The cultural and theological impact of the Protestant Reformation cannot be overstated. Augustine's views on original sin and depravity, which framed salvation in light of divine grace, prevailed again. As sinners, humanity is in no position to merit the righteousness of Christ. It must be divinely imputed and freely received by faith. The influence of Semi-Pelagianism was being eradicated from the church.

While Augustine's views on original sin and salvation by grace were rising in influence, not everyone agreed with his (or Calvin's) views on eternal predestination. A Dutch theologian and professor at University of Leiden by the name of Jacobus Arminius (1560–1609) was among these critics. While Arminius originally ascribed to Calvin's doctrine on predestination (given that he was a student under Calvin's successor, Theodore Beza), his views began to change in 1589 during the Dutch Renaissance. Like the Reformers, Arminius did not believe himself to be saying anything new about predestination and election. He appealed to early church fathers, medieval Scholastic theologians, and Protestants like Philip Melanchthon to support his views.[1] Still, when Arminius said what he did, it associated his name and followers (the Remonstrants) with a particular perspective on divine election, which we will now explore.

Eternal Predestination and Human Sinfulness

As observed in the preceding question, the Reformers rejected conditional election because proponents of the *via moderna* like Gabriel Biel sourced people's salvation in natural ability and goodness rather than God's

1. Roger Olson, *Arminian Theology: Myths and Realities* (Downers Grove, IL: IVP Academic, 2006), 22.

grace. Arminius was well familiar with these Semi-Pelagian heresies of the *via moderna*, and while false rumors circulated that he embraced that movement, he expressly rejected it.[2] Belief in original sin was necessary for orthodoxy, claimed Arminius, and predestination is clearly taught in Scripture. However, the genuineness of faith and the goodness of God had to factor into the equation somehow. Could there be a way to hold to authentic faith, a good God who cares for the salvation of all people, and eternal predestination? Before Arminius posed an answer, he first wanted to assure his critics that he was on solid, orthodox ground.

Arminius began his discourse on predestination much like the Reformers, by sourcing election in God's eternal decrees. These decrees begin with the absolute decree of the Father to appoint Jesus Christ as the Savior over sinful humanity. Second, God precisely and absolutely decreed to set the means of salvation (as through faith in Christ and repentance of sins) while also decreeing to leave certain sinners under wrath. Third, God sufficiently and efficaciously determined according to his perfect wisdom and will the means necessary for repentance and faith to be expressed. Finally, God decreed to save and condemn individuals based upon his foreknowledge from eternity past of who would (through prevenient grace) believe and persevere.[3] These decrees are immutable and from everlasting.

Arminius further addressed his Calvinistic critics who claimed that he minimized divine election. In strong language, Arminius said predestination is synonymous with the gospel itself. He did not believe election was the work of a person but the work of God, and in his fourteenth sentiment, Arminius stated that predestination shows God is the cause of all humanity's goodness and salvation. The only thing a human can bring about is sin and just condemnation.[4]

Additionally, Arminius wanted to disassociate himself completely from the Pelagian heresy. On his sentiment on humanity's free will, he clearly affirmed the sinful state of humanity, which (although not as bad as they could possibly be) is by nature corrupt, fallen, and incapable of thinking, willing, or doing what is pleasing to God. God must take the initiative in the salvation experience before a person can respond in faith.[5] With these points firmly established, and believing himself to be on common ground, Arminius began to articulate his positions on election and reprobation.

---

2. James Arminius, "The Apology or Defense of James Arminius," art. 16, 17.
3. "My Own Sentiments on Predestination," in *The Works of James Arminius*, trans. James Nichols and W. R. Bagnall, 3 vols. (Spring Valley, CA: Lamp Post, 2009), 1:185.
4. Arminius, "My Own Sentiments on Predestination," 187.
5. Arminius, "My Own Sentiments on Predestination," 189–90.

Prevenient Grace, Conditional Election, and Synergism

Election of people either to salvation or rejection is sourced in God's omniscience, claimed Arminius. God knew before the foundation of the world who would respond to the gospel and persevere to the end, as well as who would freely reject the gospel or apostatize along the way. Humanity must have a role as it pertains to election, and that begins with prevenient grace.

Prevenient (or *preventing*) *grace* is divine activity that precedes the will of a person whereby the effects of the fall are overcome through the calling, convicting, illuminating, and enabling work of the Holy Spirit. This grace allows a person to cooperate with God in repentance and faith leading to salvation.[6] For Arminius, original sin rendered humanity incapable of responding to the gospel naturally (hence, he was not a Pelagian). God's grace, however, precedes human initiative, enabling them to respond freely to the gospel in repentance and faith.[7] This prevenient grace is given to all people everywhere, and it does not sway people to believe or disbelieve. Rather, it enables a person to exercise free choice.[8] Therefore, God is sovereign over election as far as limitations and boundaries go while also not responsible for the fates of people who reject salvation. Each person must decide what to do with the gospel, a choice only possible because God overcame the sinner's depravity.

Election, then, is conditional in Arminius's theology. The condition to be met is faith, which all people (because of prevenient grace) are capable of rendering.[9] Faith is not a gift given only to some people, claimed Arminius in his first and second articles of his *Defense*. Indeed, many people do express faith in Christ but are not among the elect. Saving grace is always resistible. From eternity, God would never have seen the merit of Christ reckoned to persons who refuse grace or fail to persevere in meeting the condition of faith;

---

6. Olson, *Arminian Theology*, 159–60.
7. Arminius, "My Own Sentiments on Predestination," 185, 189; J. Matthew Pinson, "Will the Real Arminius Please Stand Up?," *Integrity: A Journal of Christian Thought* 2 (2003): 134. It should be noted that, for Arminius, this prevenient grace falls short of full regeneration. Faith leads to regeneration in his view.
8. Alrick George Headley, *The Nature of the Will in the Writings of Calvin and Arminius: A Comparative Study* (Eugene, OR: Wipf & Stock, 2017), 61–62.
9. Even people who do not hear the external call of the gospel preached may still respond to the internal call of the Holy Spirit leading to salvation. See Headley, *The Nature of the Will*, 62–63. This view was also held by John Wesley, who (although desiring to see the gospel preached to all people) believed that people who never hear the gospel will be judged by the light revealed to them (making it possible for them to be saved). See John Wesley, "On Charity," in *The Complete Sermons* (San Bernardino, CA: CreateSpace, 2013), 457–58. We should not suppose that Arminius or Wesley were universalists. See J. Matthew Pinson, "The Nature of Atonement in the Theology of Jacobus Arminius," *Journal of the Evangelical Theological Society* 53, no. 4 (2010): 781–82. Rather, God has revealed enough of the gospel to all people everywhere whereby all people can embrace or reject Christ as Savior.

thus, they were never among the elect.[10] Even still, Arminius was clear that God supplies people with grace to remain in the faith (though he permits some people to fall away by their own volition).

What is more, there is *synergism*, or cooperation between God and a person whereby salvation is a work between both. In his fourth sentiment on predestination, Arminius spoke of the continued aid rendered by the Holy Spirit that excites, infuses, and inspires people to will and work together with God. God's work, then, is to intervene preveniently and provoke continually in the life of a person, and the work of a person is to persist and prosper in the faith. As already mentioned in Arminius's beliefs on divine decrees, the reprobate are people who either resist altogether the workings of God or fail to cooperate with him unto the end.

The Goodness of God

Arminius and his followers were not out to champion human accomplishment with their views on human cooperation. Rather, they were trying to defend God's goodness. If salvation and reprobation were eternally determined, humans would not be capable of changing their trajectory. Thus, God would be the author of evil and human faith would be meaningless.[11] People would not be in heaven because of faith nor in hell because of their sin, but because of God's unchanging purposes. Arminius found such views unacceptable and unbiblical. He said eternal reprobation of the condemned "is also repugnant to the Goodness of God. . . . [H]e wills the greatest evil to his creatures; and that from all eternity he has preordained that evil for them, or pre-determined to impart it to them, even before he resolved to bestow upon them any portion of good."[12] By holding to conditional election that is dependent upon cooperation by faith, humans (not God) are responsible with what they do with the grace of God in salvation. God would be vindicated from charges of evil.

Articles of the Remonstrants

Upon Arminius's death in 1609, his followers drafted a statement known as the *Remonstrance* to summarize their views and protest to the States of Holland. This document, formalized in 1610, elaborated their views on election and predestination, and adherents were eventually known as Remonstrants. Portions of the five statements of the *Remonstrance* are below.

---

10. Headley, *The Nature of the Will*, 63–64.
11. William Den Boer, "Jacobus Arminius: Theologian of God's Twofold Love," in *Arminius, Arminianism, and Europe: Jacobus Arminius (1559/60–1609)*, eds. Th. Marius van Leeuwen, Keith D. Stanglin, and Marijke Tolsma, Brill's Series in Church History (Boston: Brill Academic, 2009), 26–34. See also Olson, *Arminian Theology*, 97–114.
12. Arminius, "On Predestination," 3.7, 166 (see 3.19). See also Mildred Bangs Wynkoop, *Foundations of Wesleyan-Arminian Theology* (Kansas City, MO: Beacon Hill, 1967), 50–57.

1. That God, by an eternal, unchangeable purpose in Jesus Christ his Son, before the foundation of the world, hath determined, out of the fallen, sinful race of men, to save in Christ, for Christ's sake, and through Christ, those who, through the grace of the Holy Ghost, shall believe on this his Son Jesus, and shall persevere in this faith and obedience of faith, through this grace, even to the end; and, on the other hand, to leave the incorrigible and unbelieving in sin and under wrath;
2. That, agreeably thereto, Jesus Christ, the Saviour of the world, died for all men and for every man . . . yet that no one actually enjoys this forgiveness of sins except the believer;
3. That man has not saving grace of himself, nor of the energy of his free will, inasmuch as he, in the state of apostasy and sin, can of and by himself neither think, will, nor do any thing that is truly good (such as saving Faith eminently is); but that it is needful that he be born again of God in Christ;
4. That this grace of God is the beginning, continuance, and accomplishment of all good, even to this extent, that the regenerate man himself, without preventing or assisting, awakening, following and co-operative grace, can neither think, will, nor do good. . . . But as respects the mode of the operation of this grace, it is not irresistible;
5. But whether they are capable . . . of forsaking again the first beginnings of their life in Christ, of again returning to this present evil world . . . of becoming devoid of grace, that must be more particularly determined out of the Holy Scripture, before we ourselves can teach it with the full persuasion of our minds.[13]

The first article affirms conditional predestination while simultaneously rejecting supralapsarianism.[14] Election is conditioned upon belief while condemnation is conditioned upon unbelief. The plan for election (to save sinners by grace through faith in Christ) is what constitutes an immutable decree from eternity past, not the specific persons of the elect. Still, God's eternal plan entailed salvation and condemnation but did not specify who belonged to which group. The second article affirms the universal scope of the atonement, namely that Christ died for the sins of all people everywhere. If atonement was made only for some people, then salvation is possible only for some (not all) people. Universal atonement makes faith and the gospel message genuine. Third, humanity is fallen and cannot believe in Christ apart from prevenient grace. Fourth, grace is essential for salvation but may be rejected. Finally, the possibility of apostasy is uncertain. While Arminius believed that people who

13. Philip Schaff, ed., *The Creeds of Christendom*, 6th ed., 3 vols. (Grand Rapids: Baker, 1998), 3:545–49.
14. For a summary of the lapsarian views, see Question 23.

once expressed faith in Christ may slip away into apostasy, the Remonstrants left this matter open to question. Further inquiry was necessary to determine their official position, leaving it possible that some people may have assurance of salvation while others may fall from grace.

Summary

Jacobus Arminius was a product of the Reformation and considered himself reformed in the broad sense. He affirmed original sin, salvation by grace, and eternal election by divine decree. He distinguished himself by emphasizing conditional election, universal prevenient grace and atonement, and synergism. His overarching concerns were to retain the integrity of the human will and preserve the moral goodness of God.

The views of Arminius and his followers were condemned at the Synod of Dort (1618–1619). For the Calvinists at Dort, if God elects based upon what a sinner does, then grace is nullified, and salvation is by works. Additionally, God then does not choose anyone to salvation. People choose God (giving them reason to boast), which resembled too much of Semi-Pelagianism. Conditional election threatened salvation by grace, the effectiveness of the atonement, and the security of someone's salvation in their view. Despite this rejection, popular preachers like John Wesley and Charles Finney embraced Arminian theology and preached it to the masses, leading to its wide embrace by many Christian churches.

REFLECTION QUESTIONS

1. How does Arminius's view of conditional election differ from that of Gabriel Biel?

2. What was the role and importance of prevenient grace in Arminius's view?

3. What is synergism, and how does it relate to election in Arminius's teachings?

4. Does conditional election, as Arminius defined it, preserve God's goodness?

5. If election is conditional, as Arminius claimed, can people have assurance of their salvation?

QUESTION 6

What Do Molinists Believe About Election?

What was initially viewed as a monk's quarrel in Germany became a sweeping movement across Europe. The Protestant Reformation was, as the name suggested, reforming Christianity in a way that could no longer be ignored by the papacy in Rome. Previous attempts to quell the Reformation and silence the Reformers proved ineffective. It was time to formally address the Reformation movement. In 1545, leaders of the Catholic Church met in Trent, Italy, to respond to the criticisms of the Reformers. For almost twenty years, the council met and deliberated Catholic beliefs and practices. The line was drawn in the sand, and no middle ground found, when it came to the doctrines of justification and authority. Salvation comes by works as well as by faith, and tradition and the magisterium are equal in authority to Scripture.

One complaint that the council was forced to concede upon, however, was the need for moral and practical reform in the church. Efforts were made to ensure clergy were properly educated, and various abuses from the clergy were addressed. A change of sorts was taking place within the Catholic Church, a movement known as the Counter-Reformation. A Jesuit priest by the name of Luis de Molina (1535–1600) embraced the church's moral and theological reform and in so doing proposed a theory of divine sovereignty and human freedom that would broaden the perspectives of Catholics and Protestants alike. Molina was well aware of the immorality within the church and sought to reconcile how humans can be responsible for their actions under an all-sovereign God.[1] Thus, his approach, later termed *Molinism*, has

1. Kirk R. MacGregor, *Luis de Molina: The Life and Theology of the Founder of Middle Knowledge* (Grand Rapids: Zondervan Academic, 2015), 16–18, 75, 133. This section will explore Molinism as a whole and not solely the thought of Molina.

been adopted and adapted in many ways, providing a fascinating perspective on human responsibility and divine sovereignty.

Divine Providence and Knowledge

Molinism is more of a theoretical system to reconcile God's sovereignty with human free will than a theory on divine election. This framework is used to tackle many philosophical and theological problems that arise when holding to divine providence and creaturely freedom (issues like the problem of evil, the inspiration of Scripture, and the effectiveness of prayer, to name a few). Still, this framework is particularly helpful when analyzing divine election, and it should be appreciated that there are a variety of perspectives within Molinism on this topic. Despite some differences, all Molinists ascribe to some central tenets. To begin, we will analyze their view of providence.

Providence, in this sense, refers to God's detailed control over his creation through his knowledge, love, and power.[2] This providence reflects his incommunicable attributes, such as omniscience (perfection in knowledge), omnibenevolence (perfection in love), and omnipotence (perfection in power). Because God is sovereign, he is in perfect control over all events while simultaneously directing them to accomplish his plan for the world. Out of his omniscience, God has perfect knowledge of all events (past, present, future, and hypothetical). He knows not only what is but what was, what will be, and what could be.[3]

The hypothetical occurrences are called *counterfactuals*, conditional statements of contingent events. God knows how people would freely act in any possible situation.[4] The term *counterfactuals* is used because the antecedent or consequent clause is typically contrary to fact, but the consequent expresses what would be true if the antecedent were true. For example: If Steve were to have a million dollars, then he would retire. Because Steve does not have a million dollars, the conditional statement describes what is not actually the case but what would be the case (thus counterfactual). Theologically applied, God possesses infinite knowledge of how any possible creature would act in any possible situation at any possible time even in a different world other than the world that currently exists.[5]

---

2. Thomas P. Flint, *Divine Providence: The Molinist Account* (Ithaca, NY: Cornell University Press, 1998), 12.
3. Flint, *Divine Providence*, 12–13.
4. William Lane Craig, "God Directs All Things: On Behalf of a Molinist View of Providence," in *Four Views on Divine Providence*, ed. Dennis W. Jowers, Counterpoints: Bible and Theology (Grand Rapids: Zondervan Academic, 2011), 79–80.
5. William Lane Craig, "The Middle-Knowledge View," in *Divine Foreknowledge: Four Views*, eds. James K. Beilby and Paul R. Eddy, Spectrum Multiview Books (Downers Grove, IL: IVP Academic, 2001), 119–20; Flint, *Divine Providence*, 38.

Collectively, all God's knowledge of all necessary truths and possibilities is called *natural knowledge*. This natural knowledge is essential to God's being (hence the name).[6] Relatedly, God possesses exhaustive knowledge of everything that will happen. This knowledge is logically posterior to his decision to create any world, a knowledge in which he knows what will happen in the world he chooses to create. This type of knowledge is God's *free knowledge* because it reflects God's free, sovereign decision to bring into existence the actual world.[7] Finally, there is God's *middle knowledge*, a collection of all possibilities that would happen by free creatures in any given world. This knowledge is located (in a sense) between God's natural and free knowledge. Middle knowledge, for Molinists, best explains how God exercises absolute sovereignty while allowing his creatures to be free and responsible.[8] Thus, concerning God's knowledge, Molinists distinguish between what could happen (natural knowledge), what will happen (free knowledge), and what would happen (middle knowledge). It is here where we understand the role of libertarian free will.

Libertarian Free Will

Libertarian free will, also known as libertarianism, is the belief that human actions are free in the sense that they are not determined or controlled by external agents or causes.[9] It contrasts *determinism*, which is the belief that all human choices and actions are determined in a way where there is no freedom to act any other way (*causal necessity*).[10] What makes people morally responsible for their actions, according to libertarianism, is that their free actions are exclusively a product of causal powers that originate within themselves such that they typically could have chosen to act otherwise in the exact same circumstances.

Molinists reconcile free will with predestination through God's middle knowledge. God's middle knowledge allows him to know how every free creature would respond in any world he would choose to make. Importantly, God foreknows how he would graciously intervene in any given world while also knowing how people would respond to such grace (whether accepting or rejecting it). Predestination, then, entails God's sovereign choice to bring about the world he did (the actual world) in light of his certain and exhaustive foreknowledge of all things, including the outcome of the free choices of his creatures. God remains sovereign while humans remain free.[11]

---

6. William Lane Craig, "A Calvinist-Arminian Rapprochement?," in *The Grace of God and the Will of Man*, ed. Clark H. Pinnock (Minneapolis: Bethany House, 1995), 146.
7. Craig, "A Calvinist-Arminian Rapprochement?," 146.
8. William Lane Craig, *The Only Wise God: The Compatibility of Divine Foreknowledge and Human Freedom* (Eugene, OR: Wipf & Stock, 2000), 129–38; Flint, *Divine Providence*, 44.
9. Flint, *Divine Providence*, 24.
10. Craig, *The Only Wise God*, 14.
11. Craig, "A Calvinist-Arminian Rapprochement?," 156–158.

Election and Reprobation

Having defined God's knowledge, providence, and predestination with their relation to libertarian free will, we are now in a position to understand how this theoretical framework approaches divine election and reprobation. For Molina, divine election is based upon this premise:

> Through His natural knowledge God comprehends Himself, and in Himself He comprehends all the things that exist eminently in Him and thus the free choice of any creature whom He is able to make through His omnipotence. Therefore, before any free determination of His will, by virtue of the depth of His natural knowledge, by which He infinitely surpasses each of the things He contains eminently in Himself, He discerns what the free choice of any creature would do by its own innate freedom, given the hypothesis that He should create it in this or that order of things with these or those circumstances or aids.[12]

This view sets the platform for election and reprobation. God foreknows how people will freely respond to the gospel (whether by faith or by rejection). Their actions are truly free, yet as the one who determined which world to create, God sovereignly and eternally knows the outcomes of these free creatures.

Kenneth Keathley has proposed a modern Molinistic construction on election. In what he calls *sovereign election*, God rules over and controls all things (even in election and condemnation) but does not cause all things.[13] In this model, God ordained the salvation of the elect (defined as all who freely choose to believe in Christ as savior) but permitted the condemnation of those persons who reject the gospel. When applying the principles of divine knowledge (mentioned above) to divine election, God knows what could happen in any given world with the gospel (his natural knowledge). From all those possibilities, God knows how each person would freely respond to the gospel (his middle knowledge). Finally, in God's free knowledge, he freely and sovereignly chooses which world to bring about, thus predestining all events but not violating libertarian free will.[14]

Theoretically, a Molinist could hold to either conditional or unconditional election. Molinists holding to conditional election affirm that people's

---

12. Luis de Molina, *On Divine Foreknowledge: Part IV of the* Concordia, trans. Alfred J. Freddoso (Ithaca, NY: Cornell University Press, 1988), 4.49.11, 119.
13. Kenneth Keathley, *Salvation and Sovereignty: A Molinist Approach* (Nashville: B&H Academic, 2010), 138–63.
14. Keathley, *Salvation and Sovereignty*, 152.

eternal destination depends upon how they freely respond to the gospel. God set the condition that elect persons are people who he foreknew would freely place their faith in him. God's election is dependent upon the will of people but known logically prior to the creation of the world. God chose the world in which he knew what would happen, but he did not causally determine which people exercise saving faith. Salvation or reprobation is due to libertarian free will, whereby things could have been otherwise.[15] Other scholars, like Keathley, claim election is unconditional in that God sovereignly decided to create people whom he knew would not accept the gospel. Thus, election is not conditioned upon faith.[16]

Additionally, Molinists could theoretically hold to either individual or corporate election (or both simultaneously). Monilists generally agree that God corporately elects the church as a whole (with the church being those who freely chose to place their faith in him for salvation). God knew who the elect were prior to the foundations of the world and chose to save these people who place faith in Christ. Still, election may be viewed individually with some nuance. Addressing 1 Peter 1:1–2 and Romans 8:29, William Lane Craig affirms that God elects and foreordains individuals to election. This election, however, is based upon knowledge of foreseen faith, and from that group he individually elects.[17]

Contrasting the elect are the reprobate. The predominant Molinist view is that the reprobate are people God saw from eternity past who would not exercise saving faith in Christ. Reprobation, then, is conditioned upon a person's free rejection of the gospel and not causally determined. Keathley refers to this rejection in terms of divine permission. While desiring things to be otherwise, God permits individuals to resist the grace offered to them.[18] The reprobate may be viewed corporately in that God rejects people who do not place faith in Christ without appointing them to that destruction. Election and reprobation ultimately depend upon what people do with the grace offered to them. Thus, God controls all things but does not cause all things, even the final appointments of people.

---

15. See Craig, "A Calvinist-Arminian Rapprochement?," 156–61. Prevenient grace is given to all people, enabling everyone the opportunity to exercise saving faith. Molina (according to Craig) viewed it as heretical that God would only allow certain persons the opportunity to believe while leaving the non-elect in their sin. People have to choose to be saved, making faith a condition to becoming elect.
16. Keathley, *Salvation and Sovereignty*, 11, 153–54. Additionally, he gives the term *overcoming grace* to God's work of overcoming the effects of the fall and leading a person to a place where faith can be expressed (*Salvation and Sovereignty*, 104). This overcoming grace resolves concerns of original sin and Pelagianism.
17. Craig, *The Only Wise God*, 34–35. This is also the view of Keathley, *Salvation and Sovereignty*, 141–42. As one can see, it is difficult to avoid (even for Keathley) making election conditioned upon faith despite claims to the contrary.
18. Keathley, *Salvation and Sovereignty*, 139–42.

Molina viewed it as heresy if anyone's eternal outcome did not involve freedom of choice. The reasons for maintaining human responsibility were many, but important to the issue was his concern for higher moral standards among the clergy during the Counter-Reformation. For Molina, there can be no moral culpability in humanity without freedom of choice. Moreover, without creaturely freedom, God would be the cause of evil. Additionally, it would be difficult to reconcile God's universal love for all people and his desire that everyone be saved if there were not creaturely freedom of choice.[19] Keathley essentially asserts the same. For him, Molinism best demonstrates God's will that all people be saved, though many are not. He also believes Molinism best upholds election apart from foreseen merit or faith while also conditionally permitting the rejection of unbelievers. He also believes it gives the best (and most biblical) explanation of God's foreknowledge in election.[20]

Molinism is often described as an alternative view between Calvinism and Arminianism. Thus, Molinists have critics on both sides. Reformed theologians like Paul Helm have argued that Molinism and middle knowledge make it impossible for God to have true providence over his creation since many people resist his will. God, then, can only bring about what free agents (through middle knowledge) choose to do.[21] Additionally, many Arminians find that middle knowledge leads only to a compatibilist free will, where human will is compatible with determinism, given that individuals could not actually do anything other than what they do.[22] Still, this perspective is active today and provides an intriguing perspective on divine election that wrestles with historic issues like the sovereignty of God, the ability for all to be saved, and Molina's original concern of human responsibility.

Summary

A less familiar perspective on divine election is Molinism. Here we have explored the basic tenets of this view and its various understandings of the knowledge of God. In this view, creatures have libertarian freedom to accept or reject the gospel, and God has perfect knowledge of how such free creatures will act. Molinists find their view best reconciles the difficulties of divine sovereignty in salvation with creaturely freedom.

---

19. Molina, *On Divine Foreknowledge*, 4.53.24–25, 232.
20. Keathley, *Salvation and Sovereignty*, 152–55.
21. Paul Helm, *The Providence of God*, Contours of Christian Theology (Downers Grove, IL: IVP Academic, 1994), 49, 161–91. John Feinberg's work *No One Like Him*, Foundations of Evangelic Theology (Wheaton, IL: Crossway, 2006) is likewise critical of Molinism, finding libertarian free will presents many problems to the nature of God.
22. Roger E. Olson, *Arminian Theology: Myths and Realities* (Downers Grove, IL: IVP Academic, 2006), 197.

REFLECTION QUESTIONS

1. What are the various types of divine knowledge in Molinism?
2. How do these types of knowledge relate to election and reprobation?
3. How do Molinists attempt to reconcile divine sovereignty and human freedom?
4. What problems does Molinism attempt to resolve?
5. Do new problems arise under this model?

QUESTION 7

How Did Karl Barth Understand Election?

While it would be a mistake to say there were no significant developments on the doctrine of election from the time of the Reformation to the nineteenth century, it is fair to say those developments and debates remained mostly within traditional boundaries. The publication of the Westminster Confession and the rise of Puritanism helped champion unconditional individual election and reprobation in traditional Reformed fashion throughout the seventeenth century. John and Charles Wesley, through their popular revivals, helped make the conditional election found in Arminian theology popular throughout the eighteenth century. On the whole, these debates concerned which Christian position was superior based upon Scripture and reason. With the rise of modern liberalism, however, such debates were undercut by the question of how much Christianity itself was true.

At the turn of the nineteenth century, Protestant liberals who were prepared to abandon traditional orthodoxy for contemporary relevance were deconstructing foundational Christian beliefs that undergird the doctrine of election (discussed in question 2). Among these scholars was Friedrich Schleiermacher (1768–1834), who denied the preexistent divine nature of Christ while also radically redefining the meaning of salvation. Albrecht Ritschl (1822–1889) believed that Greek philosophy so heavily influenced the church fathers that he felt forced to reject their doctrine of original sin and the absolute divinity of Christ. His student, Adolf von Harnack (1851–1930), followed suit, reducing the Jesus of history to a popular moral teacher.

It was against such liberalism that the works of the most notable twentieth-century theologian, Karl Barth (1886–1968), were penned. Seeking to reestablish doctrinal orthodoxy, Barth's works are popularly known as *neo-orthodoxy*. Although Barth wrote tomes of theology, he is best known for his

Church Dogmatics, which articulates a novel perspective of divine election that radically redefined the debate.

God Revealed

The problem with modern liberalism, according to Barth, was its human-centered theology. Particularly in his 1922 edition of *The Epistle to the Romans*, Barth expressed how wrong nineteenth-century liberals were to think that human experience, reason, and nature disclose God. The world cannot know the divine unless God condescends to the world, revealing himself as he truly is. Humans cannot ascend to God, for the essence of the gospel is God's descension to humanity. What was once hidden, above and beyond, has been made known to us in the person of Jesus Christ.[1] Barth does not dismiss Scripture and the teachings of the church as modes for revealing God. However, these mediums are secondary, not primary, because they are the mediators through which Christ, the true revelation, is known.[2] Thus, for Barth, before we can understand what God does in election, we must first understand him as the gracious and loving triune God who is seen in Christ (something scorned for ages by liberalism).

Christ, then, is the center of Barth's theology, for Jesus is Immanuel, God with us. In the incarnation, divinity was united with humanity (despite humanity's sin and fallenness) because God still desired a relationship with people (something only possible through Jesus). Barth said, "Once for all God became Man and so His Word reached the ears of us men, and so we men were reconciled to God."[3] Thus, any knowledge or revelation of God must be accomplished through Christ. It is against this Christocentric backdrop that Barth articulated a novel perspective on divine election.

The Electing God and the Elected Man

Despite being a Reformed theologian, Barth sought to disassociate himself from a traditional Calvinistic view of election. According to Barth, Calvin reduced Christ to merely an instrumental role. Jesus, for Barth, was more than just a means through whom the electing God chooses to bring certain people to salvation; he is the "Subject of election."[4] Barth's doctrine on elec-

---

1. Karl Barth, *The Epistle to the Romans*, trans. Edwyn C. Hoskyns (New York: Oxford University Press, 1968), 91–92, 330–35.
2. Jonathan Hill, *The History of Christian Thought* (Downers Grove, IL: InterVarsity Press, 2003), 269. See also T. F. Torrance, *Theology in Reconstruction* (Grand Rapids: Eerdmans, 1965), 109–13.
3. Karl Barth, *Church Dogmatics*, eds. G. W. Bromiley and T. F. Torrance, 5 vols. (Peabody, MA: Hendrickson, 2010), 1.2, 165.
4. Barth, *Church Dogmatics*, 2.2, 66–67. The incarnation was an eternal plan among the Trinity, and as the Son, Christ shared in that plan, thus identifying him as the electing God.

tion may be summed up in two general statements, provided here in his own wording:

> The first is that Jesus Christ is the electing God. This statement answers the question of the Subject of the eternal election of grace. And the second is that Jesus Christ is elected man. This statement answers the question of the object of the eternal election of grace. Strictly speaking, the whole dogma of predestination is contained in these two statements.[5]

Election is not merely an activity of God; it is the person of God in Christ. This belief relates to the essence of Christology mentioned above, namely that God condescends to humanity in Jesus. Election and revelation go hand in hand. To be the electing God means that it has always been the eternal and unconditional plan of God to appoint Jesus Christ as the divine-human (thereby making him the subject of divine election). God elects himself with humanity, thereby electing humanity to fellowship with God.[6] Still, he is the elected man because he is the object of divine election. God's intentions were always to reconcile the world through the incarnate Christ, and, as the predestined one, he is the elect man who secures salvation for all people.[7]

Christ the Rejected

However, Jesus is not the electing God and elected man only in positive ways. His own election negatively entails an election of obedience, suffering, and rejection. While sinful humans deserve God's wrath, God's election of Christ entailed that he be stricken and rejected by God for human sin.[8] As the elected man, he was chosen to bear the punishment of humanity's wickedness and, consequently, be the rejected man who completely extinguished God's wrath on behalf of all humanity. Here marks another significant departure from Calvin. Whereas Calvin believed we cannot know who is reprobate (for such mysteries belong to the hidden knowledge of God alone), Barth claimed to know precisely who is reprobate—none other than Jesus Christ himself. Barth stated:

> God, by the decree He made in the beginning of all His works and ways, has taken upon Himself the rejection merited by

5. Barth, *Church Dogmatics*, 2.2, 145. For a critique of Barth's claim, see David Gibson, *Reading the Decree: Exegesis, Election and Christology in Calvin and Barth*, T&T Clark Studies in Systematic Theology (New York: T&T Clark, 2009), 39–41.
6. Gibson, *Reading the Decree*, 80.
7. Bruce L. McCormack, *Orthodox and Modern: Studies in the Theology of Karl Barth* (Grand Rapids: Baker Academic, 2008), 185–86.
8. Barth, *Church Dogmatics*, 2.2, 318–19. See also Geoffrey W. Bromiley, *An Introduction to the Theology of Karl Barth* (Grand Rapids: Eerdmans, 1979), 88.

> the man isolated in relation to Him; that on the basis of this decree of His the only truly rejected man is His own Son; that God's rejection has taken its course and been fulfilled and reached in its goal, with all that that involves, against this One, so that it can no longer fall on the other men or be their concern.[9]

Christ, then, is the reprobate, for only he could provide God the Father with the adequate sacrifice for human sin. Apart from the person of Jesus, there can be no other reprobate. Thus, understanding people's election as predestination to salvation or damnation is a categorical mistake because it fails to understand the essence of Jesus Christ. Jesus was eternally elected to be the revelation of God to humanity, displaying the love of God toward the whole sinful human race. In the incarnation, divinity met humanity in accordance with that foreordained plan. That plan, however, entailed that the Father reject Christ, who became the reprobate on behalf of all humanity, suffering both physical and spiritual death.[10] Christ the divine, who took on human flesh, defeated sin's power over humanity and subsequently brought people into fellowship with God once more, rising from the dead victorious.

Predestination, in Barth, may rightly be thought of as double, given that Christ was (from all eternity) appointed to be incarnate as the divine-man while also being predestined for reprobation and death on behalf of humanity.[11] However, through these predestined roles, there came to be a new and better humanity for all people. This conclusion (matched with other features of Barth's theology) raises questions of universal salvation that must now be explored.

Universalism in Barth

It should be clear that for Barth, election is about God rather than humanity. In the fullness of time, God unfolded his eternal plan to reconcile humanity through the revelation of Jesus, who is the God-human. God is thus free to enact his grace-filled plan in a moment of time on behalf of humanity. Grace is universal in this view because of Christ's role as the elected man who took the wrath of God for all. Jesus is the man that God appointed on behalf of all people to show his grace.

The question then becomes whether Barth's view necessitates *universalism*, the belief that all people are saved. The answer to this question is more complex than it may first appear, and it is a matter of ongoing cordial debate among scholars, partly because Barth never fully committed himself on the

9. Barth, *Church Dogmatics*, 2.2, 319.
10. McCormack, *Orthodox and Modern*, 189–92.
11. Barth, *Church Dogmatics*, 2.2, 162.

issue. What is more, Barth would certainly repudiate any idea of universal salvation by default. Any universal salvation would have to be in Christ.

To answer the question, we first must understand that, for Barth, all human beings are elect in Christ (whether they are conscious of it or not). Election, as said above, is about God's eternal plan as electing God and elected man. Christ suffered the rejection that all people deserved. He also has placed himself as the new head of all humanity.[12] Because of his humiliation and exaltation, the rejection and glorification of Christ belong to all people, and no further work on the part of a person is needed to make Christ's work effective.[13]

With that said, some scholars have pointed to passages in Barth's writings where he seems to allow some people to reject the grace given to them in Christ.[14] Barth said, "To the man who persistently tries to change the truth into untruth, God does not owe eternal patience and therefore deliverance."[15] Barth's theology, they claim, prohibits an absolute universalism. However, other scholars find that while Barth's writings allow for the non-salvation of some persons, his logic necessitates it.[16]

Secondly, because of Christ's already established work mentioned above, the Holy Spirit does not need to make the salvific work of Christ effective in the life of a person. While the Spirit does awaken people to belief, and the church is commissioned to call all people to faith in Christ, the Spirit merely enables people to see what Christ has already done for them.[17] The work of Christ and the work of the Spirit cannot be separated but are a unitary act for Barth. There are some people who do not put their faith in that work, but they are merely failing to live out their true humanity provided to them by Christ. That is to say that Barth believes them to be saved despite them not knowing they are saved. Even if people fail to place faith in Christ consciously (something Barth believed is not naturally possible for people to do), they do exercise such faith because they are (like all people) in Christ. Humanity, then, cannot ultimately choose against Christ because Christ is the God-man who

---

12. Barth, *Church Dogmatics*, 2.2.
13. McCormack, *Orthodox and Modern*, 268.
14. See Michael O'Neil, "Karl Barth's Doctrine of Election," *Evangelical Quarterly* 76, no. 4 (2004): 311–26.
15. Barth, *Church Dogmatics*, 4.3i.
16. See Oliver D. Crisp, "The Letter and the Spirit of Barth's Doctrine of Election: A Response to Michael O'Neil," *Evangelical Quarterly* 79 (2007): 53–67. See also David W. Congdon, "Apokatastasis and Apostolicity: A Response to Oliver Crisp on the Question of Barth's Universalism," *Scottish Journal of Theology* 67, no. 4 (2014): 464–80, who says that Barth's theology necessitates universalism while his logic permits him to deny it.
17. See Bruce L. McCormack, "*Justitia aliena*: Karl Barth in Conversation with the Evangelical Doctrine of Imputed Righteousness," in *Justification in Perspective: Historical Developments and Contemporary Challenges*, ed. Bruce L. McCormack (Grand Rapids: Baker Academic, 2006), 179–180. See also Barth, *Church Dogmatics*, 4.3ii.

is the electing God and elected man on behalf of all people.[18] These positions from Barth lead many scholars to suggest that Barth did hold to universal salvation for all people given their universal election in Christ.

Summary

Karl Barth sought to reestablish orthodoxy against the modern liberals who preceded him by reestablishing a high view of Christology and Trinity that took seriously the life, death, burial, and resurrection of Jesus. In the process, he presented ideas that radically reframed the election debate. For him, the cross of Jesus was God's "No" whereby Christ took all humanity's works and became the reprobate on behalf of everyone. However, the resurrection was God's "Yes" in which he secured salvation for all people. No longer was the debate merely between individual or corporate election, which dominated the debate for centuries. Since the time of Barth, consideration has been given to whether Christ was the electing God and elected man who was chosen for reprobation as well as glorification, providing salvation to all people.

Barth has not been without his critics. Even though his writings are expositions of texts like John 1 and Romans 9–11, his views are often criticized for a lack of scriptural support. Other scholars, like Emil Brunner, criticize Barth on natural theology. Many evangelicals find fault in where Barth's theology inextricably leads, namely universalism and the apparent nonnecessity of personal faith in Christ for salvation. Still, Barth's theology was immensely popular and secured its place in the literature on the doctrine of election.

REFLECTION QUESTIONS

1. Do you agree or disagree with Barth that God cannot be known by history and nature?
2. What is meant by Christ being the electing God and elected man?
3. Did Jesus become the reprobate of God as Barth contended?
4. Did Christ secure universal salvation for all people? Why or why not?
5. Are all people elect in Christ, in your view?

---

18. Barth, *Church Dogmatics*, 2.2.

QUESTION 8

What Are Other Alternative Views on Election?

As we close out this historical overview of divine election, we may make a few summary statements. It should be evident that election is a firmly biblical doctrine that has consumed the attention of the church for some two thousand years. The early church wrestled seriously with heresies and the Scriptures, out of which came doctrines about the person and work of Christ and the nature of the Trinity that formed and framed the election debate. Somehow, creaturely freedom and spiritual inability had to reconcile with God's sovereignty and his eternal decrees. Some theologians, like Pelagius and adherents of the *via moderna*, sacrificed divine sovereignty for absolute libertarian free will. On the other hand, historic thinkers like Gottschalk were prepared to reject human responsibility altogether for an all-sovereign God who does not consider human will at all in the matter of reprobation. Finding the right balance between divine sovereignty and human freedom in election remains a persistent challenge in Christian doctrine, and occasionally the framework is reshaped altogether by views like Molinism and Barth's neoorthodoxy.

The question now remains, What other views are out there? Here we are not looking at different points of emphasis within the traditions mentioned already. Rather, we are looking at altogether different systems of thought. Naturally, not every alternative view can be relayed here. Most alternatives, however, can be categorized in one of the following ways: God has limitations, God requires works, and God elects everyone. As will hopefully become evident, the larger question for these views goes beyond who is finally saved. The more pressing issue is how to reconcile divine sovereignty with human freedom and responsibility.

God Has Limitations

In an attempt to avoid the extremes of Pelagianism or Gottschalk, some theologians try to reconcile divine sovereignty and free will by limiting divine sovereignty. There are two primary views that argue God has limits on absolute sovereignty so that human beings can be free (with regards to salvation and other things). The first view, popularly argued by Bruce Reichenbach, argues that God limits his power.[1] Human beings must be free, and God must be omnipotent. Both human freedom and divine omnipotence are held as truths, but both cannot simultaneously exist at the same time. God, in his sovereignty, created human beings with freedom of choice. Naturally, there are some limitations to human freedom (where the choices have to be actual possibilities), but God himself does not cause a human to act in a particular way. In order for humans to exercise their freedom, God must limit his power. Comparing God's sovereignty and human freedom to a puzzle, Reichenbach states:

> Our omnipotence puzzle piece has an important appendage which connects it to the human freedom piece, namely, that it is not inconsistent with God's omnipotence that he limit himself or his activity. God cannot, without destroying our freedom, control us or compel us to choose to act in ways that accord with his will or plan. If God has created us free to choose to love and serve him, then God cannot cause us to do so. It is up to us to accept or reject the grace offered us through the redemptive act of Christ.[2]

Notice that this view does not deny God's omnipotence (an essential divine attribute) but rather denies God's full use of it. Additionally, Reichenbach does not deny that God saves the world through Christ. He merely affirms it is up to people to use the freedom God has given them to accept the gospel. This view does hold to a conditional perspective of election, where God accepts people who accept him; however, it does so under unique terms. In this belief, God's omnipotence is limited by God himself so that human beings can truly be free. As it pertains to election, the elect freely place faith in Jesus Christ, exercising the freedom that God (through self-imposed limitations) gave them.

The second primary view that entails God's limitations is called *open theism*. Popularized by theologians such as Clark Pinnock, John Sanders, and

---

1. See Bruce R. Reichenbach, *Divine Providence: God's Love and Human Freedom* (Eugene, OR: Cascade, 2016).
2. Bruce R. Reichenbach, "God Limits His Power," in *Predestination and Free Will: Four Views*, eds. David Basinger and Randall Basinger, Spectrum Multiview Books (Downers Grove, IL: IVP Academic, 1986), 108.

Gregory Boyd, open theism is a theological system that rationalizes divine sovereignty and human responsibility through the limitation of God's knowledge. As the term *limitation* can have negative connotations, adherents of this view prefer the term *openness* because, in their view, God is open to what his creatures choose to do while also being open to the future that those choices present.[3] God has exhaustive knowledge of what can be known (the past and present) but does not know what cannot be known (the future) because it has not happened. As an infinitely intelligent being, God can certainly surmise what will happen in the future. The future, however, is not certain, and he learns what his creatures do in real time.[4] Because God does not know the future, he takes risks and his plans are often thwarted in this view.

As it relates to divine election, God does know who the elect are (in terms of knowing those persons who have faith in Christ during their lifetime), but he does not know who the elect will be. In other words, God did not predetermine a specific group of people to be the elect from eternity past, for that would take away from creaturely freedom. Instead, God has (from the foundation of the world) elected a plan with certain conditions to be met in order to become elect (namely faith in Christ), but he does not determine who is elect.[5]

God Requires Works

Another alternative view to divine election is the belief that God saves people who do good works. This view is nothing new, yet it remains popular. While any belief system that claims salvation depends on human activity may accurately be described as conditional election, this approach far exceeds the traditional view where faith alone, not faith plus works, is the condition to being saved. Here we will explore two different examples of a faith-plus-works view.[6]

Robert A. Sungenis has argued that salvation is not by faith alone but through faith and obedience. Citing James 2:24, where James says that a person is justified not by faith alone but by works, Sungenis claims that a

---

3. Richard Rice, "Biblical Support for a New Perspective," in *The Openness of God: A Biblical Challenge to the Traditional Understanding of God*, ed. Clark H. Pinnock (Downers Grove, IL: InterVarsity Press, 1994), 15–16.
4. See Clark Pinnock, "God Limits His Knowledge," in Basinger and Basinger, eds., *Predestination and Free Will*, 157. See also Gregory A. Boyd, who argues that God does possess exhaustive knowledge of future events but that those events are not certain ("Christian Love and Academic Dialogue: A Reply to Bruce Ware," *Journal of the Evangelical Theological Society* 45, no. 2 [2002]: 233). For an excellent critique of open theism, see Bruce A. Ware, *God's Lesser Glory: The Diminished God of Open Theism* (Wheaton, IL: Crossway, 2000).
5. John Sanders, *The God Who Risks: A Theology of Divine Providence* (Downers Grove, IL: InterVarsity Press 1998), 102. While sharing some common points of agreement, this view is largely rejected by Arminians.
6. The views mentioned here are the views of a respective author which may not necessarily reflect the views of their faith tradition. Moreover, these authors tie justification and election so closely that the two can be correlated for analysis.

sinner must have faith and works combined in order to be acceptable to God. These works are not to the exclusion of faith, nor are they merely good deeds. The particular works Sungenis, a Roman Catholic theologian, has in mind are obedience to God's commands and participation in the sacraments. To be clear, Sungenis does not believe salvation is by works of the Mosaic law. For him, when Paul condemned justification by works of the law, Paul as condemning Jewish customs and rituals as a means of righteousness, not the need for obedience to God's commands. Through faith, holy conduct, and participation in the sacraments, someone may become the elect of God.[7]

Another view that holds to faith plus obedience may be found among adherents of *theosis*. The view of theosis dates back to the early church fathers and was coined by Gregory of Nazianzus. Also known by its English cognates *deification* and *divinization*, theosis refers to a believer's transformation into God's likeness.[8] While *theosis* may sound similar to sanctification, deification refers to much more. One author states:

> *Theosis* is our restoration as persons to integrity and wholeness by participation in Christ through the Holy Spirit, in a process which is initiated in this world through our life of ecclesial communion and moral striving and finds ultimate fulfilment in our union with the Father—all within the broad context of the divine economy.[9]

To understand this view, we must first understand the human condition as this tradition views it. Sin is primarily viewed as a break of the divine likeness, not a break of the divine law leading to guilt and condemnation. When human beings were made in God's image in Genesis 1:27, they were made both with God's image and his likeness (with the two being distinguishable). When humanity sinned through Adam in Genesis 3, they lost the likeness of God but retained the image. As Cyril of Jerusalem stated, "At that time God said, *Let us make man after our image and after our likeness*. And the *image* he received, but the *likeness* through his disobedience he obscured."[10] Thus, what humanity needs is to be restored to the likeness of God. This line of thinking

7. Robert A. Sungenis, *Not by Faith Alone: The Biblical Evidence for the Catholic Doctrine of Justification* (Goleta, CA: Queenship, 1997), 1–3, 8–16, 38–39.
8. Stephen Finlan and Vladimir Kharlamov, eds., "Introduction," in *Theōsis: Deification in Christian Theology* (Eugene, OR: Pickwick, 2006), 1.
9. Norman Russell, *Fellow Workers with God: Orthodox Thinking on Theosis* (Crestwood, NY: St Vladimir's Seminary Press, 2009), 21.
10. Cyril of Jerusalem, "Lecture XIV.10," in *The Catechetical Lectures* in *Nicene and Post-Nicene Fathers*, Second Series, eds. Philip Schaff and Henry Wace, 14 vols. (Peabody, MA: Hendrickson, 2012), 7:96 (italics original).

led to the famous quote from Athanasius: "For He [Jesus] was made man so that we might be made God."[11] It is this notion of "be made God" or *becoming God* that concerns *theosis*/deification.

While space does not permit us to exhaust this perspective, it should be stated clearly that adherents of theosis do not mean that deification leads to someone becoming a literal god. This view, popular in Eastern Orthodoxy, remains monotheistic. Rather, the believer experiences a transformation of the self and a new life such that he or she shares, in a spiritual sense, the same qualities of God.[12] In other words, believers in Christ are immersed into divinity, in which they are cleansed from sin and receive the likeness of God (because Jesus brought together humanity and divinity), leading to a new and better humanity.

The question now is, How does theosis happen?[13] The answer is twofold. Efficiently, theosis happens through the incarnation of Jesus. Therein, divinity joined with humanity, allowing humanity to partake of the divine nature (2 Peter 1:4). The incarnation, then, allows humanity to be restored into the likeness of God. However, instrumentally, theosis is a synergistic activity between God and a person. God reveals Jesus (the divine man) to people, leading them to faith while renewing the mind and heart to the likeness of God. Believers, on the other hand, must actively cooperate with the Spirit through emptying themselves of all things that are unlike God.[14] Additionally, by belonging to and participating in the sacraments of the church, believers can engage in prayer, asceticism, and service in a way that leads to deification.[15]

As it relates to divine election (which is not a major point of emphasis in this perspective), theosis is the means by which someone becomes elect. Through cooperation with God, a person may become so consumed with the divine that he or she becomes divine (in a spiritual, not ontological sense), leading to salvation from sin. Through such works, God will save.

God Elects Everyone

A final alternative to discuss is *universalism*, the belief that God elects everyone to salvation. As mentioned in the preceding question, Karl Barth never committed himself on this issue and insisted that God's freedom meant

11. Athanasius, *Incarnation of the Word*, in Schaff and Wace, *Nicene and Post-Nicene Fathers*, vol. 4, §54, 65.
12. Finlan and Kharlamov, "Introduction," 1.
13. For a more thorough treatment on this view, see Daniel Kirkpatrick, "An Analysis of Synergistic Theosis and Deification in Light of Monergistic Perspective," *Southwest Journal of Arts and Sciences* 1, no. 1 (2021): 12–15, 22–42.
14. Russell, *Fellow Workers with God*, 40–41.
15. Veli-Matti Kärkkäinen, *One with God: Salvation as Deification and Justification* (Collegeville, MN: Liturgical Press, 2004), 31.

it was beyond the duty of the church to speculate about universal reconciliation. Other theologians, however, fully embrace the notion of universal election, albeit in differing ways. Important to this discussion is that these authors differ from Unitarians in that they affirm that any universal salvation must be done in Christ.

A common cause for holding to Christian universalism is based upon assumptions of what a good God would do. Thomas Talbott, for example, argues that God's love and goodness, displayed as a loving father, would never torture his children for all eternity.[16] If love is not the primary motif, then appealing to justice will also do. Gregory MacDonald, for example, highlights that if eternal retribution is the consequence for temporary disobedience, the punishment does not fit the crime.[17] In Christian universalism, hell may be a reality for some people, but it would not win out over and against God's love and redemption in Christ. Thus, all people will eventually be saved and among the elect.

Summary

This chapter has explored alternative views of election under three main categories: God has limitations, God requires works, and God elects everyone. Many of these views are questionable as to their orthodoxy, yet remain important in the discussion of divine election.

REFLECTION QUESTIONS

1. Does God place limitations upon his power or knowledge so that people can be free?
2. Where do religious works come into play with regard to divine election?
3. If God is good, would he not elect everyone to salvation?
4. Are the alternative views mentioned here orthodox options for Christians?
5. What other alternative views of election might exist?

---

16. Thomas Talbott, *The Inescapable Love of God,* 2nd ed. (Eugene, OR: Wipf & Stock, 2014).
17. Gregory MacDonald, *The Evangelical Universalist,* 2nd ed. (Eugene, OR: Cascade, 2012), 11–15.

PART 2

Biblical Evaluation of Election

SECTION A

The Workings of Election

QUESTION 9

Is Election Rooted in the Divine or Human Will?

As we begin to consider the intricacies of divine election, we must explore where election is sourced. Virtually all Christian traditions agree that God is the agent doing the actual choosing; however, what motivates God to choose as he does? That question, and the implications its answer brings, requires deeper examination and will be explored over the next several questions. If divine election is based merely upon the will of God, what is to be said of the will of human beings? If, on the other hand, God chooses based upon what he knows about people, then perhaps the reason some people are chosen and others are not lies in the will of humans. To this issue we now direct our attention, and we begin by understanding the biblical term of predestination.

Defining Predestination

Broadly speaking, *predestination* is a term referring to what God, from eternity past, chooses or decides to do.[1] For example, Peter and John viewed Jesus's death as the predestined purpose of God (Acts 4:27–28). Paul said all things work together for good to those who are called according to God's purpose, for those whom God predestined to be conformed to Christ (Rom. 8:28–30). Additionally, Paul said to the Ephesians that God predestined us to adoption as sons through Christ, according to the kind intentions of his will (Eph. 1:4–5). We can see from these texts that predestination refers to God's choice and determination to do something from eternity past; thus, it is

1. Walter Bauer, *A Greek-English Lexicon of the New Testament and Other Early Christian Literature*, eds. and trans. William F. Arndt, F. Wilber Gingrich, and Frederick W. Danker, 3rd ed. (Chicago: University of Chicago Press, 2000), s.v. προορίζω.

closely associated with the term *election*.[2] On this matter, there is agreement between Reformed and non-Reformed traditions. What is not agreed upon by these traditions, however, is what God's eternal choices are based upon.

For the Reformed tradition, God's predestination is based upon what he sovereignly wills to come to pass. Michael Horton gives this helpful description: "Predestination is an exercise of the divine will, which in turn is the free expression of the divine nature."[3] That is to say, God's will is eternal, just like the divine nature. As a complete and changeless being, God in infinite wisdom decreed things to be as he desires. While many things may be said to be predestined (such as the incarnation, the crucifixion, and the glorification of Christ), there is a predestination of individuals for eternal salvation (and possibly condemnation) in this view that is all sourced in the sovereign will of God.[4]

Consider again Romans 8:28–29:

> We know that for those who love God all things work together for good, for those who are called according to his purpose. For those whom he foreknew he also predestined to be conformed to the image of his Son, in order that he might be the firstborn among many brothers.

God works all things together to fulfill his purposes, according to this text. Naturally, these purposes would be rooted in the divine will, and they shall certainly prevail. This predestination also entails, in the Reformed tradition, that people are chosen to be saved and conformed to the image of Christ from eternity past.[5] Additional textual support for this view includes Romans 9:6–33, 1 Corinthians 2:7, and Ephesians 1:5, 11.

Bringing everything together, Martin Luther, commenting on Romans 9:15, said on divine predestination:

> [God] will give grace, in time and life, to him concerning whom [God] purposed from eternity to show mercy. On him will [God] have compassion and forgive his sin in time and life whom [God] forgave and pardoned from all eternity.

---

2. We might say that *predestination* is a broader term referring to what God has willed to do in all his affairs, whereas *election* is narrower in focus, particularly dealing with his work in salvation.
3. Michael Horton, *The Christian Faith: A Systematic Theology for Pilgrims on the Way* (Grand Rapids: Zondervan Academic, 2011), 311.
4. Horton, *The Christian Faith*, 311. We should not assume that predestination unto salvation assumes, negatively, a double predestination where the non-elect are foreordained to eternal retribution (or reprobation), though some adherents to eternal election hold to such a view (see Question 13).
5. For elaboration, see Gordon H. Clark, *Predestination* (Phillipsburg, NJ: P&R, 1987), 66–68.

> In doing this, God is not unjust, for so He willed and was pleased to do from eternity, and His will is not bound by any law or obligation.[6]

This quote is helpful in understanding the Reformed view. Election and predestination are from eternity past, yet in real time (upon conversion) God brings a person to faith and forgiveness. Such a decree will absolutely come to pass because God willed it to be so (from eternity past). Drawing from Augustine, John Calvin likewise believed eternal predestination in salvation belongs to God's eternal will. Granted, not everything that happens on earth is good; however, nothing occurs (even the salvation of the elect or the condemnation of sinners) apart from God's active or permissive will.[7] If God were not in control over his universe, and if things continually happened that were not caused or permitted by him, then (according to this view) he would cease to be God.[8] Therefore, even the salvation of the elect is predetermined from eternity past as part of God's sovereign will.

Unlike the Reformed tradition that understands predestination as rooted in God's eternal will, the Arminian tradition understands predestination as rooted in God's foreknowledge. Specifically, predestination refers to what God foresees (or foreknows) that free creatures will do (a view sometimes called *prescience*). As a timeless and omniscient being, God knows the willful responses of his creatures even before they make them. He knows from all eternity who will accept Christ by faith and who will reject him by disbelief. Thus, the elect were predestined to salvation from eternity not because God chose their final state but because God foreknew they would believe the gospel. Consider Jacobus Arminius on this matter:

> God decreed to save and damn certain particular persons. This decree has its foundation in the foreknowledge of God, for which he knew from all eternity those individuals who would, through his preventing grace, believe, and, through his subsequent grace would persevere . . . and, by which foreknowledge, he likewise knew those who would not believe and persevere.[9]

---

6. Martin Luther, *Commentary on Romans*, trans. J. Theodore Mueller (Grand Rapids: Kregel, 1985), 139.
7. John Calvin, *Concerning the Eternal Predestination of God*, trans. J. K. S. Reid (Louisville: Westminster John Knox, 1997), 66–67.
8. R. C. Sproul, *Chosen by God* (Wheaton, IL: Tyndale, 1986), 25–28; see also Westminster Confession of Faith, chapter 3.
9. "My Own Sentiments on Predestination," in *The Works of James Arminius*, trans. James Nichols and W. R. Bagnall, 3 vols. (Spring Valley, CA: Lamp Post, 2009), 1:185.

According to Arminius, God has decreed to save and damn persons, but he has not specifically chosen who those persons are. He foreknows how people will respond, which is the basic meaning of predestination. Similarly, Roger Olson said, "God elected those he foreknew would enter Christ by faith to be his people and damned those he foreknew would reject Christ as not his people."[10]

Scriptural support for this view includes 1 Peter 1:1–2, where Peter wrote to the "elect exiles . . . according to the foreknowledge of God the Father." Additionally, this tradition points to the many passages that affirm God's desire for all to be saved (1 Tim. 2:4, 2 Peter 3:9) along with thorough alternative interpretations to the passages used by their Calvinist counterparts.[11]

What God Predestines

While we can certainly accept that God foreknows the future, including whether people will accept or reject the gospel, this is not the meaning of predestination. Below, we will provide three reasons why we believe predestination refers to the eternal will of God to elect persons to salvation and not foreknowledge of people's choices.

First, the Scriptures affirm that predestination is rooted in God's eternal will or desire, not knowledge of creaturely actions. To be clear, we should not separate God's will from his knowledge nor set one before the other. What is at question here is not whether God's knowledge precedes his will. Rather, the question is whether predestination is ultimately rooted in the divine will (his intrinsic desire) or his knowledge of the human will (humanity's intrinsic desire). If predestination means that God elects people based upon his foreknowledge of human choices, we must assume that predestination is ultimately based upon what is in humanity rather than in God. However, Ephesians 1:5 affirms that God "predestined us for adoption to himself through Jesus Christ, according to the purpose of his will." It continues in verse 11: "In him we have obtained an inheritance, having been predestined according to the purpose of him who works all things according to the counsel of his will." Additionally, Peter and John recognized the will and responsibility of evil persons such as Herod, Pontius Pilate, the Gentiles, and the people of Israel who crucified Jesus; however, they had done what God's hand purposed and predestined to occur (Acts 4:27–28), thus reaffirming that predestination is rooted in God's will, not his foreknowledge of people's will. Additionally, we would have to radically alter the biblical terms for predestination if it were equivocal to foreknowledge. The Greek word for *predestination* is *proorizō*, and, as mentioned above, it means to decide or choose beforehand. As Romans 8:29 helpfully demonstrates, there

10. Roger E. Olson, *Arminian Theology* (Downers Grove, IL: IVP Academic, 2006), 185.
11. See Robert E. Picirilli, *Grace, Faith, Free Will* (Nashville: Randall House, 2002), 65–84.

is a difference between *predestine* (*proorizō*) and *foreknow* (*proginōskō* and *prooida*). The two are simply different terms, which is why applying foreordination as foreknowledge does not work in most references to predestination (e.g., Acts 4:28; 1 Cor. 2:7; Eph. 1:5, 11). Biblically, predestination has to be rooted in the divine will, not in knowledge of the human will.

Second, what was foreknown and predestined was people, not choices. Romans 8:29–30 does not say "*that which* he foreknew he also predestined," as if God merely foreknew information. Rather, it states: "*Those* whom he foreknew he also predestined. . . . And *those* whom he predestined he also called, . . . justified, and . . . glorified."[12] God foreknew and predestined people. This predestination makes divine election personal, not informational. God chose people not as an afterthought of human choices but as a priority in his will. Humanity, being in the flesh and not of the spirit, does not choose God, nor can they please him in the flesh (Rom. 8:5–8). God, however, can choose them beforehand (*proorizō*) and predestine them for eternal salvation. Because God's choice preceded human choice, salvation remains all of grace and not of human merit. While we will explore the relation between divine election and human choice in Questions 12, 19, and 30, we conclude that Scripture affirms the priority of divine choice over human choice.

Third, predestination from eternity past ensures God's plans and purposes do not fail. Frequently mentioned in the book of Revelation is the Lamb's Book of Life. This book has the names of the elect written in it from the foundation of the earth (13:8; 17:8). Their names will never be erased from this book (3:5), assuring not only their salvation but God's cosmic victory (21:27). There are names not written in this book, for reasons we will explore throughout this volume. However, Revelation gives Christians hope that, despite the fallenness of the world and the egregious rise of evil, God's plans and purposes will prevail. His victory is sure because it was ordained before both the foundations of the world and sin's entry into the world. Thus, John's theology in election ensures that God's saving mission does not fail.[13] Indeed, God's purposes in salvation cannot fail, as Paul affirmed in Romans 9–11. Despite the Jews largely failing to trust in Christ as Savior, and despite God's desire for all people to be saved, God's plans in salvation have not failed (9:6) and his purposes in election will continue (9:11).[14] Thus, it is people who deserve to be pitied when they reject the gospel, not God. Our salvation

---

12. See Michael Horton, *For Calvinism* (Grand Rapids: Zondervan Academic, 2011), 58. Arminians recognize the relational dynamic of the elect's union with Christ, where God foresees faith and their relation to Christ; see J. Matthew Pinson, *40 Questions About Arminianism* (Grand Rapids: Kregel Academic, 2022), 287. However, election in the Arminian view is still predicated upon foreseen faith.
13. D. A. Carson, *Divine Sovereignty and Human Responsibility: Biblical Perspectives in Tension* (Eugene, OR: Wipf & Stock, 2002), 198.
14. Horton, *For Calvinism*, 55.

is owed to God's own purposes and grace granted from all eternity, said Paul in 2 Timothy 1:9, and as one who is faithful to his eternal purpose, we can be confident that the sovereign God will prevail, as all his promises are sure.

Summary

We have discussed how the Reformed and non-Reformed traditions understand predestination and election differently. The Reformed tradition bases predestination in the eternal will of God, while the non-Reformed tradition places it in God's foreknowledge of human actions. We have concluded that the biblical evidence sides with a view that sees God's predestination to be bound within his eternal will, giving certainty that God's plans will prevail. We may conclude that human salvation has been predetermined from eternity past based upon God's sovereign will. If that is the case, we may then ask, Is election individual, comprised of the members of God's choosing, or is it corporate, comprised of the people who believe in Christ for their salvation? It is to that question we turn next.

REFLECTION QUESTIONS

1. What is the relationship between predestination and election in salvation?
2. Is predestination sourced in what God wills or what he foreknows?
3. If predestination is relational rather than informational, how does that affect our view of God's relation to the elect?
4. Can God's purposes in salvation fail to come to pass?
5. What implications are raised if someone chooses election to be rooted in God's will or his foreknowledge of human choices?

QUESTION 10

Is Election Individual or Corporate?

One of the persisting questions of the Christian church is whether divine election is corporate or individual in nature. Arminians are often viewed as the party holding solely to corporate election, while the Calvinist tradition is viewed as holding solely to individual election. However, these perceptions are not altogether accurate.[1] While there are some exceptions and nuances, Arminians do hold to individual election, and Calvinists do not deny the corporate nature of election.

The real issue, in our view, is not whether God elects the church corporately for election (which is true) or whether he elects individuals unto salvation (which is also true), but whether God unilaterally elects persons to eternal salvation apart from human choice. Because Arminians and Calvinists view the basis for divine election differently (discussed in Question 9), they naturally have a very different perspective on the makeup of the elect, and it is that issue we will now explore.

Corporate Election

As the name might suggest, *corporate election* is a view that believes that God chooses to save a particular group of people. The view differs from universalism because it affirms that there are indeed some people who are not saved, namely unbelievers. We have affirmed that corporate election of this type generates little disagreement between strongly Reformed and non-Reformed Christians. What is debated is whether God's choice to save that group implies that he has specifically and unilaterally determined who is in that group from eternity past. That distinction is the locus of the debate.

1. For a thorough treatment on the Arminian system of individual and corporate election and the distinctions within that tradition, see J. Matthew Pinson, *40 Questions About Arminianism* (Grand Rapids: Kregel Academic, 2022), 283–91.

Most people within the non-Reformed tradition (comprised of Arminians, certain Baptists, Pentecostals, and others) hold to the primacy of a corporate view of election where God sovereignly elects to save the church (the community of Christians) but does not unilaterally determine the members of it. There are a variety of ways by which this view is understood, but all adherents of this perspective believe that God's plan is to save the church, whose enrollment is open to anyone.[2]

We should be clear, however, that there is an individualistic component to this election. In the Arminian system, God foreordains to eternal life the specific individuals who he foresees will believe in him. Relatedly, he conditionally and individually reprobates people who he foresees will reject the gospel. On this matter, John Wesley viewed individuals as belonging either to the elect or the reprobate. In divine omniscience, God foreknows how people will respond to the gospel. If they choose to believe, they are part of the foreknown elect, the corporate body of Christ whom God will save. Should they respond in disbelief, they are among the reprobate (and subsequently are not elect).[3]

How corporate election relates to individual election is a matter of nuance within this perspective. William Klein, an Arminian scholar, argues that God has elected to save a corporate body of believers, namely the church, in something he calls *corporate solidarity*. For him, election means that God has chosen to save the church, the chosen body, and those who exercise saving faith receive the gift of eternal life. However, the church is not comprised of individuals who have placed faith in Christ; thus, there is no individual election to salvation. Rather, just as God chose the Israelites as his chosen people (with emphasis upon the community and not the individual), he has chosen the church to be the corporate people of the redeemed (and not individuals within it).[4] Other Arminian scholars, like Robert Picirilli, affirm that election is individual and eternal in nature; however, there is some nuance. God is outside of time, and out of his foreknowledge he knows who will belong to the corporate body of the elect.[5] One final view that fits within this category is that God individually elects Christ, but those who belong to Christ become

---

2. Brian Abasciano, "Clearing Up Misconceptions About Corporate Election," *Ashland Theological Journal* 41 (2009): 59–90.
3. John Wesley, *Calvinism Calmly Considered* (Salem, OH: Schmul Publishing, 2001), 23.
4. William W. Klein, *The New Chosen People: A Corporate View of Election* (Eugene, OR: Wipf & Stock, 1990), 257–65.
5. Robert E. Picirilli, *Grace, Faith, Free Will* (Nashville: Randall House, 2002), 51–57; see also Pinson, *40 Questions About Arminianism*, 283–91. For another nuanced perspective, see Richard Land, "Congruent Election," in *Whosoever Will: A Biblical-Theological Critique of Five-Point Calvinism*, eds. David L. Allen and Steve W. Lemke (Nashville: B&H Academic, 2010), 53–59.

the elect of God (corporately) as his one body.[6] In this view, election is limited only to Christ, and all people may become elect in Christ.

Despite some differences, the corporate election view asserts that election to salvation refers to God's choice to save the body of believers in Christ, that he does not unilaterally determine who belongs to that body of believers, and that he foreknows from eternity past how each person will respond to the gospel. Scriptural support used for the corporate election view largely coincides with texts used to support unlimited atonement and God's universal love for humanity. F. Leroy Forlines, for example, looks to John 3:16 to support corporate election. Against the backdrop of Jewish nationalism where Jews assumed their salvation by virtue of the Abrahamic covenant, Forlines argues that in John 3:16 Jesus introduced the radical notion that election is now corporate, encompassing "whosoever will believe."[7] Other scholars, pointing to Romans 9–11, argue that election, for Paul, is God's choice to bring salvation to the entire world, making all people savable if they choose to place their faith in Christ.[8]

Individual Election

Contrasting corporate election is individual election. This view, in this instance, believes God has from eternity past predetermined the specific individuals he will save through Christ. Unlike corporate election, which believes election is up to the will of a person, this view believes election is up to the will of God alone from eternity past (discussed in Question 9). The precise number of the elect is set and determined, and it is comprised of certain individuals over and against others, all by divine motive.

John Calvin thought individual election was both the clear teaching of Scripture and the only way salvation could be of grace, not merit. He stated:

> God separated out from others certain men as seemed good to Him. It is this that is expressed by the word predestinating. . . . To make faith the cause of election is quite absurd and at variance with the words of Paul. For, as Augustine wisely observes, he does not call them elect

---

6. See William G. MacDonald, "The Biblical Doctrine of Election," in *The Grace of God and the Will of Man*, ed. Clark H. Pinnock (Minneapolis: Bethany House, 1989), 207–29.
7. F. Leroy Forlines, *Classical Arminianism: A Theology of Salvation*, ed. J. Matthew Pinson (Nashville: Randall House, 2011), 188.
8. See Eric Hankins, "Commentary on Article 6: Election to Salvation," in *Anyone Can Be Saved: A Defense of "Traditional" Southern Baptist Soteriology*, eds. David L. Allen, Eric Hankins, and Adam Harwood (Eugene, OR: Wipf & Stock, 2016), 98–100; and Eric Hankins, "Romans 9 and the Calvinist Doctrine of Reprobation," *Journal for Baptist Theology and Ministry* 15, no. 1 (2018): 62–74.

> because they are about to believe, but in order that they may believe.[9]

Notice that, for Calvin, individual election is rooted in God's separation of people according to his own will, not the foreseen will of sinners. Faith does not cause someone to become elect; it is a sign that a person is elect.

Michael Horton similarly argues for individual election when he comments this way on Romans 9: "God is not arbitrarily choosing some and rejecting others. Rather, he is choosing some of his enemies for salvation and leaving the rest to the destiny that all of us would have chosen for ourselves."[10] Horton acknowledges that God elects the church as the corporate body of the elect; however, he individually saves some people out of their own willful rebellion. Citing Romans 9, Ephesians 1, and 2 Timothy 1:9, Horton affirms that Scripture teaches God's election from eternity past of specific individuals to salvation, not individuals who are elected by their will or exertion.[11]

A Survey of Scripture

As we have seen, the locus of the debate is not whether election is individual or corporate in nature, nor is it ultimately about whether it is *primarily* individual or *primarily* corporate in nature. The question, to both Arminian and strongly Reformed traditions, is whether God unilaterally elects individuals to salvation or merely foreknows human choice. Below, we will survey select texts, not in an attempt to produce more proof texts than the counterview but to determine whether God elects individuals and the wider community unilaterally or in light of foreseen faith.

It is significant to note that across both Testaments, God's people are called the "chosen ones" (1 Chron. 16:13; Ps. 105:6, 43; Isa. 65:22; Luke 18:7; Col. 3:12; 1 Peter 2:9), not the choosing ones. What made these individuals part of the elect community was not their choice of God but God's choice of them. Their response always followed divine covenantal grace. God did not merely make a covenant pathway; he made a covenant people.

We see divine initiative before human initiative in the gospel of John where Jesus affirmed that those who come to him for eternal life are those whom the Father has given him (6:37–44). These people did not choose Christ, but he chose them (15:16) and referred to them as his "sheep" who have eternal life because the Father gave them to him (10:27–29). Moving to Paul, we find the apostle closely tethered faith in Christ to election in places such as 1 Thessalonians 1:4–5 and 2 Thessalonians 2:13. However, in both of

---

9. John Calvin, *Concerning the Eternal Predestination of God*, trans. J. K. S. Reid (Louisville: Westminster John Knox, 1997), 68–69.
10. Michael Horton, *For Calvinism* (Grand Rapids: Zondervan Academic, 2011), 57.
11. Horton, *For Calvinism*, 60–62.

these texts we see that a believer's faith was preceded by God's choice of them. Their faith was evidence of their election, not a condition to it. Additionally, Paul said that "he chose us," "he predestined us," and "we have obtained an inheritance, having been predestined" (Eph. 1:4–5, 11). The focus at this juncture should not be on "us" as individuals or "us" as community but on God as the one who chose. Election is God's choice of persons, not foreknowledge of people who choose him.

While faith and obedience are of utmost importance in relation to membership within this community, there are multiple examples throughout Scripture of God electing persons who failed to have faith and obedience (at least initially). While we will explore this issue more in Question 11, here we affirm that it is the will of God alone that calls people into fellowship with the elect community (1 Cor. 1:9). That is, the will of God brought someone into the elect community, not the will or anything intrinsic within the individual (1 Cor. 1:26–29). The church is not a human institution brought about by the common will of individuals but a divine institution brought about by divine will (Rom. 11:5–7). It is individual in nature but not because of any individual other than God. Likewise, it is corporate in nature not because of corporate consensus but because of God's ultimate purposes for that community.

Summary

Upon exploring the individual and communal nature of divine election, we have made the following conclusions. First, God has chosen specific individuals to fulfill a predetermined plan that aligns with his saving promises in Christ. These people and their salvation were divine appointments, not possibilities. God did not hope that people would become his people (suffering the disappointment that many people would never actually be his). Rather, he created a people for his own possession. While the examples above entailed each person's will and obedience, membership into God's community was based upon God's initiative, not that of the person. Second, election of individuals comprises the community of God. With Christ as the chosen one and central head, the many parts come together to form the one body (Rom. 12:4–5; 1 Cor. 12:12–27). Thus, election is both individual and corporate. Third, God's election of persons and communities was, both in conception and construction, based upon the will of God alone. It was not dependent upon or caused by the will or working of any mere mortal. Some models of divine election make it where God does not ultimately choose anyone to salvation; people choose him. All God determines is the plan or agency of salvation, not persons.[12] Such a view misses the many Scripture passages that speak of God, out of his will, choosing individuals for salvation. Thus, we

12. Carl Bangs, "Arminius: An Anniversary Report," *Christianity Today*, October 10, 1960, 18.

conclude that election is of individuals who compose a community that has been formed and sustained by the will and working of God alone.

REFLECTION QUESTIONS

1. Is election solely corporate or both individual and corporate, in your view? Explain.
2. How does your understanding of the individual or corporate nature of election affect your view of where election is sourced?
3. What biblical support can you give for your view on the makeup of the elect?
4. What are the main underlying concerns of those who hold the view opposite yours?
5. How would you respond to those concerns given from the opposing perspective?

QUESTION 11

Is Election Conditional or Unconditional?

The past two questions have been closely related, and the current one is just as connected. If divine election is sourced in God's will, then he has determined the members of the elect. If, however, election is sourced in God's foreknowledge of how free creatures will act, then God has merely determined that there will be a corporate body of the elect. Let us consider further implications of whichever view we hold. If election is primarily corporate and not individual, then God merely sets the conditions to become members of the elect community while foreknowing whether or not people meet those conditions. This view aligns with many within the Arminian tradition. However, if election is sourced in God's will alone from eternity past, there are no conditions to be met in order to become part of the elect. God elects whoever he wills from eternity past for reasons known only to him. The issues at hand have been historically framed around the conditionality or unconditionality of divine election, and they are ultimately trying to understand why some people are chosen for salvation while others are not. We will explore both sides of this issue, beginning with the view of conditional election.

Conditional Election

Conditional election means that God has placed some type of condition or qualifier a person must meet in order to become a part of the elect community. What that condition is has been debated throughout church history and was particularly pressing for some early church fathers. As discussed in Question 2, Origen believed God's election is based upon foreknowledge of future piety and holiness.[1] John Chrysostom similarly believed God elects

1. Origen, "On First Principles" in *Ante-Nicene Fathers*, compiled by A. Cleveland Coxe, ed. Alexander Roberts, et al., 10 vols. (Peabody, MA: Hendrickson, 2012), 3.1.20.

people out of his foreknowledge of who will be worthy of salvation, namely people who possess a great pearl (goodness) lying in their nature.[2] For these individuals (and others), the condition of becoming elect is holiness, good works, and merit.

After the works of Augustine and the Pelagian controversy, however, the belief that humans had to meet the condition of obedience and worth became scarcer (though not altogether extinct). The more common condition to be met, found today in Roman Catholicism and the Arminian tradition, is faith in Jesus Christ. According to the *Catechism of the Catholic Church*, God's predestination in salvation entails how each person will freely respond to the grace offered in Christ (§600). Such predestination is not absolutely determinative because it is merely knowledge of how each person will choose to respond to grace (see §1037).

The Arminian tradition shares a similar view. God, out of his foreknowledge, predestines salvation for people he knows will believe.[3] In their view, in order for God to maintain his innate goodness and for human beings to be responsible for their actions, election must be conditioned upon how how people use their free will to respond to the gospel invitation. If election is not based upon a person's response to the gospel but is merely at the whims of God, then God would desire the greatest evil against some of his creatures by punishing them eternally for rejecting a salvation never truly offered to them (thus implicating God with evil and denying his love for all humanity).[4]

When this tradition affirms faith as the condition of election, they affirm that such election is owed all to grace and not human merit. Granted, a person has to believe in Christ in order to be among the elect, but coming to a point of belief is the work of God alone (thus, this view is not Pelagian). However, many adherents to this tradition also believe salvation may be lost if the condition of faith is not continually met.[5] Biblical support for conditional election is scarce, as some scholars in this tradition admit,[6] yet it appears to be the best way to reconcile what they see to be the clear teaching of Scripture regarding God's love for humanity, the universal atonement of Christ, the freedom of people, and the goodness of God.

---

2. John Chrysostom, "Homily XVI on Rom ix.1" in *Nicene and Post-Nicene Fathers*, ed. Philip Schaff, 14 vols. (Peabody, MA: Hendrickson, 2012), 466.
3. "My Own Sentiments on Predestination," in *The Works of James Arminius*, trans. James Nichols and W. R. Bagnall, 3 vols. (Spring Valley, CA: Lamp Post, 2009), 1:185. See also article 1 of the *Articles of the Remonstrants*.
4. Mildred Bangs Wynkoop, *Foundations of Wesleyan-Arminian Theology* (Kansas City, MO: Beacon Hill, 1967), 51–57.
5. Jerry L. Walls and Joseph R. Dongell, *Why I Am Not a Calvinist* (Downers Grove, IL: IVP, 2004), 80–84. See also *Catechism of the Catholic Church*, §162.
6. See F. Leroy Forlines, who stated, as an Arminian, that the Bible does not say that foreknown faith is the condition to be met for election (*Classical Arminianism: A Theology of Salvation*, ed. J. Matthew Pinson [Nashville: Randall House, 2011], 186).

Unconditional Election

Contrasting conditional election is *unconditional election*, the belief that God's choice of who to save resides entirely within himself and is not conditioned upon any action or trait on the part of people. As there are no conditions to be met by a person in order to be chosen for salvation, God simply chooses anyone he wants to save.

This definition, however, only pushes back the question of the why in election rather than addressing it fully. If unconditional election merely means that God chooses some persons to be saved without consideration of human action or merit, then why did he choose the ones he chose? Charles Hodge, the great Reformed scholar and Princeton theologian, provided a helpful response on this matter, of which we will explore six of his points. First, the final cause for all God's decrees, including election in salvation, is his glory. Citing 1 Corinthians 1:26–31 and Ephesians 2:8–10, Hodge saw everything from the creation of the world to the salvation of sinners as ordained by God for his glory alone. Second, God could have created a different universe with different outcomes, but for reasons known only to him he created the one he did. Third, his decrees are eternal (Eph. 3:9–11; 1 Peter 1:20–21). Knowing the end from the beginning, it is impossible for any of his plans to fail, and they are unified in his purpose of glorifying himself. Fourth and fifth, his decrees are immutable (Isa. 46:9–10; James 1:17) and free (Rom. 11:34). They cannot be changed or altered by human beings. Sixth, God's decrees are efficacious. Whatever he foreordains will surely come to pass (Isa. 14:27) by God either causing or permitting it.[7] Bringing everything together, God has chosen to create the universe he has with the determined outcomes he has set in place in order to bring himself the most glory. The elect are appointed to salvation because God has determined it to be so (for his glory). Therefore, there are no conditions to be met by people.

Unconditional election claims that if election were conditioned upon human action, salvation would no longer be of grace but human merit (Rom. 9:9–18). Augustine, commenting on John 15:16, said:

> We had not yet come to believe on Him, in order to lead to His choosing us; for if it were those who already believed that He chose, then was He chosen Himself, prior to His choosing. But how could He say, "Ye have not chosen me," save only because His mercy anticipated us? Here surely is at fault the vain reasoning of those who defend the foreknowledge of God in opposition to His grace, and with this view declare that we were chosen before the foundation of the

7. Charles Hodge, *Systematic Theology*, 3 vols. (Peabody, MA: Hendrickson, 2013), 1:535–45. See also Question 16.

> world, because God foreknew that we should be good, but not that He Himself would make us good. So says not He, who declares, "Ye have not chosen me."[8]

Addressing the Problems of the Why in Election

As mentioned above, the main objections against unconditional election include God's foreordaining the demise of the unsaved, his denying the opportunity for all people to be saved, and his actually not loving all people (which seems to go against the clear teaching of Scripture). In response, we may make the following assertions. First, affirming unconditional election to salvation does not necessitate affirming double predestination (or double, unconditional election) where God predestines not only the salvation of some people but the condemnation of others.[9] Again, unconditional election means that God has appointed certain persons to *salvation* for reasons known only to him, not that he has appointed certain persons for *condemnation*. The broadly Reformed tradition has never affirmed that God holds people back from believing in Christ. Sinners reject Christ and his gospel through their own willful, voluntary sin and disbelief. Unconditional election means that God has chosen to save certain persons apart from people meeting certain demands. It does not necessitate double predestination.

Second, the non-Reformed tradition claims that unconditional election denies the well-meant offer of the gospel, for some people are incapable of believing because they are non-elect (see Question 37). However, the Reformed tradition does not claim that sinners refrain from believing because they were not elect. Rather, sinners do not believe because of their own sin and disbelief. The gospel is to be spread to the ends of the earth (Matt. 28:19–20; Acts 1:8). The call to salvation is for everyone. People who respond with rejection and hardness of heart will be condemned, but they are in such a state by their own actions. Granted, the elect are in a similar state until God changes their hearts, enabling them to believe. Simultaneously, he sovereignly chooses, for reasons known only to him, to let some people remain in their own willful defiance. However, they are responsible for their own sin and disbelief. God is under no obligation to change anyone's heart, nor is he obliged to save anyone. For reasons known only to him, he changes the hearts of the elect, enabling belief, while leaving others in their own willful state of rebellion (see Questions 12 and 30).

Third, in the unconditional election view, God still loves all people and desires their salvation (see Questions 25–26). Because of unconditional election, we may say there is unconditional love. God does not love or save people

---

8. Augustine, "On the Gospel of St. John," in *Nicene and Post-Nicene Fathers*, 86.2, 7:353.
9. See D. A. Carson, *Divine Sovereignty and Human Responsibility: Biblical Perspectives in Tension* (Eugene, OR: Wipf & Stock, 1994), 196. See also Question 13.

who meet certain conditions. He loves—and elects—unconditionally without consideration of foreseen worth or achievement. To affirm unconditional election is to affirm that God has chosen to love and save people apart from what they have done, whether negatively in their sin or positively in their faith. Election is owed all to God, who has shown unconditional grace and love to the least deserving. As Charles Spurgeon once said:

> I believe the doctrine of election, because I am quite certain that, if God had not chosen me, I should never have chosen Him; and I am sure He chose me before I was born, or else He never would have chosen me afterwards; and He must have elected me for reasons unknown to me, for I never could find any reason in myself why He should have looked upon me with special love. So I am forced to accept that great Biblical doctrine.[10]

A few more points are in order. If election is based upon humans meeting a condition, we may rightly say that salvation is a work between God and people (a view called *synergism*; see Question 12). There are many problems with such a view;[11] however, among the highest is that humans may then take partial credit for their salvation. Said another way, our election is due, in part, to what we have done. While adherents to conditional election claim that salvation is owed all to grace, that grace would be nullified, we believe, if it were acquired through human activity (even a divinely enabled human activity). Furthermore, people would have little reason to believe their election (and salvation) were secure if it hinged upon their meeting conditions.

On the contrary, Scripture abundantly describes God's electing activity as based solely upon his choices and not the choices of others. Consider God's election of people. Why did God choose Adam and Eve to be the first parents of the human race? Apparently, it was not anything intrinsic within them, given that they failed to give God the obedience he commanded. Rather, we may assume that God had his own reasons that resulted in his own glory (Gen. 1:31). Consider why God chose Abram to be the father of his covenant people, the nation of Israel, through whom the Messiah would come (Gen. 12–13; 15; 17; 22). Despite Abram serving other gods (Josh. 24:2), he was chosen individually, and his descendants (who constantly resorted to idolatry) were chosen corporately to be God's chosen people over and against others. The line passed through Isaac (not Ishmael) and Jacob (not Esau) to fulfill God's chosen plan

---

10. "A Defence of Calvinism," in *C. H. Spurgeon Autobiography*, rev. ed., 2 vols. (Carlisle, PA: Banner of Truth Trust, 1981), 1:166.
11. See Daniel Kirkpatrick, *Monergism or Synergism: Is Salvation Cooperative or the Work of God Alone?* (Eugene, OR, Wipf & Stock, 2018), 77–83.

(1 Chron. 16:13–18; Ps. 105:6–10; 135:4; Isa. 41:8–9; Rom. 9:11). Moses stated that these people were chosen as the Lord's treasured possession not because of their number (or anything intrinsic) but because of the Lord's love for them (Deut. 4:37a; 7:6–8; see also Ezek. 16:3–6). If election were conditioned upon what is in people, no one would be elect because no one can meet God's standards of perfection. In reflection, we conclude that God elects people unto himself based upon his sovereign choice, not the choice of sinners. Not even faith is a condition to becoming elect. This does not mean faith is irrelevant in the Reformed tradition. Rather, it is the sign that someone is elect, not the means by which someone becomes elect.[12]

Summary

We have explored one of the most pressing questions concerning the doctrine of election: Is it conditional or unconditional? It is intricately related with the source of election. Arminians hold to election being conditioned upon foreseen faith, while the Reformed hold to unconditional election owed to the desires of God alone. We have concluded that election is best understood as unconditional in nature. If such is the case, where does human will come into play? To that important question we shall now turn.

REFLECTION QUESTIONS

1. How does the conditionality of election, explored here, relate to the previous two questions?
2. What questions or concerns are raised in an unconditional election view?
3. What questions or concerns are raised in a conditional election view?
4. Which view do you hold?
5. What scriptural support can you give for your view?

---

12. Michael F. Bird, *Evangelical Theology: A Biblical and Systematic Introduction*, 2nd ed. (Grand Rapids: Zondervan Academic, 2020), 570.

QUESTION 12

How Does Human Will Reconcile with Divine Will in Election?

The previous three questions have been intricately related, and what connects them is more than mere logic. There is an ethical dynamic that must be considered when dealing with divine election, particularly concerning human free agency. Preserving the integrity of the human will and the validity of choices has been of central concern to the Christian church. Fatalism is a pagan, not Christian, notion, so Christians have often sought to understand *how*, not *if*, their will fits under an all-sovereign God. It is beyond question that Scripture calls people to believe in the Lord Jesus for their salvation and to turn away from evil (Mark 1:15; John 1:12; 3:16; 14:1–2; 20:31; Acts 16:31; Rom. 10:9). However, if election is of specific individuals ordained from eternity past and is not conditioned upon the will of people (as has been argued), is that faith real and genuine? Is that not inauthentic and forced faith from the elect, where they were irresistibly saved apart from their own desires?

As we have already discussed and will develop further, the non-Reformed tradition believes a person may accept or resist membership into the elect community, whereas the Reformed tradition believes that God's election is not contingent upon (though it is in correlation with) human will. Each tradition's views are natural consequences of the logical ordering of things described in the previous questions, yet more is at stake. As we will find, the issue of the role of people's will extends to whether God's saving intentions can fail or ultimately be thwarted by mortal beings. To begin our discussion on the involvement of the human will, we will define self-determinism.

Self-Determinism

Because the non-Reformed tradition believes election is voluntarily entered into when the condition of faith is met, they naturally assume that someone cannot be elect apart from personal consent. Again, in this view, election is rooted in God's foreknowledge of how people will respond to the gospel and not predetermined from eternity past by the will of God alone. If such is the case, how is the will specifically involved in this view?

Given the depraving effects of sin, the Arminian tradition fully affirms that faith in Christ is not possible without prevenient grace (see Question 5). Such prevenient grace, however, has been given to all people everywhere, enabling everyone to believe or disbelieve the gospel and allowing anyone the opportunity to become part of the elect community. Prevenient grace brings people to a crossroads of sorts, enabling people to make a free choice either to become saved or not. Should they believe, the results include regeneration, justification, and glorification (and for many within this tradition, only if they persist in the faith). Should they persistently refuse to believe, they remain in sin and will face eternal judgment.[1]

There are various nuances on how to understand the precise function of the human will under this viewpoint. Some scholars adhere to libertarian free will (discussed in Question 6) while others adhere to *moral self-determinism*, a belief where moral acts are caused by oneself and not by something else (God or otherwise).[2] Again, it should be reasserted that without prevenient grace, sin would cause a sinner to act or choose in a particular way. Prevenient grace, however, enables a person to exercise free choice with God only knowing, not causing, the outcome. As it relates to election, a person may freely choose to accept the gospel and become saved or otherwise reject it and not be saved. Believers who persist in such faith were foreknown and foreordained as the elect. God's role is to enable people to choose, and their choice determines their membership into the chosen people of God.

Congruent Will

Although the Reformed tradition fully affirms that elect persons can and do resist the gospel (at least initially—see Question 19), it simultaneously believes that the basis for election resides in God's will, not the human's. This belief is rooted in their understanding of individual, predestined, unconditional election. In this view, the elect were chosen individually before the foundations of the world, independent of their meeting specific conditions such as faith in Jesus Christ. This tradition does not mean that faith in Jesus is absent or superfluous. Rather, their election is based upon the graciousness of God

1. Robert E. Picirilli, *Grace, Faith, Free Will* (Nashville: Randall House, 2002), 153–59. The Reformed Arminian view holds to a nuanced view from Wesleyan Arminians whereby depravity itself is not lessened. See J. Matthew Pinson, *40 Questions About Arminianism* (Grand Rapids: Kregel Academic, 2022), 194–96.
2. Norman Geisler, "God Knows All Things," in *Predestination and Free Will: Four Views of Divine Sovereignty and Human Freedom*, ed. David Basinger and Randall Basinger, Spectrum Multiview Books (Downers Grove, IL: InterVarsity Press, 1986), 75–76.

rather than their own choices. If such is the case, where does the function of the will come into play?

There are a variety of views and nuances within the Reformed tradition on the relation between election and the will; however, they all have a few commonalities. First, humanity's will has been corrupted by sin and is not self-determining. It needs regeneration in order to believe in Christ. Second, faith itself is a gift given to the elect and is a sign that someone is elect, not the means by which someone becomes elect. Third, faith in Christ, when it is expressed, is real and genuine, not forced or insincere. Finally, God's election is efficacious; it will not fail. None of God's immutable decrees, including his will to save, can be thwarted by human beings.

Jonathan Edwards treated this matter at some length in his book *The Freedom of the Will*. He accepted that the will is free, in a limited sense, to do as it desires. However, Edwards then explored why the will desires what it does. In short, the will chooses based upon its strongest motives (which are naturally sinful). Morally impotent, the human will cannot desire the things of God and is itself not self-determining. The divine will, however, is absolute, eternal, and efficacious even over the human will. In God's providence, he orders (by positive influence or permission) all events that will surely come to pass. Through sovereign grace, God changes the hearts of certain sinners (the elect) whereby they begin to believe in and love God. Thus, the conversion of the elect is very real and genuine. Most importantly for Edwards, God's sovereign purposes in salvation are certain and do not fail.[3]

This view is often called *determinism*, the belief that conditions exist upon the human will that incline it to act in a particular way whereby things cannot be. Determinism is not to be confused with *fatalism*, the belief that things are the way they are so there is no other possible way they could be otherwise. Fatalism assumes an inherent necessity where things are as they are because there is no universe that could possibly exist whereby things could be different. Determinism, on the other hand, affirms that things could have been different than they are; however, given that things are as they are, there are consequences that necessarily follow.

One way of understanding determinism may be called *hard determinism*, a belief where people are forced to act against their will because of constraints placed upon them (by God or something else). In this view, God may have forced people to act in a way which goes against what they naturally want to do. The alternative view may be called *soft determinism* or *compatibilism*, the belief that people act in accordance with their own desires in a way that is

---

3. "The Freedom of the Will," in *The Works of Jonathan Edwards*, 2 vols. (Carlisle, PA: Banner of Truth Trust, 1979), XIV, 1:87–89.

genuine and true to what they desire; however, those desires render people's choices and actions certain.[4]

As it relates to sin and salvation, a compatibilist view would affirm that the sinful heart always chooses what is evil. The will lacks the capacity to do what is good and pleasing to God, including exercising faith. This inability does not excuse people from doing what they ought to do, so they are all morally culpable for their sins, which they freely desire to do. God, however, changes the inward disposition of people to desire something other than what they naturally desire. He effects this change in the hearts of the elect while leaving the rest to do what their hearts naturally desire to do—namely, disbelieve the gospel and remain in sin.

Arguments for Compatibilist Election

Our view is that the involvement of the human will in divine election is best understood through a compatibilist perspective. This view affirms that people act in accordance with what they truly desire to do. Therefore, it gives the best rationale for why depraved sinners act in rebellion to God freely and with full responsibility for their actions (John 3:20; Rom. 8:7–8; 1 Cor. 2:14; 2 Cor. 4:4; Eph. 2:3). Sinners act in accordance with their nature, and God does not force (nor is responsible for) sin or unbelief on the part of sinners. It further gives strong rationale to the genuineness of faith among the elect, for it is what they want to do.

Moreover, this view best explains salvation by grace. In this view, God changes the hearts of undeserving sinners through regeneration and gifts them with faith (John 6:29; Acts 16:14; Eph. 2:8–9). The moral self-determinism view, on the contrary, believes people are elect because they choose it. Simply put, some people had the foresight (originating within themselves as a response to prevenient grace) that salvation in Christ would be better than condemnation. If all things are equal (and all people are under prevenient grace), then self-determinism means that certain people made better decisions than others, giving them grounds for boasting. However, election (rooted in the will of God, not the will of people) ensures election is all of grace, giving no grounds for human boasting (Eph. 2:8–9).[5]

Granted, a self-determinism view affirms both the corrupting powers of sin and prevenient grace. That grace, however, only brings a person to a state of neutrality where faith is intrinsically summoned, which causes a person to become saved (meeting the condition of election).[6] The problems sur-

---

4. For an overview, see John Feinberg, "God Ordains All Things," in Basinger and Basinger, *Predestination and Free Will*, 19–43.
5. See D. A. Carson, *Exegetical Fallacies*, 2nd ed. (Grand Rapids: Baker Academic, 1996), 121–22.
6. As mentioned above, Pinson believes that prevenient grace does not lessen depravity; however, this does not resolve the issue. Pinson speaks of prevenient grace as God drawing

rounding such synergism in election will be explored in Question 14. We may here highlight some issues with this view of prevenient grace. First, Scripture nowhere indicates that someone is in a state of complete neutrality. Someone is dead in trespasses and sin or alive in Christ, in darkness or in the light, enslaved to sin or free in Christ. There is no third state. Second, the Arminian tradition wishes to assert that faith must precede regeneration and election lest God impose his will on the unwilling. That assertion, however, falls short. A compatibilist view, as argued for here, does not claim God forces people to will something other than what they desire. Rather, it asserts that people's choices are determined by a controlling influence leading them to will what they will. Sin controls the appetites of the depraved, leading them to will what they will. God must change people's hearts (through full regeneration) so that they can will for something different, even to believe in the gospel.[7] Here, Arminians say that God would then be violating the human will, forcibly changing its desires. Arminians, however, admit just as much with their doctrine of prevenient grace whereby God superseded their natural depravity and hostility.[8]

What should thus be clear is that a regenerated heart does not make faith insincere; it makes it possible. Having the heart of stone replaced with a heart of flesh does not negate the sincerity of saving faith. Rather, it makes sincere faith possible. In this framework, people do what they truly want to do, but if people are to believe, their will must be regenerated.

Finally, and significantly, a compatibilist understanding of faith and the human will ensures that God's purposes in salvation never fail. It is true that the Lord does not desire for anyone to perish but for all to come to repentance (2 Peter 3:9). Regrettably, that very thing fails to happen every day as sinners perish into eternity. This retribution is not God's desire. Human rejection of the gospel, however, does not mean the saving purposes of God have failed (Rom. 9:6). The continual testimony of Scripture is that the Lord never fails to accomplish his purposes, nor can mere mortals thwart divine plans (Job 42:2; Isa. 14:24, 27; 46:10; Acts 5:38–39). Rather, God sovereignly permitted certain persons to do exactly what they wanted to do (sin and disbelieve), making them responsible for their actions while changing the hearts of some persons

---

and illuminating people in their depravity. But Scripture presents depraved people as spiritually dead and blind. In such a condition, they cannot respond to the drawing or see the illuminating light of the gospel unless God first changes their condition through full regeneration.

7. See Question 31, and Daniel Kirkpatrick, "An Exegetical and Theological Argument for the Priority of Regeneration in Conversion," *Mid-America Journal of Theology* 31 (2020): 89–101.
8. For a thorough evaluation of prevenient grace, see Daniel Kirkpatrick, *Monergism or Synergism: Is Salvation Cooperative or the Work of God Alone?* (Eugene, OR: Pickwick, 2018), 116–25, 150–53.

(for reasons known only to him) to desire Jesus Christ as Savior. In a non-Reformed view, the plans and purposes of God are constantly frustrated as God fails to achieve what he desires for human salvation. In the view argued for here, God has and will always have the victory, having saved those whom he purposed to save. He gives every consideration to the human will either by permitting them to remain in their willful rebellion or by changing their affections and gifting them faith.

Summary

Understandably, there are difficulties in understanding how divine election relates to the human will, and the issue is far more complex than what can be treated here. However, we have presented two major perspectives on this issue. The non-Reformed tradition, holding to libertarian free will or self-determinism, believes that sin has indeed corrupted the will but that prevenient grace liberates it, enabling people to express faith freely, which leads to election. Their view of prevenient grace was questioned here, and a compatibilist view was suggested instead. In that view, a person's will acts according to its own desires in a way that is real and genuine yet determined by influences. Some people's will remains controlled by sin, leading them to act in sin and disbelief, while the elect's will is transformed and faith is given so that new genuine desires emerge. In this way, the will of humans is genuinely involved in the salvation process while God's eternal decrees are sure to prevail.

REFLECTION QUESTIONS

1. What is the difference between moral self-determinism and compatibilism?
2. Are there reasons why the human will chooses what it does?
3. Can faith be sincere if God has to transform the human heart?
4. Do you agree or disagree with the non-Reformed view of prevenient grace? In either case, why?
5. Can the plans and purposes of God be thwarted by people?

QUESTION 13

Does God Elect Some People to Hell?

There has been a logical flow of thought explored over the past several questions that almost necessitates the response of all subsequent questions. If God elects only a community of people (namely the church) and not specific persons, then he merely foreknows how people will respond to the only condition for entry, namely faith in Christ. These views, found in the non-Reformed tradition, logically flow one to the other. By holding to such views, they escape the next logical implication much easier than their Reformed counterparts, which concerns double predestination and reprobation. In the non-Reformed view, God would certainly not predetermine to unconditionally reprobate someone to hell from eternity past, just as he does not unconditionally elect someone to heaven. Each person is able to accept or reject the gospel, making each person responsible for his or her eternity.

The Reformed tradition, on the contrary, holds to individual, predestined election based solely within the will of God apart from any conditions being met by the person (including faith). If that is the case, would not that logically mandate that God foreordains the demise of the non-elect? Would sinners, in this view, not be in hell because of their sin and disbelief but because they were appointed to such an end with no possibility for things to be otherwise? These objections have been prevalent throughout church history and are among the most difficult to answer. Below, we will explore the issue in greater detail.

Understanding Reprobation

The Greek noun for *reprobation*, *adokimos*, is rarely used in the New Testament.[1] The term is translated as "unqualified, worthless, base," and its

1. See Rom. 1:28; 1 Cor. 9:27; 2 Cor. 13:5–7; 2 Tim. 3:8; Titus 1:16; and Heb. 6:8.

antonym, *dokimos*, refers to "testing" and "certifying" something to be true.[2] *Adokimos* often refers to faith that did not stand the test of time or trial or was otherwise shown to be disingenuous.[3] As for a general definition of *reprobation*, Peter Sammons states: "Reprobation is defined as the eternal, unconditional decree of God for the non-elect. In this decree, he chooses to exclude the non-elect from his electing purposes of mercy and to hold them accountable to the strict standards of justice to display the glory of his righteous wrath."[4] Thus, by an eternal, unconditional decree, God excludes the non-elect from mercy and salvation because of his purposes and choice while also holding them accountable for their sin.

There are two elements within the decree of reprobation. The first part is called *preterition*, a belief that God predestines the non-elect to remain in their depraved state, abandons them in their willful rebellion, and passes over them with saving grace. This view entails an active and eternal decree from God but is passive in its execution; he merely passes over them while distributing mercy. This is the view of Wayne Grudem who, like the Canons of Dort, defines reprobation as, "the sovereign decision of God before creation to pass over some persons, in sorrow deciding not to save them, and to punish them for their sins, and thereby to manifest his justice."[5]

A second element of reprobation that is more active in nature is called *precondemnation* (or *predamnation*), a belief that God determines that certain individuals be held to standards of justice without consideration of their actions.[6] Precondemnation is so called because it is a decision made by God before (pre-) a life lived. Note that precondemnation is merely a determination from eternity past (which will surely occur) and not the application of holding someone to justice (which occurs at condemnation). Sinners are condemned based upon their sin in this view. Yet God sovereignly and unilaterally appointed them to that end from eternity past without any offense having yet been done. Romans 9 is often used as the primary proof text for these views.

Alternative Viewpoints

With reprobation explained, we may now seek to determine various viewpoints on reprobation to determine if God elects some people to hell. For

---

2. Walter Bauer, *A Greek-English Lexicon of the New Testament and Other Early Christian Literature*, eds. and trans. William F. Arndt, F. Wilber Gingrich, and Frederick W. Danker, 3rd ed. (Chicago: University of Chicago Press, 2000), s.v. ἀδόκιμος, δόκιμος.
3. Gerhard Kittel, ed., *Theological Dictionary of the New Testament*, 10 vols. (Grand Rapids: Eerdmans, 1978), s.v. δόκιμος.
4. Peter Sammons, *Reprobation and God's Sovereignty: Redeeming a Biblical Doctrine* (Grand Rapids: Kregel Academic, 2022), 47.
5. Wayne Grudem, *Systematic Theology: An Introduction to Biblical Doctrine*, 2nd ed. (Grand Rapids: Zondervan Academic, 2020), 834.
6. Sammons, *Reprobation and God's Sovereignty*, 123.

the sake of focus, we will summarize four alternative views: a non-Reformed view, an equal ultimacy double predestination view, an unequal ultimacy double predestination view, and a single predestination view.[7]

As we have explored the Arminian view at length throughout our study, we will merely summarize it here. In this perspective, God does predestine, in a sense, a person to heaven or hell based upon what he foresees as a person's free response to the gospel. People whom God sees as accepting the gospel are the elect and are predestined for glory while people who reject the gospel are predestined to condemnation.

An *equal ultimacy double predestination* view is a belief where God predestines both the elect to heaven and the non-elect to hell while also working actively in the lives of both elect and reprobate to bring about that end. God is the sole (or ultimate) agent, who works equally in the hearts of the elect and reprobate to bring about either belief or unbelief in accordance with his double, predestined will (hence the name). This view is often called *hyper-Calvinism* and is rejected by most Calvinists and adherents of the Reformed tradition, given that God would be working unbelief and disobedience into the hearts of the non-elect (which raises moral concerns).[8]

The next alternative is *unequal ultimacy double predestination*, a belief that God predestines people either to heaven or hell but only works positively in the hearts of the elect to bring them to belief, negatively leaving the non-elect to themselves (not creating unbelief in their hearts or coercing them to sin). This view is unequal in that God works in the hearts of the elect and non-elect differently (with the elect getting active involvement and the non-elect getting passed by), yet it is still ultimate in that God has eternally decreed to predestine both the elect to heaven and the non-elect to hell. This view is widely accepted within Calvinism.[9]

The final alternative we will explore is *single predestination*, a belief that God predestines the elect to salvation yet leaves the rest to their own willful sin and disbelief, resulting in their just condemnation. In this view, reprobation (as defined above whereby God foreordains from eternity past the demise of the non-elect) is rejected because God only predestines the elect to salvation, not the rest to condemnation (hence the predestination is only single).

Evaluating the Perspectives

The overarching question here is why certain sinners are in hell. The two pillars that orthodox Christianity must hold to is that people are in hell because of their sin and disbelief (Luke 13:27–28; John 3:18; Rom. 2:6–8; 6:23;

7. See Sammons, *Reprobation and God's Sovereignty*, 112–14.
8. R. C. Sproul, *Chosen by God* (Wheaton, IL: Tyndale House, 1986), 142–43. Sproul rejects this view.
9. Sammons, *Reprobation and God's Sovereignty*, 113; Sproul, *Chosen by God*, 142–48.

Rev. 21:8) and that God's judgment over them is just (Deut. 32:4; Ps. 145:17; Rom. 9:14). Thus, we may reject any notion of reprobation that asserts that sinners receive eternal retribution solely because of God's ordination. Such retribution would deny that sinners are in hell because of sin and unbelief while also denying that God's judgment over them is just. Although an equal ultimacy double predestination view would affirm that sinners commit sins worthy of eternal judgment, we must consider that such sin was caused not solely by their own will, but by God's. This sin would be coerced, leading to moral ramifications on the character of God. We find that Scripture attributes all sin to the corrupted will of people, making them alone culpable for their actions and deserving of judgment (James 1:13–15). Thus, we reject equal ultimacy double predestination.

The Arminian tradition wishes to equate predestination with foreknowledge of the free actions of creatures. Biblically, however, foreknowledge is primarily an intimate knowledge of persons, a relational knowledge more so than a factual knowledge of people's actions.[10] The clearer teaching of Scripture in our view is that there is at least election and predetermination of individuals from eternity past unto salvation based solely upon the will of God (Luke 12:32; John 13:18; Rom. 9:15–16; Eph. 1:4–5; 2 Thess. 2:13; 1 Peter 2:9). Thus, we reject the Arminian view.

In our analysis, the best alternatives are between unequal ultimacy double predestination and single predestination. Both views affirm the positive side of election (as unto salvation). What must be considered now is whether God's election is double, entailing the condemnation of the non-elect.

Despite objections to the contrary, an unequal ultimacy double predestination view, with its elements of preterition and precondemnation, is an orthodox option because it does not, by default, make God unloving or responsible for human sin. This view fully affirms God's perfect goodness and justice along with human responsibility, primarily through its understanding of secondary causes. Here, humans have the ability to cause things to happen, and they are responsible for their actions. God is not the efficient cause of all events or actions. In other words, he is not the agent who carries out the actions; thus humans are responsible for their own actions. Even still, God is sovereign over all things, and nothing happens without his being the ultimate cause and determiner over all things that ever have existed, including the predestination of the elect to heaven and the reprobation of the non-elect.[11] The primary proof text used to support this view is Romans 9. Exhausting that passage is beyond our scope here, yet we acknowledge that this view of reprobation is an orthodox alternative that merits consideration.

10. See Michael F. Bird, *Evangelical Theology: A Biblical and Systematic Introduction*, 2nd ed. (Grand Rapids: Zondervan Academic, 2020), 565–70.
11. See Sammons, *Reprobation and God's Sovereignty*, 193–204.

In our view, the better alternative is single predestination, whereby God foreordains the salvation of the elect yet leaves the non-elect to their natural devices (thus not foreordaining their demise through precondemnation). The Reformed tradition has interpretations of Romans 9 that do not require preterition or precondemnation.[12] In the unequal ultimacy double predestination view, the non-elect are in hell by God's determination, and while it accounts for God passing by the non-elect with saving grace in a way similar to single predestination, it also affirms that God predestined the non-elect to such an end. In a single predestination view, God permits the sin and disbelief that voluntarily arise within the hearts of the non-elect, leading to certain condemnation without predetermining their eternity in hell before they live. We believe this view preserves God's universal love for the world and desire for all people to come to salvation (Isa. 55:1; Matt. 11:28; John 3:16; 1 Tim. 2:3–4) better than the alternative views. Additionally, we believe it best explains how condemnation over sinners may be just with no culpability being assumed by God. Moreover, this view upholds the notion that the saving intentions of God prevail, as he saves precisely those elect he foreordained to save.

A view of single predestination still has a deterministic view of divine sovereignty and predestination (as mentioned in Question 12) where God is absolutely sovereign and self-determining in all affairs (including human salvation). God's sovereignty, however, is compatible with the human will. Humans act in accordance with their desires, yet their desires are determined outside of their control. Sin and disbelief arise naturally from the human heart. No divine causation is needed there. Thus, people are in hell because of divine consequence, not divine cause.[13] Said another way, the non-elect are left to their own devices, which will result in their certain condemnation. Nevertheless, they are responsible for their sin and disbelief. The elect, while being in a similar condition, have their hearts transformed by the predetermined will of God from eternity past in a moment in time, resulting in a new heart and acceptance of the gospel by faith. The elect were predestined to this end apart from any merit within them, while the non-elect were passed over in this process.

Peter Sammons (an advocate of compatibilism) observes, "The chief objection to compatibilism is that God is still responsible for human sin because he is in control of the factors which influence a person's choice."[14] This objection is partially true, though it is not reason to reject compatibilism. God is, indeed, in *control* of the factors that influence choices because not even sin is

12. Bruce Demarest, *The Cross and Salvation: The Doctrine of Salvation*, ed. John S. Feinberg, Foundations of Evangelical Theology (Wheaton, IL: Crossway, 2006), 135–38; A. H. Strong, *Systematic Theology* (Philadelphia: Judson, 1954), 790; see also William G. T. Shedd, *Dogmatic Theology*, 3 vols. (Grand Rapids: Zondervan, 1969), 1:430.
13. G. C. Berkouwer, *Divine Election*, Studies in Dogmatics (Grand Rapids: Eerdmans, 1960), 183–86, 215–17.
14. Sammons, *Reprobation and God's Sovereignty*, 138.

outside of his control; however, God is not the *cause* of the controlling influence. He controls (or in our language, *determines*) through divine decree all that happens. Yet humans can (and do) act freely in accordance with what they desire to do. They do not act contrary to their wills, nor does God force them to act contrary to what they desire. As sovereign God, however, he is in control of what controls the desires of the human heart and may change them any way he wishes upon whomever he wishes. Additionally, as a self-determined being, God ordains not only his desired ends but also the means necessary to reach those ends in such a way that humans are not fatally forced to act contrary to their wills. Thus, the non-elect are responsible for their sin and are condemned according to it without God being a causal agent that determined that end.

Summary

This difficult question asked whether God reprobates sinners to hell by immutable decree and whether people who hold to individual, unconditional election must hold to such a view. We have explored various viewpoints on this issue, in which some traditions affirm reprobation while others deny it. Our view is that God only predestines the elect unto salvation without being a causal agent to the demise of the non-elect. This approach, we believe, best preserves the moral nature of God while also ensuring the responsibility of people.

REFLECTION QUESTIONS

1. Does predestination of some people to salvation necessitate predestination of others to condemnation?

2. What is the difference between preterition and precondemnation?

3. Which view on reprobation do you hold to and why?

4. Is reprobation compatible with God's love and desire for all people to be saved?

5. Does reprobation cause additional concerns about the character of God in your view?

QUESTION 14

How Does God Elect?

In the non-Reformed system, because God elects corporately based upon foreknowledge of how free people will respond to the gospel, it assumes people take an active role in their election. There is cooperative action that involves God's choice of people and people's choice of God. God does his particular work in designing the plan of salvation along with working in the hearts of people (through prevenient grace) while people do their part in accepting the gospel message and believing in Christ for salvation. This cooperation between God and people is called *synergism*, a belief that salvation (or a particular aspect of salvation) is a work between God and people.[1] The alternative view is *monergism*, the belief that salvation (or a particular aspect of salvation) is solely the work of God.[2] This belief is held by the Reformed tradition, based upon their view that God elects individuals for reasons based solely within his own will from eternity past, apart from any conditions being met by people. Monergists, unlike synergists, believe becoming elect is entirely passive on the part of people and that such people accept and believe that they are recipients of God's election, not that their faith makes them elect.

In this question, we will explore the non-Reformed and Reformed understandings of synergism and monergism as they relate to divine election in order to determine best how God elects. A helpful starting place for this discussion will be understanding divine and human action in terms of cause and effect.

Cause and Effect

Before we discuss causation, we will first define the term *effect*. An effect is the outcome or result of previous actions. It is the product of the operations of some type of causal process. If we were to ask why something is what it is, we can say that it is what it is because someone or something made it that way.

1. *Synergism* comes from the Greek terms *syn* ("with") and *ergos* ("worker").
2. *Monergism* comes from the Greek terms *mono* ("one") and *ergos* ("worker").

If we were to look at a house, for example, we can say that the house is the outcome or effect of builders who made it.

Causation itself is a bit more complex and has a rich history dating back at least to the ancient Greek period within Western philosophy.[3] Put simply, a *cause* is something that produces an event or outcome (whether partly or wholly). There is an *efficient cause* (the primary agent or agents that brings about a change or effect), an *instrumental cause* (a secondary cause that produces an effect that owes its efficacy to the efficient cause), and a *material cause* (the materials out of which the effect is composed). Returning to the analogy of the house, the outcome (or effect) is the house, but the causes are many. There were the builders (the efficient cause), the materials used for the house (the material cause), and the tools to shape those materials into a house (the instrumental cause). Without these causes, there would be no house.

We may utilize this framework as we approach the notion of works, actions, and grace. If an action is causative, it is a contributing factor that a person does. We may understand this type of action as a *work*, an activity done by someone that causes an effect, outcome, or accomplishment that merits a wage. Without such action, the outcome would not be realized nor the goal achieved. In the illustration of the house, the construction crew (efficient cause) and the tools (instrumental causes) must work in order for there to be the outcome (or effect) of the house. The crew and tools, then, can take credit for their work and the outcome.

Contrasting works are *non-causative activities*, actions done by someone that do not cause an effect. Passive and typically receptive in nature, non-causative activities are actions that people do that are neither meritorious nor causative. When applied to the analogy above, the construction team may do everything to build the house yet choose to give that house freely to a person. The person receiving the keys to the house contributed nothing to the house's construction, meaning that person may not take credit for it (though that person may be a grateful recipient). A person's action of receiving the house remains real and authentic, yet that action did not contribute anything to the existence of the outcome. We may apply this framework to synergism and monergism in election.

Synergism in Election

As stated above, the non-Reformed tradition holds to synergism, in which there is cooperation between God and people that leads to election.[4]

3. For an overview of causality, see Helen Beebee, Christopher Hitchcock, and Peter Menzies, eds., *The Oxford Handbook of Causation* (New York: Oxford University Press, 2012).
4. To be clear, many non-Reformed scholars do not identify themselves as synergists, nor do they prefer the label. See J. Matthew Pinson, *40 Questions About Arminianism* (Grand

Election, then, would be the effect, and God and people would be causes, but in what way? The primary claim in non-Reformed circles is that God alone is the efficient cause of election because they (rightly) understand God's grace as the primary cause. They also claim that people's faith is an instrumental cause that is done synergistically with God's acceptance of that faith, which leads to their election. Roger Olson says Arminians "hold a form of evangelical synergism that sees grace as the efficient cause of salvation and calls faith the sole instrumental cause of salvation, to the exclusion of human merits."[5] Thus, God is the chooser who chooses out of grace (as efficient cause), yet people must do their part in believing the gospel (instrumental cause) from their free will (material cause),[6] which meets the condition of election (the effect).

The act of believing, which again is the instrumental cause, is not an effort to champion human ability or deny the efficacy of grace in their view.[7] This tradition is concerned about preserving human responsibility and divine integrity. One author states:

> Just as God does not force a person to sin, neither does he force anyone to accept grace. A person chooses to accept grace when he decides to meet the conditions which God has established for receiving it. Of course, there is no merit in making the decision, for the condition is one of grace and not works. Nevertheless, a person is responsible for making the decision himself. If he does not make it, he has only himself to blame.[8]

Election, thus, is synergistic in this view because people must cooperate with God's grace and meet the conditions necessary in order to attain the effect of election. Everything is attributed to grace because even the act of believing is only possible thanks to prevenient grace, yet it is nevertheless a cause that leads to the effect of election.[9]

Rapids: Kregel Academic, 2022), 145–49. However, their theology that places faith as a condition and cause fits the meaning of synergism, whether they embrace the label or not.

5. Roger Olson, *Arminian Theology: Myths and Realities* (Downers Grove, IL: IVP Academic, 2006), 95. See also Norman Geisler, *Chosen but Free: A Balanced View of Divine Election*, 2nd ed. (Minneapolis: Bethany House, 2001), 69.
6. We will refer to both the human and divine wills as material causes not because there is anything physical or material about them but because they are compositional in nature and provide what is necessary for the instrumental causes to operate.
7. Olson, *Arminian Theology*, 158.
8. Jack W. Cottrell, "Conditional Election," in *Grace for All: The Arminian Dynamics of Salvation*, ed. Clark H. Pinnock and John D. Wagner (Eugene, OR: Resource, 2015), 90.
9. For further treatment, see Daniel Kirkpatrick, *Monergism or Synergism: Is Salvation Cooperative or the Work of God Alone?* (Eugene, OR: Pickwick, 2018), 74–84.

Monergism in Election

The Reformed, monergistic view, on the other hand, sees God (and his will) as the sole cause of divine election. God alone is the efficient cause in whom all electing activity is sourced. His will, expressed by divine decrees, is the material cause by which election is composed. The instrumental cause would be Jesus Christ, as people chosen for salvation were done so in him, and the effect would be the election of individuals. Therefore, election has only one worker, namely God.

This view is built upon what has already been explored throughout this book. Divine election (the effect) is predestined from the eternal will of God (efficient and material causes) of select individuals through Jesus (instrumental cause). The elect did not have to meet any conditions to become elect, including faith. While faith is very much connected to election (as was observed in Question 12), it is receptive in nature, not causative.[10]

A Case Against Synergistic Election

With both sides defined, we now come to a point of evaluation. We begin by critiquing the synergistic perspective concerning their claim that God alone is the efficient cause of salvation. To reiterate, synergists claim that God is the efficient cause of election and that faith is a secondary, instrumental cause. However, it appears that humans serve as efficient causes just as much as they do instrumental causes in this view.

The non-Reformed tradition denies that God is the only one doing the choosing. In fact, God does little choosing aside from determining the means, conditions, and boundaries of salvation, for he merely gives people the opportunity to choose him, then God chooses the people who chose him. God's role in election is to foreknow what people will choose to do out of their free will, then accept the persons who persevere in their choice of him. This view has every indication of making people the efficient causes of their election. While the non-Reformed tradition attributes the very ability to choose to grace, that does not negate the fact that people must be the choosers of God if there is to be divine election.[11] The problem with making humans efficient causes of their election is that their salvation is ultimately attributed to what they did, which nullifies grace and contradicts Scripture (Eph. 1:4–5; 2:8–9).

Additionally, we may also affirm that any form of synergism that causes any aspect of salvation turns faith into a work. Human action that causes an effect to come about and leads to a deserved benefit is rightly understood as a work. Should we claim that our human will (material cause) did the activity of believing (instrumental cause), which met the condition of becoming elect

10. See Kirkpatrick, *Monergism or Synergism*, 68–76.
11. See Geisler, *Chosen but Free*, 40–41.

(the effect), then faith has become a contributing work, with election and salvation being the deserved outcome. We find that this view contrasts with the prevalent New Testament teaching of salvation by grace. As discussed in Question 12, the non-Reformed view affirms that faith originates from within people, and there are some people who (wisely) apply it when others do not. Such independently exercised faith not only causes election, in their view, but it would also give someone grounds for boasting (Eph. 2:9).[12] This view does not seem to best reflect the teaching of Scripture on how God elects.

Figure 14.1: The Causes of Election by Tradition

	Non-Reformed View	Reformed View
Efficient Cause	God and the believer	God
Material Cause	Human's will	God's will
Instrumental Cause	Person's expression of faith	Jesus Christ
Effect	Election	Election

A Case for Monergistic Election

We believe that a monergistic view of election best reflects the teaching of how God elects. We will make this case on exegetical and philosophical grounds. First, out of the major passages of Scripture that speak of election in salvation, God is always the subject of the verb *eklegomai* ("to choose"), and humans are always its object. Said another way, God is the efficient cause and chooser; human beings are the chosen (see Rom. 8:30; 9:11; 11:5; 1 Cor. 1:27–28; Eph. 1:4; 2 Tim. 1:9; 2 Peter 1:10). Scripture attributes the choosing in election to God alone. Jesus said in John 15:16 that his disciples did not choose him but that he chose them. Humans are the recipients of the choosing, not the choosers.

Additionally, Scripture indicates that the material cause of election is the divine will, not human will (discussed in Questions 9–10). Paul said that our predestination to adoption in Christ was according to the intention of God's will (Eph. 1:5, 9–11). He also said in Romans 9:11 that Jacob was chosen over Esau not because of anything good or bad done by either of the twins, but because of God's purpose and according to his choice. Thus, we affirm that the material cause is the divine will, not the human will.

12. See Greg Welty, "Election and Calling: A Biblical Theological Study," in *Calvinism: A Southern Baptist Dialogue*, eds. E. Ray Clendenen and Brad J. Waggoner (Nashville: B&H Academic, 2008), 226.

Moreover, the instrumental cause of election, according to Paul, is Jesus (Eph. 1:5–7), not faith. People who are predestined for salvation are done so through Jesus Christ and bestowed "in the Beloved" (Eph. 1:5–6). With Jesus as the instrumental cause, the elect have no grounds to boast in what they have done through their own efforts. What they have is received by faith but not caused by faith. Should faith be causative, it would become a work that merits an outcome. However, if the instrumental cause is Christ, and the elect are chosen in him, then election is sourced in God's grace and work, not people, giving them comfort and security in their salvation while removing any grounds for boasting.

Summary

How does God elect? This question can be answered either synergistically (where humans work together with God to become elect) or monergistically (where God alone does the electing). We have explored this question by looking at cause and effect. If the effect (or outcome) is election, what caused it? Synergists say election occurs because of divine and human causation in the efficient, instrumental, and/or material causes. We have argued that this view is inadequate because it makes human faith a contributing work that causes election. We instead argue in favor of monergism, which sees God as the efficient cause, his will as the material cause, and Christ as the instrumental cause. The outcome or effect is divine election, and as we have argued elsewhere, the elect believe in Christ as a response to grace, not as something done in order to acquire it.

REFLECTION QUESTIONS

1. What are the various types of causes that lead to an effect?

2. How is God involved in these various causes?

3. Does human faith cause election in your view?

4. What are monergism and synergism?

5. Do you believe election is monergistic or synergistic?

QUESTION 15

When Are the Elect Saved?

We cannot speak of divine election without consideration of timing. As we found in Question 9, election is the predestined plan of God from eternity past that is rooted in his perfect divine will. Consider the implications of such a belief. If God individually chooses certain people to be saved out of his sovereign will and not based upon any conditions found within people, do those beliefs logically require that someone has been saved even before birth (perhaps from eternity past or at the crucifixion of Christ)? If so, what is the purpose of evangelism and conversion? If not, how can someone be elect and not saved? Now, these questions should be distinguished from another important question regarding timing and election that concerns the logical order of God's salvation decrees, which we cover in Question 19. For now, we will focus on when, in time, the elect become saved.

Saved but Not Elect

The first perspective we will explore is the Arminian position, which distinguishes between people who express saving faith and people who are elect. According to Arminius, many non-elect people believe in Christ.[1] Said another way, someone may have expressed justifying faith and be consequently saved, yet for lapses and defections in their lives they forfeit their salvation and therefore will not be among the elect. As we have already observed in Questions 5 and 9–11, election in the Arminian view is primarily understood as God's foreknowledge of how people will freely choose to respond to the gospel *and* persevere in that faith. That is, the elect are only people who God foreknows will persist in the Christian faith. We should

1. "The Apology or Defense of James Arminius," articles 1 and 2. To be clear, article five of the *Remonstrance* left the issue unsettled as to whether someone may lose salvation once it is received, and there are a few Arminian scholars who hold to eternal security in salvation, though Arminius himself rejected it.

not think, in this view, that someone becomes a part of the elect community by meeting the condition of faith, for there are some people who believe initially but fall away. Arminius was certain there are many people who believe the gospel who are not among the elect, for they in due time fall into apostasy. Rather, for Arminius, the elect are people whom God foreknew would persevere in the faith to the end of their lives. While more will be said in Question 18, this Arminian position relates to their view of *universal atonement*, where the cross makes everyone able to be saved but does not, in fact, save and secure anyone.

Eternally Elect but Temporally Saved

Another view is that it is possible to be elect but not yet saved. Found in Reformed traditions, this view affirms that election of people is based solely and unconditionally upon the will of God before time began, but the elect are only saved when they place faith in Christ for salvation at some point in their lives. Granted, people who were elected to this salvation will certainly be saved when God effectually calls them to himself in a moment in time through the proclamation of the gospel, but they are not actually saved until they respond to it in faith. Thus, there is a difference between an eternal decree for someone to be saved (election) and the application of that decree (through faith in the gospel), for only when people believe are they united to Christ and justified for the forgiveness of their sins. Faith did not make them elect. Rather, it made them saved.[2] Consider this statement against the Arminian position from the Canons of Dort: "The quickening and saving efficacy of the most precious death of his Son should extend to all the elect, for bestowing upon them alone the gift of justifying faith, thereby to bring them infallibly to salvation."[3] While election is eternal and unconditional, salvation is by faith that transpires infallibly in a moment in time.

While the Synod of Dort, after much debate, came to affirm limited atonement, some adherents of this view also ascribe to universal atonement. While the differences on the atonement's extent are significant and divisive, the unifying element is that atonement is effective only for the elect. Unlike Arminianism, which believes the cross does not effect salvation for anyone but only makes salvation possible, this view believes the cross effects and secures the salvation of the elect. Still, the benefits of that atonement are not actualized in an elect person's life until they receive the gospel.

---

2. Faith would still be receptive and not causative in this view because faith was given to the elect and only after a prior regeneration by the Holy Spirit, making salvation entirely monergistic. See Michael Horton, *For Calvinism* (Grand Rapids: Zondervan Academic, 2011), 70, and *The Christian Faith* (Grand Rapids: Zondervan Academic, 2011), 566.
3. Canons of Dort, 2.8, in Philip Schaff, ed., *The Creeds of Christendom*, 6th ed., 3 vols. (Grand Rapids: Baker, 1998), 3:587.

Eternally Elect and Eternally Saved

A final view to consider, found within hyper-Calvinism, is the belief that someone may be elect and saved prior to faith. Advocates for this view are rare, though they may be found historically in the seventeenth- and eighteenth-century writings of theologians like Joseph Hussey and John Gill and more modernly in Herman Hoeksema. This tradition believes in eternal justification, eternal adoption, and the eternal covenant of grace whereby the elect were saved prior to their expression of faith, whether that be from eternity past or at the time of Christ's death.[4] In this view, faith is an acknowledgment of the salvation the elect already possess, not a gift to be received in a moment in time for those whom God has eternally decreed to save. This view has been continually rejected by the Reformed tradition and was notably refuted by the Puritan John Flavel.

A Case for Eternal Election and Temporal Salvation

Our view is that divine election is from eternity past, though the act of salvation happens in a moment in time upon a person's conversion. We will make this case first through scriptural analysis, followed by a critique of the hyper-Calvinist and Arminian views.

Beginning with Jesus's teachings on the matter, we look to John 6. In verse 29, we hear Jesus say that God works belief in Christ in the lives of the elect, namely those whom the Father has given to the Son (v. 37). Jesus made clear in verse 40 that the eternal divine will brings these chosen ones to faith, which he reiterated again in verse 44. Here we see that belief in Christ happens in time among the elect. Additionally, in John 15 Jesus spoke of union with Christ (which is only possible by faith) in terms of branches abiding with the vine. In this same message to his disciples, Jesus affirmed that they did not choose him but that he chose them (John 15:16–19). Here we see the connection between eternal election and the need for personal faith (abiding). To abide in Christ is the work of God given to the people God has chosen, yet it is expressed in moments in time.

Peter also affirmed through his epistles that certain people were elected by God for salvation while also affirming that they were born again at a moment in time (1 Peter 1:1–5). Additionally, these people are a chosen race even before they were born, yet in a moment in time they were called out of darkness and into the light of Christ (1 Peter 2:9–10).

The Pauline writings are replete with examples of eternal election and temporal conversion. In the lengthy discourse on eternal divine election in Ephesians 1, Paul affirmed that these elect persons still had to hope in Christ, listen to the message of truth, and believe in it personally (vv. 12–15). Additionally, in

4. For an overview, see Peter Toon, *The Emergence of Hyper-Calvinism in English Nonconformity 1689–1765* (Eugene, OR: Wipf & Stock), 82, 123–24.

2 Thessalonians 2:13–14 Paul affirmed that God chose people from the beginning of time for salvation, yet they were effectually called through Paul's gospel at a moment in time to be saved. While the Colossian church was chosen and beloved of God, there was also a moment in time when they died to their sinful nature and were raised with Christ (Col. 3:1–3, 12).

These texts are critical in helping us form a full picture of salvation. While someone may be elect from eternity past for salvation in Christ, they still need to be united at a moment in time to Christ. Election ensures that the glorious aspects of salvation and the eternal plan of God will prevail in the lives of those whom God appointed to salvation. It does not, however, remove the need for these aspects.[5]

Additionally, when we affirm that people may be elect and not yet saved, we see the necessity and importance of preaching and evangelism. After a lengthy discourse on divine election in Romans 9, Paul stressed in 10:1 that his heart's desire and prayer was for Israel's salvation. However, Israel will not be able to believe in Christ for that salvation (nor anyone else, for that matter) without the gospel being preached (Rom. 10:13–15). All people, including the elect, must hear the gospel of Jesus Christ in order to be saved. Election does not replace the need for conversion. Rather, election makes conversion possible. By God's design, he has decreed not only the persons for election but the plan for saving the elect, namely, the proclamation of the gospel. Accordingly, people whom God has willed to save will hear the gospel, repent of their sins, and believe in Christ for salvation according to the eternal will of God.

The problem with the hyper-Calvinistic view mentioned above is that it fails to distinguish divine election from the other aspects of salvation. That tradition (erroneously) believes that to be elect is to be saved, justified, adopted, and redeemed. However, Scripture portrays these aspects of salvation as distinct from one another, and each aspect is necessary in order to be saved. Additionally, the hyper-Calvinistic view negates the need for conversion and the preached gospel. It renders meaningless all commands in Scripture to repent and believe in Christ. It denies the true desire of the elect to turn away from sin and embrace a beloved Savior for the forgiveness of their sins because all of that was done before they were ever born. Ultimately, it amounts to fatalism that denies human responsibility, and it calls into question the moral character of God, who would save and condemn people based upon his sovereign will alone without consideration of people's response to the gospel.

When we consider again the Arminian view in which someone can be saved without being elect, we encounter many issues. Aside from what was discussed in Questions 9–11 (that election is from eternity past and based upon the will of God) there are reasons we should not assume someone can

---

5. Donald Macleod, *Compel Them to Come In: Calvinism and the Free Offer of the Gospel* (Tain, Scotland: Christian Focus, 2020), 46–48.

be saved without being elect. Paul, in Romans 8:29–39, spoke of those who were predestined for salvation. These predestined are also those who (in time) are called to Christ, leading to their justification and glorification. Paul knew of no theology where someone can be saved apart from being elected. Those people who express faith leading to justification are those who were predestined to this end by God's will. Granted, many Arminians affirm that election is eternal and certain because of the foreknowledge of God. Even still, this tradition affirms that such people may be saved without being elect. This, however, is the opposite view of Paul, where someone may be elect without being saved but may not be saved apart from being elect. What is more, because the verdict of righteousness has been imputed on these elect people's behalf, all charges that could ever be brought before God have been dropped. Because these people were predestined and justified, there is no more condemnation awaiting them nor anything that could separate them from the love of God in Christ. The elect do not need to fear that God would change his mind on ultimately saving them because of their lack of performance, for the performance of Jesus Christ is enough (see Question 20). In the eyes of God, the predestined elect were predestined to be conformed to the image of Christ (Rom. 8:29). God sees the righteousness of Christ on the sinner's behalf leading to his or her justification and ultimate glorification. God's verdict has been made and cannot be undone, not by any created thing (Rom. 8:39)—including people. Thus, we may reject any notion that would suggest that someone may be saved without being among the elect.

Summary

This question explored an element of timing within divine election, namely when God saves the elect. We explored the three primary views on this issue, namely the Arminian view where someone can be saved but not elect, the Reformed view where someone may be elect but not yet saved, and the hyper-Calvinist view where someone may be saved prior to faith. Our conclusion on the matter is that God elects from eternity past but brings about that salvation in moments of time through the proclamation of the gospel and its acceptance at conversion.

REFLECTION QUESTIONS

1. Can someone be saved without being elect, in your view?

2. Conversely, can someone be elect without being saved?

3. Why would belief in eternal justification and eternal redemption become a hyper-Calvinist view as opposed to just a Calvinist view?

4. How is gospel proclamation related to the timing of salvation among the elect?

5. Do the elect need to fear that they may lose their salvation status, or the saved that they may lose their election status?

QUESTION 16

What Is the Ultimate Purpose of Election?

The previous several questions have explored the workings of divine election. The question that remains is, What are all these workings ultimately out to accomplish? As we might expect, there are different answers given to this question. However, unlike previous questions that have led to division and different schools of thought, the answer to the present question brings much common agreement, even if there are differences in which purpose is primary.

Put simply, there are many purposes we can find for election, though we may say that some purposes take priority over others. For example, we may (rightly) think that a purpose of election is to give salvation to sinners so they do not experience God's justice. While true, we may press that answer further on why God might want to save such sinners. An appropriate reply may be that God, full of love, cares for his creatures and desires a relationship with them. Again, while true, we may ask why God would still want to show such love to them. Might there be some ultimate reason, followed by secondary reasons, for divine election? We will explore that answer below.

Finding the Ultimate Purpose

While there are many purposes behind God electing sinners to salvation through Jesus Christ, there must be some parameters. Whatever purposes we may propose must be grounded within Scripture. As we observed in Question 3, historical suggestions include the replacement of fallen angels (per Anselm), as well as to provide a moral guide on how to treat people (per Peter Abelard). Neither of these suggestions finds adequate biblical support. Additionally, any suggested purpose must fall within the parameters of orthodoxy, particularly with regard to *aseity* (Lat. *a se*, "of himself")—the belief that God has life in and of himself as self-existent and self-sufficient Creator with no need or lack whatsoever. God is under no internal obligation (such as loneliness, boredom, or innate need) or external obligation (force, requirement, or pressure) to save anyone. Granted, God's attribute of justice does require him to punish the wicked, but he is not obligated outside himself to save the wicked.[1] Any answer to the purpose of divine election in salvation must be rooted in a desire to save as opposed to an obligation to save.

With these parameters in mind, we may begin evaluating what may be the ultimate purpose of divine election as well as whether that ultimate purpose is central to humanity or God. If we say election is primarily for the sake of human beings, we find that it causes numerous problems. Suppose someone were to say that election's primary purpose is to save as many people as possible so they do not go to hell. According to Scripture and tragic trends seen in the world today, people embracing the gospel and entering heaven are rare (Matt. 7:14). The very purpose of election would be failing daily. Additionally, if the purpose of election resides within people showing pure love to others, as Abelard said, then we may also wonder if the purpose of election will ever prevail in such a broken world as ours, where hate and violence abound. Should we say that God's purpose in election is so that people can have a better life, become better human beings, become healthier and happier, or whatever else that centers on humanity, then we would have to conclude that our greatest problem is not sin before a holy God but a lack of personal fulfillment. Our greatest need would be self-improvement, not salvation, and the purpose for our existence would reside within ourselves, not God. Given that much of the world feels unhappy and unfulfilled, we ultimately would have to conclude that election has been a colossal failure and that God's plan in election is constantly frustrated. In our view, we find that there is no biblical or meaningful way to locate the ultimate purpose of election within ourselves.

On the contrary, when we explore the purposes of divine election from Scripture, we see that they are centered around God with one ultimate, overarching purpose—his glory. The focal text that shows God's purposes in election is Ephesians 1:3–14. Paul said the following in verses 3–6 (NASB):

> Blessed be the God and Father of our Lord Jesus Christ, who has blessed us with every spiritual blessing in the heavenly places in Christ, just as He chose us in Him before the foundation of the world, that we would be holy and blameless before Him. In love He predestined us to adoption as sons and daughters through Jesus Christ to Himself, according to the good pleasure of His will, to the praise of the glory of His grace, with which He favored us in the Beloved.

---

1. The necessity of divine justice does not deny divine aseity because this attribute is *of himself*. God's eternal attribute of justice demands that he punish wickedness, but he is under no obligation to save (making such salvation based upon grace and not obligation).

Many wonderous purposes of election are found in these verses. Paul said in verse 3 that it was certainly the intention of God the Father to bless us with every spiritual blessing. Clearly, our blessing and good finds its way in the kind purposes of God's election. We also read in verse 4 that God chose us so that we would be holy and blameless before him. Clearly, our holiness and sanctification matter to God and fit within his purposes in election. Also from verse 4, we see that divine love for humanity was a driving force for election. No doubt, to express the perfect love of God unto undeserving sinners was a reason God chose to elect people for salvation and send his son to die (John 3:16).

While all these wonderous purposes may be gleaned from this text, they are not the ultimate purpose for God's predestining work in salvation, for that purpose is found in verses 5–6 (NASB) in the phrase "according to the good pleasure of His will, to the praise of the glory of His grace." Here we see that all electing activity is centered in his will to bring praise for his grace among the elect. Paul reiterated this theme of God's desire to be glorified by worshipers in verse 9 (NASB), where he said that our salvation is "according to His good pleasure which He set forth in Him," and again in verses 11–12 (NASB): "having been predestined according to the purpose of Him who works all things in accordance with the plan of His will . . . to the praise of His glory." Finally, in verse 14 (NASB), Paul reiterated that our redemption is "to the praise of His glory." Whatever further conclusions we may make as to the purpose of divine election, we must understand that the primary purpose of election is the glorification of Jesus Christ. Commenting upon this Ephesians 1 passage, the great Wesleyan New Testament scholar I. Howard Marshall wrote, "Salvation is rooted in the purpose and initiative of God. Before the world was even created he planned to have a holy people, and he further destined them to be his children. . . . And all of this redounds in Paul's eyes to the praise of the glory of God's grace."[2] The glory of God as the ultimate purpose in election and salvation is also mentioned elsewhere (see Rom. 8:29–30; 9:11, 17; Heb. 13:20–21; 1 Peter 2:9).

The Ultimate Purpose of the Ultimate Purpose

Why is God's unparalleled glory the ultimate purpose behind his decree to save? Because he has revealed to us that the glorification of Christ has been his will from all eternity. God has eternally desired to have Jesus exalted through the redemption of the world. Our most precious beliefs as Christians (such as the incarnation, the atonement, the bodily resurrection of Jesus, and the high priesthood of Christ) are the eternal plans of God, not

2. I. Howard Marshall, *New Testament Theology: Many Witnesses, One Gospel* (Downers Grove, IL: IVP Academic, 2004), 381. For additional commentary on the primary purpose of God's glory from this text, see Darrell L. Bock, *Ephesians*, Tyndale New Testament Commentaries (Downers Grove, IL: IVP Academic, 2019), 31–42.

mere afterthoughts when Adam and Eve sinned in the garden. The gospel is not some type of Plan B because God's purposes failed. It has always been God's plan to send the Son to take on human flesh, live the perfect life, serve as the atoning sacrifice, be raised by the Spirit, and reign over a restored created order. Simply put, the grand storyline of all time and history has as its central and supreme focus the coronation of the glorified Jesus, who receives a new and glorified heaven, earth, and people, all proclaiming his excellencies forever and ever.

Just as Ephesians 1:4–7 affirms that the elect were chosen to be adopted and redeemed from eternity past, it also affirms that they were chosen for that adoption and redemption in Christ *through his blood* from eternity past. Thus, the shed blood of Christ for the salvation of the elect was the will of God even before time began. The crucifixion, resurrection, and glorification of Christ were eternally planned, not afterthoughts. God has an eternal will executed in real time, all leading to Christ being before and over all things, even head over the church (Col. 1:15–18).

The author of Hebrews stated that the death and resurrection of Christ were part of an eternal covenant given to the specific "sheep" (or elect) to the praise of Christ's glory. As an eternal covenant, we therefore know that the incarnation, death, resurrection, and high priesthood of Christ were all parts of God's eternal plan that would not fail (Heb. 13:20). Thus, while Israel and the Romans who crucified Jesus were responsible for the murder of the Messiah, Peter boldly confessed that the crucifixion, resurrection, and priesthood of Christ were the predetermined and foreknown plans of sovereign God (Acts 2:22–25), all leading to the glorification of Christ (v. 28).

It is here that we become mindful that God's purposes in election are not centered around humanity but God. When we look to the great eschaton and read about what will happen at the return of Christ in Revelation 21:1–7, we see that the old heaven and earth have passed away, and the new order has come. With it comes the new Jerusalem, coming as a bride adorned for her husband. This city is filled with those whose names were written in the Book of Life from the foundation of the world (Rev. 13:8; 21:27), and there the elect from all of earth's nations will forever dwell with and for the Lord, giving him glory forever and ever (21:24, 26). Thus, salvation is more than our own comforts in heaven. It is centered around the eternal plans of God to give Jesus a new heaven and earth filled with worshipers whom he has purchased with his own blood. Salvation extends beyond human beings to the wider fallen world, a world that also was cursed by the sin of Adam (Gen. 3:17) yet redeemed and renewed by Christ.[3] God's plan was always to have a sinless man rule over

3. For more on the broader picture of salvation in Christ, see N. T. Wright, *Surprised by Hope: Rethinking Heaven, the Resurrection, and the Mission of the Church* (New York: HarperOne, 2008), 198–201.

the earth, yet the first Adam failed. Fortunately, the second and better Adam triumphed, and initially through the resurrection and ultimately at his return, Jesus rules victorious over a redeemed world.

Naturally we may wonder how God's eternal plan to save a sinful world relates to other eternal decrees and whether his foreordained plan assumes that God may somehow be responsible for humanity's disobedience (explored in Question 23). These questions, however, must not distract us from the ultimate purpose of election, which is the glorification of Jesus Christ.

The Ultimate Purpose of Secondary Purposes

With the glorification of Jesus Christ firmly established as the ultimate purpose in divine election, we may then look to the many secondary purposes. While not an exhaustive list, we can say that secondary purposes include things such as love for human beings, the security of the elect's salvation, and the holiness of the church. We must not neglect these precious secondary purposes, though we should keep them in their proper order.

To say that every other purpose in election is secondary is not to diminish the goodness of the secondary purposes. Rather, we understand that they derive their purpose from the ultimate purpose of Christ's glorification. Said another way, we can be certain that the secondary purposes will prevail because God has eternally determined the primary purpose: to see himself glorified in Christ. Every secondary purpose will infallibly come to pass because God will not fail in seeing the Son glorified. For example, God's absolute desire to see himself glorified in Christ (the ultimate purpose) ensures us that we are and always will be beloved by God (the secondary purpose). Additionally, we can be assured of our salvation in Christ because God's highest motive is to be worshiped by us whom he chose to redeem. Moreover, we can know for sure that our holiness will prevail despite our continued disobedience because God has eternally purposed to have a holy people proclaim his excellencies. Whatever secondary purpose we find, we can know it will ultimately prevail because of the primary purpose of the glorification of Christ.

Summary

For the past several questions, we have explored the workings of salvation. This question explored what all those workings are ultimately leading toward, and the answer we have found is the glorification of Jesus Christ. Far from being an afterthought in the mind of God, the eternal plan for election, salvation, and many other precious doctrines is to see Jesus Christ exalted over a redeemed creation for which he died. This primary purpose gives meaning and significance to secondary purposes such as love, a desire to save, the gift of eternal life, and more.

REFLECTION QUESTIONS

1. What is aseity, and why is it important in the discussion of the purpose of divine election?
2. What do you believe is the ultimate purpose behind divine election?
3. Is that ultimate purpose centered around God or humanity?
4. What are some secondary purposes behind divine election in your view?
5. How do those secondary purposes derive their value from the ultimate purpose?

SECTION B

Relating Election to Other Doctrines

QUESTION 17

How Is the Trinity Involved in Election?

The great British Baptist preacher Charles Spurgeon once said that any gospel without the Trinity is a rope made of sand that cannot hold together, yet a gospel with the Trinity is of such might that hell itself cannot prevail against it.[1] We agree with Spurgeon that there can be no salvation without the Trinity because, as we discussed in the previous question, election centers upon the glory and power of God, not people. The question then becomes how the Trinity is involved in election. Before we attempt to answer this question, we must first revisit an ancient controversy discussed in Question 2.

The *Trinity* refers to God as three in persons yet one in essence. When we speak of God as one, we are referring to each person in the Godhead fully and eternally possessing the same divine nature, as well as being united in will and purpose. That oneness does not mean, however, that each person of the Trinity is the same person or has the same function. Failing to distinguish between either the persons or the works of each member of the Trinity leads to the heresy of modalism. In addition to modalism being called *subordinationism* and *Sabellianism*, it is also known for *patripassianism*, a heresy that claims God the Father (*patri*) suffered (*passion*) on the cross. Notice that this same heresy of modalism is at play where there is no true distinction between Father and Son, yet also notice that the heresy moved toward the works as opposed to simply the nature of the Trinity. In other words, it is important to distinguish between not only the nature of the persons within the Trinity but also each person's work. Here we are referring to the *economic Trinity*, where we understand the specific works of the Trinity in relation to salvation history, and the *immanent Trinity*, which analyzes the nature of the Trinity's eternal being (discussed in Question 2). In regard to the economic Trinity, we must be careful not to step into misappropriation by attributing the wrong works

1. "Personality of the Holy Ghost," in *Spurgeon's Sermons*, 10 vols. (Grand Rapids: Baker, 1987), 1:55.

to respective members of the Trinity within the economy of salvation. While such precision may sound like theological hairsplitting, it is of great importance if we are to remain biblically faithful and avoid ancient heresies.

Still, because of the unity of will and collaboration in function between the Father, Son, and Spirit, it is difficult to distinguish too sharply between each member of the Trinity in election. Yet this is not altogether problematic. We must not forsake the unity of the Trinity for the sake of individuality lest we creep into tritheism. To summarize how the Trinity as a whole is involved in election, we can say that the Triune God has eternally willed to choose certain persons for salvation in moments of time through the proper workings of the Father, Son, and Holy Spirit. If this summary sounds awfully close to the definition for divine election mentioned in Question 1, that is because it is meant to be so. If election refers to who God has chosen, we must understand how God, being Triune, goes about choosing as three distinct yet unified persons. We will explore this matter below, careful to avoid misappropriation, beginning with God the Father.

The Begetting Father

To understand God the Father's relationship to election, we must understand his relationship to the Son, for to do so not only bases our understanding in divine revelation but solidifies election in a person, making it as real and personal between the Father and us as it is between the Father and the Son. God's choice in election was not some abstract divine thought, nor was it a cleverly thought-out scheme when humanity sinned. It was an eternal and deliberate decree of the triune God to be brought about in the fullness of time in the person of Jesus Christ. Here we are speaking of *eternal generation*, the doctrine that the unbegotten Father has eternally begotten the Son in whom the Holy Spirit eternally proceeds. This language may seem opaque, yet it becomes clearer in light of Scripture and confession.

Scripture tells us that the Father begot and sent the Son (John 3:16; 8:42; 20:21; Acts 13:33; Gal. 4:4; 1 John 4:9, 14). Such language of begetting and generating may sound like the Father created the Son, similar to an earthly father with his human children; yet the early church, beginning with the Nicene Creed, clarified that the Son was begotten (not made) by the Father before all ages. The apostle John made clear that the Son was in the beginning with the Father (John 1:2; 1 John 1:2). Thus, we know not only that the Father and Son have eternally existed but that they have eternally existed and related to one another as Father and Son. While distinct from one another, they share the same essence as well as an eternal relationship, one we may understand as *begetting*. The language is meant to be personal and relational with the expression of perfect love between the two; thus, we should avoid any notion of the Son (or Spirit) being a creation of the Father. Important in this line of thought is that the sonship the Son holds is his by right, for he possesses this status naturally and eternally with the Father.

As begetting Father, he has eternally elected his Son (Matt. 17:5; Mark 9:7; Luke 9:35), and the Son proceeds from the Father to carry out a redemptive purpose (John 3:16; 6:44; 12:49–50; 17:21–26; 1 John 4:9). Thus, the Son is the Father's chosen, yet there are others who are chosen, namely the elect, whom the Son saves (John 10:27–30; 17:11, 24). Important to the choosing of the elect, however, is that the elect are chosen in the Chosen One, Jesus Christ. That is, the elect are elected in Christ himself. While people may commonly picture the destination of salvation as heaven, the Scriptures portray the destination of salvation as in Christ. People were not elected so they could be in a place (like heaven) but in a person (Jesus). The place is a consequence; the person is the source. Salvation as a whole, and election in particular, means to be chosen by God, in God, and for God. Apart from the begetting Father who has eternally chosen the Son, there would be no salvation and thus no election.

Additionally, the Holy Spirit also proceeds eternally from the Father, though in a different way. It is the Son, not the Spirit, who is begotten of the Father, though both eternally proceed from the Father. The Spirit proceeds spiritly (sometimes called *spiration*) from the Father, much like breath proceeds from a person. While the procession of the Son took place in time at the incarnation, the procession of the Holy Spirit took place at Pentecost in the economy of salvation. Similar to the Son, the Spirit fully and eternally possesses the divine nature and is unified with the Father and Son in purpose and will. As he relates to the Father, however, the Holy Spirit is poured out by the Father upon the elect whereby the Spirit applies the work of Christ to their account and indwells them now and always (Acts 5:32; 10:38; 15:8; Rom. 5:5; 1 Cor. 6:19; 2 Cor. 13:14; 1 Thess. 4:8). Apart from the Father sending the Spirit, there would be no salvation for the elect.[2]

The Begotten Son

The Son is the begotten of the Father (John 1:14, 18; 3:16, 18; 1 John 4:9) sent into the world to save the elect. He lived his life on earth as the Son in flesh, never ceasing to be truly divine, and the death he died was as the eternally generated Son. That is, as the eternally begotten of God, he is elect and chosen to carry out the Trinity's plan of redemption in a moment in time within the economy of salvation. Although we disagree with much of what Karl Barth put forth on election (discussed in Question 7), we do agree that Christ himself is the elect of God according to the eternal will of the Trinity.[3] Because of the unity of will and purpose within the Trinity, we know that the

---

2. For more on eternal generation, see Fred Sanders, *Fountain of Salvation: Trinity and Soteriology* (Grand Rapids: Eerdmans, 2021), 88–28; and Fred Sanders and Scott R. Swain, eds. *Retrieving Eternal Generation* (Grand Rapids: Zondervan Academic, 2017), 260–70.
3. Karl Barth, *Church Dogmatics*, ed. G. W. Bromiley and T. F. Torrance, 5 vols. (Peabody, MA: Hendrickson, 2010), 2.2.

Son eternally willed himself to be the sacrifice on behalf of sinful people in order to redeem a people unto himself. Therefore, Jesus was not a victim at the hands of an abusive Father, as some people have perversely suggested.[4] His election to sacrifice (much like his appointment as eschatological king) was something he willed from all eternity (Acts 2:23).

Again, the salvation that the elect receive is not to an abstract reality or disconnected existence. The election of the redeemed is always *in* the Son (Rom. 8:29–30; Eph. 1:4–7, 9–11, 13; 2 Tim. 2:10; Rev. 17:14). Christ lived the perfect, sinless life (his *active obedience*) and also received the penalty for sinners as their substitute (his *passive obedience*), both of which are imputed to the elect, leading to justification and reconciliation. It is here that we see the great importance that the Son's eternal generation has to the elect. Because election is in the Son, who has an eternal relationship status with the Father (as Son to Father), so too are the elect brought into an adoption, a filial relationship, with the Father. The sonship that the Son possesses by right becomes a sonship of the elect by grace, for in the elect's union with the Son they share a common heavenly Father (John 1:12–13; Rom. 8:15–17; Gal. 4:6; 1 John 3:1). In light of this sonship, Fred Sanders says well that "in the economy of salvation, we see that by God's unfathomable grace and sovereign power, the eternal trinitarian processions reach beyond the limits of the divine life and extend to fallen man."[5]

The Son, then, serves as the atoning sacrifice for and savior of the elect (Rom. 8:29–34).[6] As substitute for the elect, on the cross he propitiated the wrath of God against sin, thereby removing the penalty and enmity that stood between God and the elect, leading to their reconciliation. Christ's righteousness is imputed (or reckoned to belong) to the elect through faith (Rom. 1:17; 3:22–26; 4:5–13).[7] Importantly, the Protestant tradition has never suggested that believers possess the inherent righteousness of the Son. Likewise, we should not think that to be righteous means the elect actually *become* righteous as if their righteousness was intrinsic within them. Rather, the elect are considered to be righteous through an external, foreign righteousness that comes by union with Christ through faith. Thus, the Son accomplishes

---

4. Steven Chalke and Alan Mann, *The Lost Message of Jesus* (Grand Rapids: Zondervan, 2003), 182–83; Brian McLaren, *The Story We Find Ourselves In: Further Adventures of a New Kind of Chrisitan* (Minneapolis: Fortress, 2019), 102. These three authors would agree that Christ's suffering on the cross was not the Father abusing the Son. However, they argue that if substitutionary atonement were true, it would be a form of cosmic child abuse by the Father against the Son.
5. Sanders, *Fountain of Salvation*, 92. See also Matthew Barrett, *Simply Trinity: The Unmanipulated Father, Son, and Spirit* (Grand Rapids: Baker Books, 2021), 155–78.
6. Whether he died solely for the sins of the elect is another issue, to be discussed in Question 18.
7. See John R. W. Stott, *The Cross of Christ* (Downers Grove, IL: InterVarsity Press, 1986), 209–12; and Leon Morris, *The Apostolic Preaching of the Cross*, 3rd ed. (Grand Rapids: Eerdmans, 1965), 269–87.

redemption for the elect and allows them to enjoy the fellowship that the Son has had from all eternity.

The Proceeding Spirit

While much has already been said about the Spirit's work to the elect, we will develop a few more points. Again, the Spirit proceeds from the Father while also being sent by the Son (John 14:26; 15:26). We see here the relation and distinction between salvation accomplished and salvation applied. The Son accomplishes salvation for the elect, yet he sends the Spirit to apply it. The Spirit thus bears witness to Christ and regenerates hearts, resulting in the elect's belief in the Son through the faith given to them. Moreover, the Spirit indwells believers as the Spirit of Christ (Rom. 8:9; 1 Peter 1:11), sealing and securing the elect's salvation in the Son, in whom they share sonship as adopted sons and daughters of the Father (Rom. 8:15; Gal. 4:6). What is more, the Spirit empowers the elect to bear witness to others about the salvation found in Christ (Acts 1:8), and in the Spirit they enjoy the sweetness of fellowship not only with God but also the whole community that he has redeemed. As Sanders rightly says, "Without the Spirit, the person and work of Christ are locked into first-century Palestine,"[8] to which we add: Without the Spirit, there would be no salvation to give to the elect.

Summary

This section has explored the economy of salvation in the Trinity in order to see how each member of the Trinity is uniquely yet harmoniously involved in election. Our hope is to reinforce what was mentioned in Question 16—namely, that our most precious doctrines as Christians in the economy of salvation, like the incarnation, atonement, election, and church, are not afterthoughts in God's mind due to sin entering into the world. They are the eternal plans of God that will surely prevail. Here, we have explored how the immanent Trinity of Father, Son, and Holy Spirit have carried out the economy of salvation in specific yet unified activities according to the eternal counsel of their will. The unbegotten Father eternally generates the Son, the begotten Son accomplishes redemption for the elect, and the Spirit applies that work to the elect, who enjoy an adoption and fellowship that has been enjoyed by the Trinity since before the very foundations of the world.

REFLECTION QUESTIONS

1. What is the immanent Trinity, and how is that distinguished from the economic Trinity?

---

8. Sanders, *Fountain of Salvation*, 143.

2. What is eternal generation, and why is it important to the doctrine of election?

3. How does the eternal generation of the Son relate to the adoption of the elect?

4. What did Christ accomplish for the elect?

5. How does the Spirit apply the work of Christ to the elect?

QUESTION 18

Did Christ Die for All People or Only the Elect?

Nothing unites Christians like knowing Jesus Christ died and rose again to save sinners. It is of such a unifying and uncompromising force that Paul called it of first importance in the church (1 Cor. 15:3–4). Indeed, we can say believing in Christ's death and resurrection for the forgiveness of sins is at the heart of what it means to be a Christian. However, few things have divided Christians like the issue of the *extent of the atonement*, or whether Christ came to die for all people or the elect only.[1]

The issue is so divisive because of the further questions and implications our answer to the atonement's extent brings. For example, if Christ died for the sins of all people, did his work on the cross actually save anyone, or did it only make people savable? Did Christ die for people who would never accept the gospel, meaning some of the blood of Christ was wasted? If Christ died for everyone's sin (not just the elect), why are people still condemned to hell? On the other hand, if Christ did not die for the sins of the whole world, what do we do with the many passages of Scripture that speak of God's love for the whole world and desire that everyone be saved?

Before we tackle those issues, it is worth noting that there is much that unites evangelical Christians in relation to the extent of the atonement. All evangelicals believe that Christ died to pay for the sins of the elect and that the gospel should be preached to everyone everywhere. With few exceptions, we all believe that God loves the world that he made and truly desires everyone to be saved. Moreover, while there is some distinction between Calvinists and Arminians on this point, both traditions agree that the cross itself is perfectly

1. For a full-length treatment of the atonement, see Channing L. Crisler, *40 Questions About the Atonement* (Grand Rapids: Kregel Academic, 2025).

sufficient to pay for the sins of every person and that it must be applied by faith. These points of agreement should not be overlooked.

Despite areas of agreement, we can still see that there are significant implications for whichever view we hold. People who hold to unlimited atonement side historically with the Arminian position, which has long held that Christ died for the sins of everyone everywhere. People who believe Christ died for the sins of the elect only side historically with the Calvinist tradition. These two alternatives make up the primary viewpoints on the extent of the atonement, since evangelical Christians have rejected universalism. Below, we will survey these views, along with any alternatives, in hopes to understand better for whom Christ died.

Limited Atonement

Limited atonement refers to the view that Christ died solely for the elect. The term is something of a misnomer, as advocates of this view stress that the atonement is limited only in scope, not efficacy. Adherents sometimes prefer terms like *particular redemption* or *definite atonement* to stress that the atonement is never limited in potency or efficacy, only in whom it reaches. The cross atones and saves only those whom it intends (and does so without fail) according to this view.

To be clear, all Christians agree the scope of the atonement has to be limited in some way if we are to deny universalism. The question becomes whether it is limited by God or by people. The Calvinist tradition believes the atonement is limited in scope by God himself while, as we shall see, the Arminian tradition believes it is limited by people's unbelief. Historic roots for limited atonement can be found in the writings of Augustine and Basil of Caesarea. There is debate as to whether John Calvin held to limited atonement,[2] though he most certainly did in our view.[3] It was widely held to by the Puritans and in historic confessions like the Synod of Dort and Westminster Confession.

Adherents of this tradition see limited atonement as the clear teaching of Scripture. Jesus said he laid his life down for his sheep (John 10:11, 15, 26), his church (Acts 20:28; Eph. 5:25–27), and those whom the Father draws to Christ (John 6:37, 44). Sometimes the biblical authors use limiting language like *us* or *many* to refer to those for whom Christ died, rather than collective words like *all* or *everyone* (e.g., Isa. 53:11; Matt. 20:28; John 17:2–9; Rom. 5:8–11).

---

2. Kevin Dixon Kennedy, *Union with Christ and the Extent of the Atonement in Calvin*, Studies in Biblical Literature 48 (New York: Peter Lang, 2002); R. T. Kendall, *Calvin and English Calvinism to 1649*, Studies in Christian History and Thought (Carlisle, UK: Paternoster, 1997), 13–18.
3. Roger R. Nicole, "John Calvin's View of the Extent of the Atonement," *Westminster Theological Journal* 47, no. 2 (1985): 197–225.

Additionally, this tradition affirms that the atonement did not make people savable; it actually saved them (Isa. 53:10–11; John 10:15, 26–28; 17:2, 4, 9; Rom. 5:8–11; 8:1, 30–32; Titus 2:14; Heb. 2:11; 9:12–15; 10:14). The atonement was effectual, not potential, in its working. To be clear, affirming that the work on the cross actually saves the elect is not the same thing as the eternal salvation view found in hyper-Calvinism (discussed in Question 15). The need persists both for the Spirit to apply Christ's atoning work on the elect and for the conversion of sinners. Rather, this view looks to the eternal council of the Trinity, where the Father chooses the elect, gives them to the Son (John 10:29) who is sent to die for them, and sends the Spirit to apply that work through regeneration, effectual calling, and the grace-filled conversion of the sinner.[4]

The limited atonement tradition further argues that unlimited atonement must imply universalism, which cannot be. Said another way, if Christ died for all sins for every person, then that must include the sin of disbelief. Everyone's sins would thus be forgiven, and everyone would go to heaven (which also makes gospel proclamation meaningless). However, there are people in hell, and if they are in hell despite Christ having satisfied the penalty for their sins, they are there unjustly.[5] On the contrary, Christ died solely for the elect, none of his blood was wasted, and only their sins are forgiven (Matt. 20:28; John 3:36; 10:11, 16, 26; Eph. 5:25; Titus 2:14).

Unlimited Atonement

The contrasting view to limited atonement is *unlimited atonement* (sometimes called *universal atonement*), which holds that Christ died an atoning death for every person who has lived or ever will live. Similar to the view above, unlimited atonement (in evangelical circles) refers to the scope of Christ's atoning work on the cross, not its application, meaning Christ died for the sins of everyone but each person must appropriate the gospel through faith in order to be saved. While the scope of the atonement is unlimited in the eyes of God, it is limited in efficacy by people when faith in Christ is refused. As it relates to election, this tradition can affirm that Christ died for the elect (that is, those whom God foreknew would accept the gospel by faith), but he died for more than just them. Christ died for everyone, making everyone savable. Historically, this view was held to by some early church fathers and Scholastics, Arminius, the Remonstrants, Free Will Baptists, and the Wesleyan tradition.[6]

4. Michael Horton, *The Christian Faith: A Systematic Theology for Pilgrims on the Way* (Grand Rapids: Zondervan Academic, 2011), 518.
5. John Owen, *The Death of Death in the Death of Christ* (1852; repr., Carlisle, PA: Banner of Truth Trust, 2007), 124–61, 232–33.
6. For an excellent historical overview, see David L. Allen, *The Extent of the Atonement: A Historical and Critical Review* (Nashville: B&H Academic, 2016).

The Arminian viewpoint emphasizes God's perfect love for all humanity and the texts that state that Christ died for the world (John 1:29; 3:16; 2 Cor. 5:14–15, 18–19; 1 Tim. 2:3–6; 4:10; Titus 2:11; Heb. 2:9; 2 Peter 3:9; 1 John 2:2; 4:14). God cannot truly be someone who loves everyone if he only died for some of them. Moreover, if limited atonement were true, God would also be redeeming people without consideration of their response to the gospel, which violates the human will and makes God (rather than people) culpable for their punishment in hell.[7] Furthermore, as there is a real possibility of apostasy, and the elect are comprised only of people who persevere to the end of life, unlimited atonement best explains (in their view) how someone may possess the saving benefits of the atonement (forgiveness of sins) yet may forfeit them, leading to their condemnation.[8] In sum, salvation is available but not automatic in Arminianism, and it may be compared to someone who committed a heinous offense deserving condemnation, is offered a presidential pardon, and yet refuses to accept it. Forgiveness must be accepted in order to be effective.

Historically, the two views above have been the primary viewpoints of the church, and various debates exist within these traditions, such as over whether God has one will or two wills, the meaning of *all* and *world* in passages like John 3:16 and 1 John 2:2, and whether or not Christ's death is sufficient for all but efficient only for the "elect." Most of the debate has centered on these issues. There is another viewpoint, called *Amyraldism* (also known as *Four-Point Calvinism*), that upholds total depravity, unconditional election, irresistible grace, and perseverance of the saints yet holds to unlimited atonement. As a hybrid view, it is criticized by Calvinists and Arminians alike, and the chief criticisms against it are the arguments mentioned above.

Our Case for Definite Atonement

Christians trying to navigate these difficult theological issues today may be wary of embracing historic labels like "Calvinist," "Arminian," and "Amyraldist." Often, such avoidance is because all these traditions make valid points affirmed by Scripture. God does love all humanity. Christ is said to die for the elect and the world. Christians are called to preach the gospel to everyone everywhere, calling everyone to salvation in Christ. Just how are we to reconcile all of these scriptural truths?

Our view aligns with the Reformed tradition that believes the atonement of Christ is particular to the elect. We ascribe to this position because Scripture affirms that the Son was sent to die for and save the elect (Matt. 1:21;

---

7. Jerry L. Walls and Joseph R. Dongell, *Why I Am Not a Calvinist* (Downers Grove, IL: InterVarsity Press, 2004), 50–57.
8. Robert E. Picirilli, *Grace, Faith, Free Will* (Nashville: Randall House, 2002), 115.

John 10:11, 15; Acts 20:28), that his sacrifice was said to be for "many" (Matt. 20:28; 26:28; Heb. 9:15, 28), and that the atonement makes sinners saved rather than savable (Acts 13:48; Rom. 5:10; 2 Cor. 5:21; Eph. 5:25–27; 1 Tim. 1:15; Heb. 2:17, 9:12; 1 Peter 3:18).

What do we make of all the many verses that speak of Christ dying for the world (mentioned above)? Here we must understand that context determines meaning, and the word *world* (Gk. *kosmos*) can mean many things. John 1:29, 4:42, and 12:47 are but a few texts that describe Jesus as the Savior of the world. However, John the apostle also used the word *world* to refer to the earth (John 1:10; 10:36), to everything that is hostile to God and depraved in nature (John 8:23; 12:25, 31; 13:1; 16:11), and to humanity in general (John 8:26; 12:19). We believe that references to Christ taking away the sins of the world or being the Savior of the world must have limitations in order to avoid universalism, and the best way to understand such statements is that Christ is the cosmological redeemer who defeats sin and saves people from all over the world, not just ethnic Israel.[9] When John wrote his gospel, he emphasized that Jesus's death was not for one nation only (namely Israel) but for the children of God who are scattered abroad (John 11:51–52). His point was that the atoning work of Christ was not limited to the Jews, not that all people's sins are atoned for. The same principle applies to the usage of the word *all* (Gk. *pantas*).[10] John (who also wrote the book of Revelation) believed there would be people from every tribe, language, people, and nation (Rev. 5:9) grafted into the saving plans of God. He did not mean to imply that all people were redeemed or that all sins of all people were atoned, for such teaching would imply universalism.

Consider again what was mentioned above. If the payment for all people's sin has been made, why are certain sinners in hell? Someone will answer, "Because they did not accept this payment by faith." While true, we respond, "But is not it a sin to reject the gospel in disbelief?" Most certainly, people will affirm it is. If so, did Christ pay for that sin as well? If so, then there is no just cause for sending anyone to hell. If not, we affirm that Christ did not pay for all sins of all people. Naturally, someone may reply, "But if Christ died for all the sins of the elect, including their unbelief, then are they not saved at the moment Christ died, thus negating the need for true conversion?" Our response, aligning with the historic Reformed tradition, is that redemption

9. J. Ramsey Michaels, "Atonement in John's Gospel and Epistles," in *The Glory of the Atonement: Biblical, Theological, and Practical Perspectives*, eds. Charles E. Hill and Frank A. James III (Downers Grove, IL: InterVarsity Press, 2004), 106–18; Michael Horton, "Traditional Reformed View," in *Five Views on the Extent of the Atonement*, ed. Adam J. Johnson, Counterpoints: Bible and Theology (Grand Rapids: Zondervan Academic, 2019), 131–32.
10. See Shawn D. Wright, *40 Questions About Calvinism* (Grand Rapids: Kregel Academic, 2019), 182–86; Owen, *Death of Death*, 231–47.

for the elect was accomplished at the cross, thus securing objective forgiveness for all their sins, though such redemption is applied through faith upon a sinner's genuine conversion wrought by effectual calling and regeneration.

If our views above hold—and centuries worth of Reformed Christian witness affirm they do—then the main criticisms against limited atonement would have to do with God's universal love for humanity, his desire all people be saved, and the free offer of the gospel. We will explore these important topics in subsequent questions.

Summary

The atonement unifies Christians for good reason. There is no salvation apart from the cross. On the supremacy and sufficiency of the work of Christ on the cross, Christians stand now and always united. However, we must consider how to reconcile the atonement and its extent with divine election. We have surveyed limited and unlimited atonement views with the nuances both sides bring. Our view is that Christ died for the sins of the elect alone, in accordance with Scripture, that such a view explains why sinners are in hell and why there can be no universalism, and that the cross actually saves sinners.

REFLECTION QUESTIONS

1. What points of unity do all evangelicals share about the atonement?
2. What are the major points of disagreement concerning the scope of the atonement?
3. Do you believe the atonement is limited by God or by people?
4. Does the cross save or make people savable, in your view?
5. What is Amyraldism?

QUESTION 19

How Does Election Relate to Conversion?

It would be difficult for a reader of the New Testament to miss the clear and urgent command for people everywhere to repent and believe in Jesus Christ in order to be saved (Mark 1:15; Luke 7:50; John 3:16–18; Acts 2:38; 3:19; 8:22; 16:31; 17:30; 26:20; Rom. 10:9). Calling sinners to repentance and salvation in Christ through the power of the Holy Spirit is the Great Commission Christ gave to his disciples (Matt. 28:19–20; Acts 1:8), and until our Lord returns this is the task the church is called to fulfill.

Yet how does the church calling people to be saved in Christ relate to God calling people to be saved in Christ? If God has unconditionally, unilaterally, eternally, and individually appointed people to salvation in Christ (our view of election as presented in this book), then how does that relate to people willfully and sincerely repenting of sin and believing in Christ for their salvation? While we have covered some of these matters in previous questions (especially Questions 12 and 15), more must be said to address some of the concerns of people who hold to a different view of election. For example, C. Gordon Olson finds individual, unconditional election from eternity past (our view) to be irreconcilable with true, meaningful conversion because that view of election makes gospel proclamation incoherent and insincere, mocking the non-elect who cannot believe the gospel while also saving the elect coercively and against their will.[1] Olson is not alone. Many people struggle to reconcile the intersection between sovereign divine will and human will in salvation (explored more in Questions 30–31). If only one of these wills existed, we would have little tension. As it is, Scripture affirms God's sovereign will in salvation along with people's need to repent and believe. Just how are we to

1. C. Gordon Olson, *Getting the Gospel Right: A Balanced View of Salvation Truth* (Cedar Knolls, NJ: Global Gospel, 2005), 317–18.

reconcile this question? To begin, we will begin by looking at the Latin phrase *ordo salutis*.

Ordo Salutis

Salvation is made up of many aspects. Scripture uses terms like election, justification, redemption, conversion, regeneration, and more to speak of salvation. While we may be tempted to think that these terms are synonymous, they hardly refer to the same thing. Each of salvation's aspects correlate to the effects of sin. Sin and the fall have caused complex problems in humanity, meaning that people need a complex salvation. To illustrate, because people are dead in their trespasses and sin, they need regeneration. Because people are guilty according to the law, they need to be justified. Because people are enslaved to sin, they need redemption. On we could go. The question then becomes, if salvation is made up of many parts, or aspects, how do they relate to one another and in what order should we place them? Here, we come to the meaning of *ordo salutis*, the Latin term for the ordering of salvation's aspects.

When we speak about ordering the aspects of salvation, we are not necessarily speaking of when in time each aspect of salvation occurred (though there is a timing element for some of the aspects). Rather, we are mainly considering what aspects would precede others logically. Naturally, the non-Reformed tradition orders salvation's aspects differently than the Reformed, largely because the former sees human choice as preceding other aspects like election, regeneration, and redemption. For the non-Reformed tradition, salvation would begin with God's eternal plans to save sinners in Christ, prevenient grace to overcome sin, conversion (repentance and faith), and then regeneration, justification and redemption, and sanctification, with those persons who finally persevere in faith being the foreknown elect.[2] Calvinists, on the other hand, would place election and other divine decrees as first priority, followed by regeneration and effectual calling, conversion, and then justification, redemption and adoption, sanctification, and glorification.[3] Some people are critical of trying to order salvation's aspects because they (rightly) find no exhaustive *ordo salutis* articulated in Scripture (though Rom. 8:29–30 is often used). Also, critics think that if salvation's aspects are placed into an order, we then divide the whole of salvation. However, as all aspects of salvation are found in Scripture and certain factors like eternal decrees, depravity, and human response must be accounted for, it is perfectly acceptable

---

2. For an overview, see Robert E. Picirilli, *Grace, Faith, Free Will* (Nashville: Randall House, 2002), 170–81. More aspects could be mentioned. The point is that this tradition views faith as preceding all saving activity.
3. For an overview, see Matthew Barrett, *40 Questions About Salvation* (Grand Rapids: Kregel Academic, 2018), 73–76.

to attempt to order the aspects in a logical manner without compromising or separating the parts that make up the whole of salvation.

Regeneration and Effectual Calling

Having already argued that salvation is rooted in the divine will of the immanent Trinity and accomplished in redemptive history, we now turn our attention to the application of salvation among the elect. As sinners are in a state of spiritual depravity, no force of effort by sinners or evangelists is sufficient to bring about conversion. As we have said before, the Holy Spirit applies the salvation the Son accomplished, meaning that any reception of salvation must begin with the Spirit rather than the sinner. On this matter, Reformed and Arminian traditions are agreed. As we discussed in Question 12, they disagree regarding the extent the Holy Spirit must prevene upon sinners. As we have already said, sinners need to be brought from spiritual death to spiritual life, not to a spiritual crossroads for personal decision-making. The human heart needs to be made new for the depraving effects of sin to be washed away, yet how is that done in real time? Romans 8:29–30 is sometimes called the "golden chain" of salvation, for it gives us a helpful (though not exhaustive) progression of salvation's outworking. There, Paul said that among the predestined (i.e., elect), God "called," "justified," and "glorified." Salvation moves from divine intent to human application.

Paul began by saying that the predestined were called by God, something known as *effectual calling*. Jonathan Hoglund gives this excellent definition of effectual calling: "The *effectual call* is an act of triune rhetoric in which God the Father appropriates human witness to Christ the Son in order to convince and transform a particular person by ministering, through the presence of God the Spirit, understanding and love of Christ."[4] Said another way, the triune God calls, or summons, certain people to himself for salvation. Hoglund rightly states that such calling is appropriated by human witness (which is the gospel proclamation for everyone everywhere to acknowledge and honor their Creator and to believe in Jesus Christ for the forgiveness of their sins, called here the *general call*). However, we may also understand the general call in accordance with general revelation (Lat. *vocation realis*, see Ps. 19:1–4; Rom. 1:19–21), which itself is a divine call for people to acknowledge God and pursue him in faith, removing any excuse for disbelief and sin. Nevertheless, this general call, extended to all people, is not effectual in its working given that not all people are saved. For salvation to occur, the general call must be accompanied by the effectual call, something only given to the elect.

The effectual call is solely from God and is specific only to the elect. Paul referred to the recipients of the letter of Romans as those "called to belong to

---

4. Jonathan Hoglund, *Called by Triune Grace: Divine Rhetoric and the Effectual Call*, Studies in Christian Doctrine and Scripture (Downers Grove, IL: IVP Academic, 2016), 4.

Jesus Christ" (Rom. 1:6), the Corinthian church as those who were called into fellowship with Christ (1 Cor. 1:9, 24), and the Thessalonians as the elect called by God to salvation through human proclamation (2 Thess. 2:13–14). These people were called by divine summons through human witness, leading to the regeneration and conversion of the elect. While the general call for everyone to be saved in Christ goes to all people, only the elect are effectually called (Rom. 8:28–29; 9:24–29; 1 Cor. 1:24; Gal. 1:15; 1 Thess. 1:4–5; 2 Thess. 2:13–14).[5]

Subsequently, when the elect are effectually called to salvation through the general call, there is an accompanying activity of *regeneration*, the monergistic and instantaneous work of the Holy Spirit whereby he raises a sinner from spiritual death into new life, replacing a heart of stone and its controlling influences with a heart of flesh, enabling a person to repent and believe in Jesus Christ for salvation. Regeneration overcomes the depraving effects of the fall and enables people to see the testimony of the Holy Spirit to Jesus Christ and hear the summons of the Father in a way that leads to genuine repentance and faith, or *conversion*. The Father's calling precedes any activity on the part of a sinner, and the Holy Spirit's work of regeneration allows a person the very ability to respond to that calling with the faith gifted to them. Said another way, what God calls the elect to do in conversion, he enables them to do by regeneration.[6]

To further clarify, God's calling to the elect is effectual, meaning it will certainly come to pass. While the elect may initially resist the general call, God's purposes in salvation prevail. Effectual calling is overcoming grace, and though tradition has called this doctrine *irresistible grace*, the point is not that people can never resist it or that their will is irresistibly coerced. Rather, God's saving purposes prevail even over defiant sinners. All Christians who reject Pelagianism affirm that the human will is spiritually dead and unable to render to God what it should. To say that God, not sin, now orients the desires of the soul is not to deny the authenticity of faith. Rather, it is to affirm that what controlled the heart has been put to death and replaced by a willing heart that allows a person to desire what before was impossible, namely a glorious Savior in Jesus Christ.[7]

The Elect and Conversion

We should now see how the *ordo salutis* is accomplished in the lives of the elect. God's divine decree to save elect persons in Christ from eternity past through their willful faith in Christ (brought about in a moment in time

---

5. Bruce A. Ware, "Divine Election to Salvation," in *Perspectives on Election*, ed. Chad Owen Brand, Five Views (Nashville: B&H Academic, 2006), 17.
6. See John Murray, *Redemption Accomplished and Applied* (Grand Rapids: Eerdmans, 1955), 95–96.
7. For a more thorough treatment, see Matthew Barrett, *Salvation by Grace: The Case for Effectual Calling and Regeneration* (Phillipsburg, NJ: P&R, 2013), 69–123; and Barrett, *40 Questions About Salvation*, 119–33.

through human witness, regeneration, and effectual calling) that results in justification, adoption, and a lifelong journey of sanctification is, in our view, the most biblical way to understand how God goes about saving the elect.[8]

More specifically, this faith (while an activity of a person) is a divine gift (Eph. 2:8–9; Phil. 1:29; 2 Tim. 2:24–26).[9] Belief does not rise from any unregenerate heart; it must be given. With all humanity being in a state of depravity, God's divine intervention and grace, not innate ability, is the only reason some people believe while others do not. This divine grace that justifies sinners is not active only in the initial stages of awareness of sin, knowledge of the person and work of Christ, acceptance that such knowledge is true, and trust in the saving promises. Rather, grace is active throughout the lifetime of the believer, whereby all saving activity is attributed to grace. Therefore, we can and should distinguish faith from faithfulness. The elect are saved because of God's grace in the person and work of Christ through faith (trust and belief), not human obedience (faithfulness). Faithfulness is the consequence of salvation, not the cause of it. Saving faith is receptive, not causative. It is an awareness of a lack of personal worth, an assent to the sufficiency of the person and work of Christ, and a reliance upon the grace and mercy of God to save. Therefore, there are no grounds for the elect to boast in anything but the greatness of their God to the exclusion of all human merit.

Summary

Is unconditional, unilateral, eternal, and individual election to salvation inconsistent with meaningful repentance and faith? Having explored what is meant by the *ordo salutis*, we have here argued that through effectual calling and regeneration, God brings about the willing repentance and faith of the elect in a real and meaningful way, which will hopefully address some of the concerns mentioned earlier that the two are incompatible. In summary, divine election does not make conversion meaningless; it makes it possible.

REFLECTION QUESTIONS

1. What is the *ordo salutis*, and how do election and conversion fit in it?

2. What is meant by effectual calling, and how is that related to and distinguishable from general calling?

---

8. See Herman Bavinck, *Saved by Grace: The Holy Spirit's Work in Calling and Regeneration*, ed. J. Mark Beach, trans. Nelson D. Kloosterman (Grand Rapids: Reformation Heritage, 2008), 147–59.
9. Sam Storms, *Chosen for Life: The Case for Divine Election* (Wheaton, IL: Crossway, 2007), 69–75.

3. Can the elect resist God's saving grace?

4. How does someone come to a point of repenting and believing, in your view?

5. How would you order salvation's aspects?

QUESTION 20

Are the Elect Secured in Their Salvation?

Nothing quite demonstrates the practical importance of the doctrine of election like security in salvation. Granted, the doctrine of election, being a biblical teaching, should be understood in its own right regardless of any personal application we may find. It has implications, however, for other doctrines, not least of which is our security in salvation. Are the elect ensured of certain salvation, or can they forfeit it? Relatedly, though distinct, can the saved lose their election status? Do the saints persevere to the end? These questions are pressing not only to modern minds but also to the very Scriptures themselves, though there has never been universal consensus on the matter within the Christian faith.

It is not our intention here to make a broad case either for or against eternal security in salvation, for many scholars have done so masterfully.[1] As it is, these scholars have argued their case biblically by analyzing eternal security in light of doctrines such as faith, free will, and divine benevolence as well as justification, regeneration, and effectual calling (to name a few). Our intention, however, is to make a case about the security of salvation on the basis of divine election. We will explore various perspectives before concluding that divine election secures believers' salvation.

A Brief Survey

Broadly speaking, there are three primary views in relation to election and eternal security: unconditional election and eternal security, conditional

1. Other scholars addressing eternal security and the possibility of losing salvation within this 40 Questions series include J. Matthew Pinson, *40 Questions About Arminianism*, Shawn D. Wright, *40 Questions About Calvinism*, Gregg R. Allison, *40 Questions About Roman Catholicism*, and Matthew Barrett, *40 Questions About Salvation*.

election and eternal security, and conditional election and possible apostasy.[2] Nuances within these views will be highlighted here as appropriate.

Sometimes referred to as *perseverance of the saints*, the unconditional election and eternal security view affirms that those who were eternally and individually chosen by God will never lose their salvation because salvation is owed to the immutable will and saving activity of God alone. The roots of this view go back as early as Augustine, who believed that God's grace not only brings us to Christ but preserves us in Christ.[3] The view further builds upon what the Reformed tradition sees as three distinct covenants outlined throughout Scripture, namely a covenant of redemption, a covenant of works, and a covenant of grace. The covenant of redemption refers to God's eternal decree within the immanent Trinity to choose persons for redemption. Persons were chosen unconditionally, individually, and from eternity to be redeemed in Christ, and that decree will certainly prevail despite human sin. The covenant of works refers to the first covenant God made with humanity through Adam that, if upheld, would result in rewards and, if broken, would lead to sanctions (blessings and curses).[4] Finally, the covenant of grace refers to Christ's fulfillment of the covenant of works as he bore the consequences of people who failed to uphold it, thereby satisfying God's justice while gifting both repentance and faith to the elect whom he reconciles to himself. As it relates to eternal security, the elect fall into the covenant of redemption, which is not predicated upon human response. Moreover, Christ has fulfilled the covenant of works on behalf of the elect through the covenant of grace, which means that salvation rests securely in the hands of God, not people.[5]

The conditional election and eternal security view believes that election is conditioned upon faith and that salvation is secured once that faith is expressed.[6] Believers may presently have assurance that salvation will certainly occur once they meet the one condition of salvation and election, namely faith. Important in this framework, however, is that eternal security is only eternal insofar as the present and future are concerned, not eternity past. That is to say, a person is secured in salvation upon conversion (the will of the person), not eternity past (the will of God). Norman Geisler states, "Salvation

---

2. See J. Matthew Pinson, ed., *Four Views on Eternal Security*, Counterpoints: Bible and Theology (Grand Rapids: Zondervan Academic, 2002) for an overview of these views. Note that while there are differences between the Reformed Arminianism and Wesleyan Arminianism views from that work, both views hold to conditional election and the possibility of apostasy.
3. Augustine, "On the Gift of Perseverance," chs. 14 and 33.
4. See Westminster Confession of Faith, 7.2.
5. For an overview, see Michael S. Horton, "A Classical Calvinist View," in Pinson, *Four Views on Eternal Security*, 30–35. See also Westminster Confession of Faith, 7.3–6 and 17.2.
6. See Norman Geisler, *Chosen but Free: A Balanced View of Divine Election*, 2nd ed. (Minneapolis: Bethany House, 2001), 101–3, 120–21; and Norman Geisler, *Systematic Theology*, 4 vols. (Minneapolis: Bethany House, 2004), 3:300–345.

of the believer is eternally secure from the very first moment of salvation,"[7] namely upon conversion.

The third and final view we will survey is conditional election and possible apostasy. This view is found in Jacobus Arminius, John Wesley, and those of a Wesleyan-Arminian theology.[8] It should be stated that there is no singular Arminian position on eternal security, as even the *Articles of the Remonstrants* left the matter open to various opinions. Nevertheless, this conditional election and possible apostasy view affirms that election is conditioned upon continuous faith and that believers may lose salvation through their action(s).[9] Several points of clarification are necessary here. First, we have made the case in numerous parts of this book that election, in the Arminian view, concerns God's foreknowledge of those persons who would continue in the faith to the end of their lives. Relatedly, this view affirms that people may have faith in Christ yet not be elect (discussed in Question 15). Put together, someone may have faith in Christ, be subsequently saved, and then abandon the faith, resulting in a loss of salvation. Notice, however, that this loss of salvation does not mean that a person lost election status. In the view of most Arminians, people who apostatize never were among the elect, for Christ foresaw their lapse of faith and never reckoned them into the foreordained elect. Thus, there is no loss of election status, for they never had it to begin with (even if they once had faith). Second, while adherents to this view affirm that election is conditioned upon faith and that loss of salvation is possible, there is disagreement on the types of apostasy and whether the apostate could ever return to the faith. One view of apostasy is that when someone renounces faith in Christ altogether, it is unforgiveable and irremediable. A person who commits such apostasy may never be saved again, for that person cast aside the only means by which sinners can be right with God, namely faith (Heb. 3:7–4:13; 6:4–8; 10:26–31).[10] A second type of apostasy, adhered to by Wesleyan Arminians, occurs whenever a person, through backsliding, engages in unrepentant sin

---

7. Geisler, *Chosen but Free*, 103.
8. Adherents to the New Perspective(s) on Paul would also fit under this category, though such a view is too vast to be treated here. Simply put, under this perspective, Paul is less concerned with justification and imputed righteousness than he is with including Gentiles in the people of God. The view ultimately concludes that entry into the covenant is by grace yet staying in the covenant is a matter of works. See E. P. Sanders, *Paul and Palestinian Judaism: A Comparison of Patterns of Religion* (Philadelphia: Fortress, 1977); N. T. Wright, *Paul: In Fresh Perspective* (Minneapolis: Fortress, 2005); and Wright, *What Saint Paul Really Said: Was Paul of Tarsus the Real Founder of Christianity?* (Grand Rapids: Eerdmans, 1997).
9. See I. Howard Marshall, *Jesus the Saviour: Studies in New Testament Theology* (Downers Grove, IL: InterVarsity Press, 1990), 306–24.
10. See J. Matthew Pinson, *40 Questions About Arminianism* (Grand Rapids: Kregel Academic, 2022), 360–62.

to the forfeiture of salvation. This type of apostasy is remediable should the sinner repent.[11]

Eternally Elect and Secure

How we understand eternal security largely depends on how we understand the workings of election discussed in previous questions. If we understand the elect to be people who meet the condition of faith, with their faith serving as the instrumental cause of their election, we might conclude that people can lose their salvation. However, if we believe election is sourced solely in the divine will from eternity past and not conditioned upon belief, we may conclude that the elect are eternally secure. Said another way, if people's beliefs or actions caused or contributed to their salvation, it makes sense that their lack of belief or actions could remove salvation. However, if salvation is not caused by people but is solely the work of God, then a person's salvation is as secure as the faithfulness of God. Because we have made the case that election is rooted in the divine will from eternity past and not conditioned upon faith, we believe that God will continue his saving purposes for the elect that he willed from before time began, thus seeing the saint through in the faith, leading to certain glorification. Below, we will make this argument from Scripture based upon three overarching points: election is of God, election is in Christ, and election is from eternity.

As we observed in Question 9, our view is that divine election is sourced solely in the will of God, not his foreknowledge of human actions. Jesus said in John 6:37–39 that the will of the Father who sent him is that he should have all whom the Father willed to give him, that he should lose none of them. Jesus reaffirmed the point in John 10:27–30 that his chosen sheep will never perish, nor will anyone snatch them out of his hand because the Father gave them to the Son. Ephesians 1:4–5 affirms that people who were predestined to adoption were done so according to the intentions of the divine will. Paul also said in 1 Corinthians 1:7–9 that because God is faithful, the Corinthians will be confirmed and found blameless to the end. Each of these passages, and more, affirm belief and obedience from people; however, they never base the status of salvation upon humans. Rather, we find that salvation is secure and our election is certain because it is rooted in God's will, not our own.

What is more, salvation is secured because of election in Christ. As we observed in Questions 16–17, election is not an abstract choice in the mind of God or people. Rather, it is a personal reality. Election is always *in* the Son (Rom. 8:29–30; Eph. 1:4–7, 9–11, 13; 2 Tim. 2:10; Rev. 17:14). Because election is in the Son, people who abide in him by (not because of) faith receive his atoning sacrifice (Rom. 8:29–34) and his righteous status imputed to their

---

11. See J. Steven Harper, "A Wesleyan Arminian View," in Pinson, *Four Views on Eternal Security*, 238–46.

behalf (Rom. 1:17; 3:22–26; 4:5–13). They are one with Christ and forgiven of all sins, past, present, and future, leading to an adoption and sonship that belongs to Christ by right yet to believers by grace. This union has the ultimate purpose of glorifying the Son forever (discussed in Question 16). As a result, because God's eternal plan is to see Christ exalted over a redeemed humanity, believers are secured in their salvation because God will not fail to receive the glory due his name.

A third and final point concerning election and security of salvation relates to the eternality of divine election. Not only do the elect possess election status from all eternity but they have, as a consequence, security of salvation from eternity past. Here we do not mean that Christians have eternally been saved, but rather that they have been eternally secure. Often, when people think of eternal security, they do so from the point of conversion forward. Divine election, however, requires that we also think of eternal security from before time began. The elect are eternally secure in their salvation not upon the event of salvation but in eternity past, given that their salvation in Christ was always the eternal will of God, certain to occur from eternity in a moment in time through effectual calling (Eph. 1:4–15; 2 Thess. 2:13–14; 1 Peter 1:1–5). This view extends beyond the mantra "Once saved, always saved." While true, this view might suggest that someone's eternal security in salvation is only secure "once saved" (upon true conversion) rather than from eternity past. The issue we find with this view is that salvation is secure not because of conversion (which takes place in the will of a person) but because of divine decree (which takes place in the will of God). The elect's salvation is secured from eternity past because election occurs in eternity past, is made effectual by divine calling, and is held by God for future glorification.

Summary

The doctrine of eternal security is a matter of great theological and practical importance given that humanity continually fails to render to God the faithfulness he deserves. While human frailty would lead us to despair, we can draw great hope knowing that our salvation is secure not because of our faithfulness but because of God's. In this question we have defined various alternative viewpoints on eternal security and their relation to divine election, while ultimately concluding that the elect are—and have forever been—secured of certain salvation primarily on three grounds: election is of God, election is in Christ, and election is from eternity.

REFLECTION QUESTIONS

1. How does someone's view of conditional or unconditional election relate to eternal security?

2. Is your view of eternal security one of unconditional election and eternal security, conditional election and eternal security, or conditional election and possible apostasy?
3. What biblical support can you give to your view?
4. Why is eternal security in salvation not the same thing as eternal salvation?
5. Is the phrase "Once saved, always saved" the best way to explain eternal security?

QUESTION 21

What Is Hardening of the Heart?

If the security of salvation is found to be of utmost practical importance (as discussed in the preceding question), the hardening of hearts must be of at least equal importance. Consider: Would God eternally secure the elect for certain salvation while simultaneously hardening the non-elect to certain condemnation? Who does God harden and why? What happens to a person whose heart is hardened, and is it remediable?

While it may be prudent for Christians to tread lightly on this difficult topic, the hardening of human hearts is still an issue we must tread because Scripture clearly speaks to it (Exod. 4–14; Josh. 11:20; 1 Sam. 6:6; Ps. 95:8; Isa. 63:17; John 12:38–40; Rom. 9:17–18; 11:8; 2 Cor. 3:14; Heb. 3:7–19). Before we attempt to understand what the hardening of hearts means and does, we will first explore its significance in church history.

Erasmus, Arminius, and Non-Calvinists

The matter of the hardening of hearts, both in its meaning and application, came to a head during and following the Protestant Reformation. The Dutch humanist Desiderius Erasmus, appealing to Origen and Jerome, believed divine hardening refers to God not punishing at once the sinner and, with divine forbearance, allowing someone to persist in wrongdoing.[1] For Erasmus, Pharaoh's heart was created morally neutral (a Pelagian concept) and was first hardened by Pharaoh himself without divine causation, yet God turned that wickedness to his own purposes to accomplish salvation for Israel. Thus, hardening of hearts is ultimately done by people, and God merely permits it.

The language of Jacobus Arminius was altogether different and stronger than that of Erasmus. God does harden the hearts of individuals; however,

1. Desiderius Erasmus, *On the Freedom of the Will* in *Luther and Erasmus: Free Will and Salvation*, eds. E. Gordon Rupp and Philip S. Watson (Louisville: Westminster John Knox, 2006), 65–67.

he does so conditionally as punishment and consequence for people's own sinful rebellion. Truth is offered to people, prevenient grace makes it possible to respond to that truth, yet people reject that truth, leading to God giving them a reprobate mind. Through their continued rebellion, God blinds them to the truth, yet only as a consequence of their willful opposition. God, then, is gracious and desires their salvation yet foreknew and permitted their sin, resulting in their deliverance into evil.[2]

John Wesley was less strong in his language yet similar in his thinking that the hardening of hearts is a result of a person (like Pharaoh) being stubborn and impenitent unto his own ruin. Important to Wesley and many non-Calvinists is that hardening of hearts is remediable upon a sinner's repentance and certainly not an eternal divine decree. The only unchangeable divine decree is that God will love believers and hate nonbelievers; yet, as he has not ordained which persons are nonbelievers, he does not have a predisposition to hate someone. Thus, Pharaoh (and others who have had the hand of the Lord against them) may have repented and believed, leading to salvation.[3] In similar veins, other non-Calvinists affirm that God does harden hearts but only in response to people first hardening themselves against the will of God. Desiring everyone to be saved yet permitting people to use their free will, God gives certain people who willfully rebel against him both a depraved mind and hardened heart as well as an opportunity to repent (though continued opportunity is never guaranteed).

Luther, Calvin, and the Strongly Calvinistic Tradition

Martin Luther (who found Erasmus, Origen, and Jerome to be quite absurd and unbiblical on this point) argued that God was the ultimate cause of Pharaoh's hardened heart, not Pharaoh himself. Hardening of hearts does not refer to indulging the wicked through forbearance; it is a direct punishment of God from his immutable will. Divine forbearance of human sin will do no good to people's hearts that are bound and sullied with sin. Rather, for Luther the key issue is election. God elects and redeems those individuals he desires to save. The rest are hardened by God in life, leading to certain and deserved condemnation at death.[4]

John Calvin aligned with Luther's view that God was the ultimate hardener of Pharaoh's heart to the praise of his own glory. Calvin emphasized (in accordance with Rom. 1:26) that God gives people over to reprobate minds because of their sins, with the consequence being that they are spiritually

---

2. *The Works of James Arminius*, trans. James Nichols, 3 vols. (Grand Rapids: Baker, 1986), disputation 9.21, 2:175–76.
3. John Wesley, *Calvinism Calmly Considered*, 2 vols. (Salem, OH: Schmul, 2001), 3:55–57.
4. Martin Luther, *On the Bondage of the Will*, in Rupp and Watson, *Luther and Erasmus*, 223–31.

blind and obstinate of heart. Like Luther, the difference between who gets hardened and who gets softened in heart is a matter of divine election. God leads the elect to certain salvation while hardening all others to condemnation.[5] Ultimately, if God hardens someone's heart, it is not resistible or remediable under this view. Nevertheless, each non-elect person willfully commits sin and is deserving of condemnation. Hardness of heart is deserved by sinners while also caused by God.

Calvinists see parallels between God's predestination of Pharaoh (namely, that he would be a vessel of wrath) and all of the reprobate. Pharaoh, like all sinners, was responsible for his actions and deserving of condemnation, yet it was God's purpose that he be reprobated. To accomplish this reprobation, there was spiritual hardening and blinding in real time that fulfilled what was decreed from eternity past. Moreover, while judgment is deserved, the ultimate basis for the hardening is God's glory.[6]

The Who, How, and Why of Hardening

Although the hardening of hearts has been understood differently in terms of its ultimate causes and effects, there is general consensus on what is meant by the phrase *hardening of hearts*, namely, the act of a person's spiritual nature becoming obstinate and calloused to God, resulting in a failure to hear, be sensitive to, or obey him. Most adherents to the major traditions mentioned above recognize that there is a both/and when it comes to hardening hearts (where it is an activity both of God and a sinner, as opposed to being strictly of one or the other). The bigger issues at stake are whom God hardens (whether all non-elect people or just select individuals), whether hardness of heart is remediable or resistible, and whether it is in response to someone's sin or lack of election status.

Naturally, how we understand reprobation (discussed in Question 13) largely determines our view on hardening of hearts. The two are intricately related yet distinct. Reprobation, in this sense, refers to the eternal and unconditional decree whereby God chooses not to save certain persons while holding them accountable to justice. Hardening of hearts, on the other hand, is an execution of that divine decree whereby he makes the reprobate callous to the gospel and other divine revelations during their lifetime. As stated before, our view of the human will is that of concurrence, and our view of election is solely single in nature (which rejects foreordination to condemnation). In light of those two premises, how do we understand the hardening of human hearts?

---

5. John Calvin, *Concerning the Eternal Predestination of God*, trans. J. K. S. Reid (Louisville: Westminster John Knox, 1997), 146. See Calvin, *Institutes*, 3.24.13–14.
6. For a modern representative of this view, see James R. White, *The Potter's Freedom: A Defense of the Reformation and a Rebuttal of Norman Geisler's* Chosen but Free (Greenville, SC: Calvary, 2009), 211–15.

R. C. Sproul gives three helpful insights that are indicative of our own view of the hardening of hearts. First, Sproul states that, though the Bible clearly teaches that God hardened Pharaoh's heart, it does not expressly state *how* God hardened Pharaoh's heart (or anyone else's, for that matter). Second, if God directly intervened in the human heart to create new evil and resistance (called *active hardening*), then God would be the author of sin and Pharaoh's condemnation would be unjust. Third, God could harden hearts *passively* by removing all restraints that common grace places upon sinful humanity, increasing their willful desires and letting them act freely to their own peril and God's glory.[7] Under this view, God is the ultimate cause of hardening. His activity, however, is mainly handing sinners over to their depraved devices, resulting in their willful spiritual blindness and insensitivity to divine revelation in accordance with God's perfect will and glory.

This passive hardening is the view we find to be the most biblical and best explanation for divine sovereignty, the culpability of sinners, and the holiness of God. From the Pharaoh narrative in Exodus, we see that there are twenty references to Pharaoh's hardness of heart. While most of the references to hardening the heart are said to be by God (or a divine passive verb is implied), Pharaoh is said repeatedly to have hardened his own heart, refused to listen, and/or refused to obey. All of these facets are important to uphold. Contrary to Erasmus, God does harden hearts and is not merely forbearing. Furthermore, God takes the initiative in the hardening process through his immutable will (Exod. 4:21; Josh. 11:20; Rom. 9:15–18). Humankind, however, is actively involved in the hardening process by being hostile toward God and pursuing evil. All people (elect and non-elect) harden their own hearts toward God, yet God (passively) hardens the hearts of the non-elect in complete synchronization with their own hardening. The elect are never hardened by God yet are effectually called and redeemed in a moment in time.

A few other passages of Scripture must be examined. In John 12:37–40, though Jesus performed many signs to observant crowds, they did not receive him in faith because God blinded their eyes and hardened their hearts, just as Isaiah the prophet foretold (Isa. 6:10; 53:1). However, we agree with D. A. Carson, who finds that the crowds were still responsible for their sin and disbelief and condemned by God in accordance with their own sinful wills for the redemptive plans of God to come to pass.[8]

In Romans 1, Paul spoke of God giving up people to their own lusts who were willfully hostile to him, who exchanged the glory of the incorruptible God for idols (vv. 24, 26, 28). Paul clearly affirmed that people who indulge their sinfulness and reject their creator are deserving of both death (v. 32)

---

7. R. C. Sproul, *Chosen by God* (Wheaton, IL: Tyndale House, 1986), 144–45.
8. D. A. Carson, *The Gospel According to John*, Pillar New Testament Commentary (Grand Rapids: Eerdmans, 1991), 447–49.

and the depraved mind God gives them (v. 28). Therefore, God's act of hardening is ultimately giving people over to their own sinful desires and natural hostility, though we also affirm that God hardens non-elect person's hearts through secondary causes (see Question 22).

Regarding Paul's commentary on Pharaoh in Romans 9, we affirm that God is not unjust or immoral in how he dealt with Pharaoh, whose will was actively involved alongside God's direct influence in the hardening process. In accordance with the Exodus narrative and Romans 9, we believe that God, not Pharaoh, is the ultimate cause of hardness of heart so that God's name might be proclaimed throughout the earth for his glory (v. 17). These observations are made by G. K. Beale, who makes another significant point concerning Romans 9 and the Exodus narrative—namely, that the hardening of hearts most likely (in our view *certainly*) affects the spiritual realm (not just cognitive and decision-making processes) of people's lives, which affects eternal destiny. Thus, hardening of hearts is not a historical and temporal issue but an ongoing reality today. Additionally, when the non-elect harden their hearts, they don't do so independently of God's simultaneous involvement in the hardening process. God is not responsible for the sinner sinning, nor does he excuse the sinner's willful actions, but he is involved.[9]

A few more observations are in order. We believe there is an unconditional and conditional aspect to hardening. Unlike Arminianism, we believe hardening to be unconditional. Why did God harden Pharaoh's heart, removing all restraints so that he acted recklessly and wickedly? The only indication Paul gave is for the glory of God (Rom. 9:17). It merely seemed to please God to harden Pharaoh's heart to accomplish the redemption of the Jews from Egypt when there were an infinite number of other possibilities afforded to him to achieve the same end. Why does God harden some people's hearts today (the non-elect) while other people's hearts (the elect) are opened? We simply cannot know. God does what is best to him. We cannot say it is because of sin on our part given that all people are sinners and deserving of condemnation. It cannot be because of foreseen goodness because then salvation would be by works and not grace. It can only be because of God's intentions.

At the same time, we can say that the reason why God hardens hearts is a deserved judgment conditioned upon people's willful rejection of him. Pharaoh set himself up as God, hardened his own heart, and refused to listen to Moses. People today harden their hearts against God and willfully refuse to acknowledge their Creator, leading to divine hardening (Rom. 1:23–24), which we find to be irremediable and irresistible. These non-elect persons do

---

9. G. K. Beale, "An Exegetical and Theological Consideration of the Hardening of Pharaoh's Heart in Exodus 4–14 and Romans 9," *Trinity Journal* 5 NS (1984): 129–54. See also John Piper, *The Justification of God: An Exegetical and Theological Study of Romans 9:1–23*, 2nd ed. (Grand Rapids: Baker Academic, 1993).

not want the lordship of Christ over their lives, nor do they want to live a life pleasing to him. God gives them over to their depravity, leading to their just condemnation. Bringing the unconditional and conditional aspects together, we conclude that God unconditionally hardens whomever he desires (namely the non-elect) for reasons known only to him, yet he does so to people who deserve such judgment because of their willful actions.

However, unlike the strongly Calvinistic position, we believe predestination to be single. God's act of hardening is primarily permissive in nature. God releases the non-elect to their own devices, not intervening like he does in the elect, for reasons known only to him. The non-elect's condemnation is deserved but not foreordained by God.

Summary

After briefly tracing how the hardening of hearts has been understood historically, we have concluded that God is the ultimate cause of hardening hearts, that he does so only to the non-elect unconditionally for reasons known only to him, that his act of hardening is primarily passive in nature, and that such judgment is fully deserved.

REFLECTION QUESTIONS

1. How did the views of the Reformers and their followers differ from others regarding hardening hearts?

2. Whose hearts does God harden?

3. Why does God harden hearts?

4. What role do sinners play in hardening hearts?

5. Is God just to condemn persons whose hearts he hardened?

QUESTION 22

What Can Satan and the Demons Do to the Elect and Non-Elect?

In the preceding question, we found that God hardens the hearts of the non-elect in a passive way, primarily leaving them to their own sinful devices and unhinging more of their natural hostility toward God, leading to unbelief and ultimately to final condemnation. While general grace keeps sin under restraint, God (to varying degrees) releases those restraints in the non-elect who all the more will act corruptly and reject divine revelation. However, this raises an interesting question. If sinners are naturally depraved, spiritually blind, and unable to come to God on their own initiative, what need is there for any demonic agents to tempt them to sin, blind them to the truth, and prevent them from coming to faith? Do not their natural wills already do these very things? Wayne Grudem, for example, says:

> Demons will try every tactic to blind people to the gospel (2 Cor. 4:4) and keep them in bondage to things that hinder them from coming to God (Gal. 4:8). They will also try to use temptation, doubt, guilt, fear, confusion, sickness, envy, pride, slander, or any other means possible to hinder a Christian's witness and usefulness.[1]

Although we agree with this statement, it raises the question why Satan must keep unbelievers from seeing the light of the gospel (2 Cor. 4:4) when the gospel is already incomprehensible and foolish to them (Isa. 6:10; Matt. 13:11; John 12:38–40; 1 Cor. 1:18–19, 23; 2:14) or why Satan and demons must tempt people (1 Thess. 3:5) when people's own souls tempt and entice

1. Wayne Grudem, *Systematic Theology: An Introduction to Biblical Doctrine*, 2nd ed. (Grand Rapids: Zondervan Academic, 2020), 536.

them to sin already (James 1:14). Why would Satan need to keep sinners in bondage to things that inhibit their coming to God whenever we are, apart from Christ, already slaves to sin and will never go to Christ on our own initiative (Rom. 6:6–20)?

Although the relation of the demonic to the elect and non-elect appears to be conflicting from the questions listed above, we will find that there is no conflict at all, for God, being sovereign, utilizes demonic entities as secondary causes to carry out his perfect will. Below we will explore the relation of the demonic to the elect and non-elect from the Scriptures.[2]

The Sovereignty of God over All Creation

The first premise to affirm when exploring demons and election is the absolute sovereignty of God over all things, including people, angels, and demons. The psalmist says:

> The LORD has established his throne in the heavens, and his kingdom rules over all. Bless the LORD, O you his angels, you mighty ones who do his word, obeying the voice of his word! Bless the LORD, all his hosts, his ministers, who do his will! Bless the LORD, all his works, in all places of his dominion. Bless the LORD, O my soul! (Ps. 103:19–22).

All works of God's hands fall under his dominion and sovereignty, declares the psalmist, and this includes the demonic. Jesus's disciples found that demons were subject to them because of the name of Jesus (Luke 10:17), for the authority Jesus has over demons was given to them (Luke 10:19–20). While there is some debate as to which fall of angels is mentioned in 2 Peter 2:4 and Jude 6 (whether at the original fall of Satan or Gen. 6:1–4), scholars agree that God's judgment over them is a sign of his sovereignty and lordship over them.

Because God is in absolute, sovereign control over all things, including the demonic, Christians should reject any notion of dualism that places Satan and the demons as equal to or outside the control of God. On this matter, John Calvin rightly said, "As for the discord and strife that we say exists between Satan and God, we ought to accept as fixed certainty the fact that he can do nothing unless God wills and assents to it."[3] Looking to the book of Job, Calvin saw Satan appearing before God to get his assignment

---

2. This section will focus on demonic activity as it relates to a person's election status. For a general book about demons from this series, see John R. Gilhooly, *40 Questions About Angels, Demons, and Spiritual Warfare* (Grand Rapids: Kregel Academic, 2018).
3. John Calvin, *Institutes of the Christian Religion*, ed. John T. McNeill, trans. Ford Lewis Battles, Library of Christian Classics (Louisville: Westminster John Knox, 1960), 1.14.17.

(Job 1:6; 2:1). He can do nothing more or less than what God assigns. When the Lord asked for Ahab to be enticed in 1 Kings 22:20–22, Calvin saw that a spirit of falsehood showed up to carry out divine commands. Saul was tormented by an evil spirit because it was the Lord's will to subject him to punishment (1 Sam. 16:14). Second Thessalonians 2:11 states that God sends deluding influences from Satan so that people will not believe the truth. All these texts (and more) said to Calvin that Satan and the demons are directly under God's power and are compelled to give service to him however he sees fit.[4]

God, Satan, and the Non-Elect

With the sovereignty of God firmly established, what does this have to do with divine election? The answer is, Everything! God uses secondary causes like demons (as well as angels and humans) to carry out his will, including his will in election and non-election. Still, he does so in perfect, sovereign control over the free agency of each agent (human and demonic). As mentioned in Question 12, our view of the human will is that of compatibilism (or soft determinism), where people act in accordance with what they desire, yet those desires act in compatibility with the sovereign will of God. With that view upheld, we say that demonic wills also act in accordance with their desires over which God maintains sovereignty. Scripture gives every indication that the demonic are doing exactly what they desire to do even if they could not do otherwise, and God directs and uses their will and activities to accomplish his determined purposes.

God's sovereignty over demons, humans, and salvation are seen well in Jesus's parable of the sower (Matt. 13:3–23; Mark 4:3–20; Luke 8:5–15). There Jesus spoke of the gospel as "seed" that is sowed by a sower on various types of ground (hearts of people). Among the elect, the gospel seed yields salvation. However, among people to whom the kingdom of God had not been revealed (the non-elect), it did not yield salvation. Jesus spoke of people who hear the word of God, but the devil takes away that word from their hearts so that they do not believe and become saved. Here we see divine, demonic, and human wills all acting in accordance with what they each desire to do. God desires to save the elect and not save the non-elect. Satan desires to remove the gospel that God determined would not bear a harvest unto salvation. The non-elect refuse to believe and be saved (Luke 8:12). All three wills (the divine, the demonic, and the human) act in accordance with their desires, with the demonic and human wills falling under the sovereign plans of God. Satan may have removed the seed, but the natural soil of their heart remained in its natural condition, leading to disbelief in the gospel and no salvation. All three

4. Calvin, *Institutes*, 1.14.17. See also See also T. H. L. Parker, *Calvin: An Introduction to His Thought* (Louisville: Westminster John Knox, 1995), 38.

wills worked in accordance with what they desired to do, which ultimately resulted in what God foreordained. Secondary causes, like Satan in this case, were used to accomplish God's will.[5]

In a similar way, Paul spoke of the gospel being veiled to the perishing (non-elect) because Satan has blinded their unbelieving minds so that they do not see the light of the gospel (2 Cor. 4:3–4). Satan, therefore, utilizes his will in veiling and blinding minds from the gospel. The objects of this activity, however, are not innocent victims. The minds that were blinded were already the "unbelievers."[6] Yet what is to be said of God's will or role? Verses 5–6 provide the answer. There, Paul said that he preached the gospel but that God has been shining the light of the glory of God into the hearts of the elect. Although evangelists, like Paul, preach the gospel to all people (v. 2), God must shine the light of the gospel into the unbelieving elect, resulting in their salvation, while utilizing a secondary cause, like Satan, to veil that light in the hearts of the unbelieving. We must ultimately conclude that God will shine gospel light to people he desires to save.

One last passage may be examined to show how the wills of God, Satan, and humans work through concurrence for the condemnation of the non-elect, namely 2 Thessalonians 2:8–12. There, Paul spoke of the man of lawlessness who comes in the embodiment of Satan's power. Matched with this coming is the deluding influence that God will send to all people who reject the truth and embrace this deceiver's lies. Paul affirmed here the willful activity of the man of lawlessness and Satan, the unbelieving hearts and responsibility of sinners who delight in evil, and the sovereignty of God in salvation and condemnation. God gives people up to the consequences of their sin, using satanic forces in the process, in a way that upholds responsibility and carries out his purposes in election.[7]

Why might God want to use Satan and the other demons to accomplish his purposes for the non-elect? We believe that the use of secondary causes, like the demonic, vindicates God from being a causal agent in the demise of the non-elect. If God blinded people's hearts, he might be said to have caused people's unbelief. If Satan blinded them, however, Satan is culpable even if it ultimately achieves God's foreordained purposes. If God were said to enslave

---

5. See David L. Turner, *Matthew*, Baker Exegetical Commentary on the New Testament (Grand Rapids: Baker Academic, 2008), 339–42; Darrell L. Bock, *Luke 1:1–9:50*, Baker Exegetical Commentary on the New Testament (Grand Rapids: Baker Academic, 1994), 728–29.
6. The Greek best reads, "blinds the minds of the unbelievers," namely people already unbelieving, not "so that they became unbelievers." See Murray J. Harris, *The Second Epistle to the Corinthians*, New International Greek Testament Commentary (Grand Rapids: Eerdmans, 2005), 329.
7. Leon Morris, *1 and* 2 Thess*alonians*, Tyndale New Testament Commentary (Downers Grove, IL: IVP Academic, 2009), 130–33.

people or remove the gospel seed, God may incur guilt and responsibility for the people's actions and response. As it is, by being sovereign over all creation, God accomplishes his perfect will through secondary causes (like demons), though both demons and humans are acting in accordance with their own wills. God, however, remains guiltless.[8]

One more brief point may be made about the relation between God, Satan, and the non-elect, though it is not limited solely to the non-elect, namely, having a demon. Although the term *demonic possession* is often used, the Bible does not expressly speak of such overruling control of demons over a human's life. Nevertheless, Scripture does speak of demonic influence and control resulting in negative influence and loss of abilities (Mark 9:17; Luke 4:33; 8:27). We affirm that apart from salvation in Christ, people may experience demonic possession to varying degrees. This possession could include some elect persons (consider Mary Magdalene in Mark 16:9 and Luke 8:2, who once had seven demons). Such possession, however, would immediately cease in an elect person's life upon true conversion as the Holy Spirit takes occupancy and no other master is over the believer (Rom. 6:14; 8:9–11).

God, Satan, and the Elect

Finally, we will consider the relation between God, Satan, and the elect. As God's saving purposes in election will certainly prevail, and there is security in the salvation of the elect (as answered in Question 20), we find that Satan and the demons' actions are different toward the elect. We will categorize demonic activities against the elect in two primary ways: afflicting Christians and afflicting Christian ministry.

As not even Jesus himself was immune to demonic temptation (Matt. 4:1; Mark 1:13; Luke 4:2), neither is the Christian (1 Cor. 7:5; 10:13). The human will is naturally drawn to sin; however, Satan desires to make sin appealing while hiding its consequences. The elect, both pre- and post-conversion, will experience temptation to sin. The good news, however, is that none of those schemes will have the final word. No one can bring a charge against God's elect (Rom. 8:33–34), for God's verdict of justification has been made. Moreover, God redeems and uses all of Satan's schemes against the elect for his greater purposes. Even as Satan entered into non-elect Judas to initiate the crucifixion (Luke 22:3), God used Satan's evil against him, leading to salvation for the elect. Whatever Paul's "thorn in the flesh" was in 2 Corinthians 12:7, it was viewed both as a messenger of Satan and an opportunity for God's grace and power to prevail. In 1 Corinthians 5:5, we read of Paul instructing the

---

8. Although our view of reprobation differs somewhat, we find agreement with this treatment of secondary causation (primarily in proximate and efficient causes): Peter Sammons, *Reprobation and God's Sovereignty: Recovering a Biblical Doctrine* (Grand Rapids: Kregel Academic, 2022), 193–204, 221–22.

Corinthian church to hand one of its members over to Satan for committing an egregious sin so that his flesh might be destroyed yet his soul saved. Paul believed Satan's activities could be used for good because God is sovereign over all Satan's activities against Christians.[9]

At various times and ways, the demonic may hinder Christian witness and ministry. This was the case for Paul, who said Satan hindered him from going to the Thessalonian church (1 Thess. 2:18). The church's struggle is not ultimately against flesh and blood but spiritual forces of wickedness (Eph. 6:12). Nevertheless, Christians have everything they need for the battle (Eph. 6:13–17), with the promise that God's purposes will prevail. God is sovereign and will have the victory.

Summary

God is absolutely sovereign over all things. In this section, we have explored his sovereignty over not only salvation but Satan's forces. We found that demons are used as secondary causes to carry out God's purposes for the non-elect and the elect. To the non-elect, God uses Satan in the hardening of heart process, yet not in a way that violates the will or responsibilities of demons or the non-elect. Moreover, we found the demonic to be true enemies of Christians and Christian ministry. Because of God's sovereignty, however, they will only lead to the advancement of God's kingdom and glory.

REFLECTION QUESTIONS

1. How should we view Satan and demons in relation to God—as equals or subordinates?

2. How could you explain God's preservation of demonic wills and human wills while carrying out his sovereign plans?

3. How have you seen demonic opposition in the Christian life?

4. How have you seen demonic opposition in Christian ministry?

5. How can God's sovereignty bring peace to people going through such opposition?

---

9. Donald Guthrie, *New Testament Theology* (Downers Grove, IL: Inter-Varsity Press, 1981), 140–41.

QUESTION 23

What Is Supralapsarianism, Infralapsarianism, and Sublapsarianism?

No discussion of divine election would be complete without exploring supralapsarianism, infralapsarianism, and sublapsarianism. What do these terms mean, and what is their significance? Before answering these questions directly, let us consider a few related questions. What did God, exactly, decree and ordain from eternity past? We may say such things as creation, the incarnation and atonement, the existence of the church, and the glorification of Christ. We may also ask ourselves what God, from eternity, permitted to occur. We could say the fall of demons, the fall of Adam, and sinners using their will immorally. Somewhere in these lists, we should also account for things like the eternal judgment of sinners and the salvation of the elect. Now, in what order did these decrees occur in the mind of God? We now arrive at the issue at hand.

In the doctrine of predestination, we must consider whether God's decree to save came before or after his decrees to create and to permit the fall of humanity. As God is outside of time, we are speaking here of a logical, rather than temporal, ordering of God's decisions. High Calvinists who followed Ulrich Zwingli, Theodore Beza, and, earlier, John Duns Scotus held to *supralapsarianism*, the belief that God first (Lat. *supra*) decreed to save the elect and condemn everyone else, then decreed to create and then to permit the fall (Lat. *lapsus*) of humanity in Adam.[1] The alternative view,

1. A fascinating alternative view of supralapsarianism was formed by Karl Barth, primarily in *Church Dogmatics* 2.2, that God's choice in election was before all other decrees (essentially affirming that supralapsarianism as defined by traditional Reformed theology was not going far enough). For Barth, in his high Christology, God ordained the elect first and

held by most other Calvinists, is called *infralapsarianism*, the belief that God first determined to create and then to permit the fall of humanity, followed by (Lat. *infra*) a decree to save the elect.

By and large, these two views are most prevalent within Calvinistic theology (with infralapsarianism being most widely ascribed to). A third option also may be found, called *sublapsarianism*. This view believes that God first decreed to create human beings, then decreed he would permit them to fall, then decreed he would provide a universal atonement sufficient for the sins of the whole world, then finally decreed that he would elect some people to receive this salvation while leaving the rest to condemnation. One major difference between sublapsarianism and infralapsarianism is whether God's decree to elect some people and reprobate the rest is *above* his decree to provide salvation (infralapsarianism) or if the decree to elect some people and reprobate the rest occurs *under* (Lat. *sub*-) his decree to provide salvation (sublapsarianism). The other major difference between the two is that sublapsarians typically hold to unlimited atonement while infralapsarians hold to limited atonement.[2] See Figure 23.1 below for a summary of each view.[3]

Further Framing the Issue

Readers may rightly assume that this debate is a nonissue to non-Reformed theologians who order divine decrees altogether differently. As we have already shown throughout this study, the non-Reformed frame predestination in terms of foreknowledge of people who will freely believe in Christ for salvation. They would certainly reject any decree to elect some people and reprobate others without consideration of their response (whether before or after a decree to permit the fall). If, however, we do not align theologically with the non-Reformed system, how are we to decide which view of God's decrees is best? If we are to attempt to side with a view, more needs to be said about each perspective and the implications each one brings.

---

foremost in his decree of the elect man, Christ Jesus, who himself was elect and reprobate on behalf of all people. See Michael Horton, *The Christian Faith: A Theology for Pilgrims on the Way* (Grand Rapids: Zondervan Academic, 2011), 317–23.

2. Augustus H. Strong, *Systematic Theology* (Philadelphia: Judson, 1954), 3:777–79. See also Millard J. Erickson, *Christian Theology*, 2nd ed. (Grand Rapids: Baker Academic, 2003), 931. Note that some theologians use infralapsarianism and sublapsarianism synonymously and contrastively to supralapsarianism. See Benjamin B. Warfield, *The Plan of Salvation: The Order of God's Decrees* (Eugene, OR: Wipf & Stock, 2000), 92, 95, who would expressly reject the sublapsarian view mentioned above.
3. For an alternative chart, see James Oliver Buswell, *A Systematic Theology of the Christian Religion*, 2 vols. (Grand Rapids: Zondervan, 1962), 2:135, who adapted it from Warfield, *The Plan of Salvation*.

Figure 23.1: The Lapsarian Views

Logical Decree Order	Supralapsarianism	Infralapsarianism	Sublapsarianism
1	To elect some people to salvation and reprobate all others	To create human beings	To create human beings
2	To create human beings (as either elect or reprobate)	To permit humanity to fall	To permit humanity to fall
3	To permit humanity to fall	To elect some people to salvation and reprobate all others	To provide universal atonement
4	To provide limited atonement	To provide limited atonement	To elect some people to salvation and reprobate all others
5	To give the Holy Spirit to apply salvation to the elect	To give the Holy Spirit to apply salvation to the elect	To give the Holy Spirit to apply salvation to the elect
6	To sanctify the elect	To sanctify the elect	To sanctify the elect

Consider this question: Was the fall of humanity predestined or merely foreknown by God? The answer will address whether or not sin was a necessity ordained by God. The three views above agree that, whether by divine predestination or permission, sin was a certainty, but how we frame this answer will determine, to a degree, who is responsible for sin. Supralapsarianism has long been criticized (despite denials from adherents) of ultimately making God the author of evil. Under this view, God created some people to be vessels of condemnation without consideration of their sin. If God's reprobation of the non-elect was first decreed without reference to the fall of humanity into sin, then their condemnation would be owed more to divine sovereignty than to divine justice.[4] Furthermore, in supralapsarianism, God decreed to elect some people and reprobate others before he decreed to create them. However, Scripture, according to the critics of supralapsarianism, teaches that God chooses people out of the world (John 15:19) and out of the same "lump" as people who would be condemned (Rom. 9:21). Thus, God's decision to elect

4. Louis Berkhof, *Systematic Theology*, 4th ed. (Grand Rapids: Eerdmans, 1976), 121–22.

had to precede people as logically created beings and in a state of sin. For supralapsarians, humans existed as possibilities (Lat. *in posse*) but not actuals as God did not yet view anyone as sinners. In other words, God first determined that there would be a definite number of people saved and a definite number of people reprobated, then he determined to create them as actual people, and then he permitted their fall, followed by a determination to redeem the elect.[5]

Infralapsarianism has more adherents because it avoids these issues. It affirms that God permitted the fall and decreed to reprobate some sinners on the basis of their sin. In convincing language, this tradition finds that there is asymmetry between God's election and reprobation. God's election is entirely of grace, apart from what people have done. God's reprobation is entirely of justice with full consideration of what people have done. For reasons known only to God, he elected certain people to be objects of his grace while also choosing to pass by others who would remain objects of justice. However, this response engenders criticism against infralapsarians. Louis Berkhof, for example, found that infralapsarians are hesitant to say that God decreed for sin to exist. Rather, they say he permitted it. However, they must then admit that because God's decree to create preceded his decree to permit the fall, humans have the power to thwart God's plans (which amounts to Arminianism). Contrastively, if infralapsarians were to say that God did ordain there to be sin in the world, but only permissively, then they ultimately arrive at the same point of view as the supralapsarians, who rendered sin to be a certainty in order to bring about God's pleasure.[6]

The sublapsarian view mentioned above is popular among people who hold to universal atonement (with the cross being sufficient to save all people yet efficient for the elect only). God thus truly desires salvation for everyone (as a decree of higher order), yet he limits salvation only for the foreordained elect (a subsequent decree). However, B. B. Warfield sharply criticized this perspective, which he called post-redemptionism, Amyraldism, and hypothetical universalism. Although he did find that the view meets the simplest definition of particular election (and Calvinism), he also found it illogical, unstable, and unbiblical. Why would the Father give his Son to die for all people when he did not intend to avail that death to all people alike and equally? If Christ was given to atone for a sinner's sin, then that person must be saved, according to Warfield (leading to universalism). If sublapsarianism is ascribed to, substitutionary atonement must then be replaced for a governmental theory of the atonement (which contradicts the main biblical motif of the atonement).[7]

---

5. R. L. Dabney, *Systematic Theology* (Carlisle, PA: Banner of Truth Trust, 1985), 232.
6. Berkhof, *Systematic Theology*, 123.
7. Warfield, *The Plan of Salvation*, 96–97.

Addressing the Issue

Clearly, these issues are complex. How then are we to respond to the ordering of divine decrees? The simplest answer is to not respond at all and consider this to be an unfruitful scholastic debate. However, there are significant implications at stake. We should attempt to address the issue as best as we can.

Before we come to any conclusions on the matter, we should acknowledge areas of common ground. First, all the traditions outlined here recognize that God's decree is singular, not plural. Said another way, God's decree is one, not many, in intention and presence. Thus, although we speak of "decrees" (plural) within these views, we recognize them not as separate from one another but as a unit with logical progression. Second, although this issue revolves around the logical ordering of decrees within the mind of God, we recognize that no one can reasonably know the mind of God with absolute certainty unless such things are revealed. There are mysteries simply too great for the human mind (Deut. 29:29). Rather, we are ultimately trying to order the decrees in our minds based upon how we understand them to be logically arranged in God's mind and thereby drawing out the implications of our own views on God's will for creation, the fall of humanity, and election. Because we are dealing with such matters, we recognize that this theological construct is the work of human beings trying to grapple with matters that (although significant) are beyond our ability to answer with absolute certainty. Thus, and third, we believe there is room for differences of opinion. Although the Canons of Dort and Westminster Confession exclude a sublapsarian view, we recognize this to be an in-house debate among Christians. Even the Protestant Reformers showed differences of thought. We, likewise, should approach this matter with grace for one another.

Our own position on the matter is that of infralapsarianism. The order, then, would be as follows: God decreed that the Son would be incarnate, to create humanity, to permit the fall of humanity, to elect some people to salvation, to provide a limited atonement through Jesus as Savior, and to save the elect while leaving the rest in their own state of willful rebellion.

The incarnation of Christ as the God-man has always been the intention of the triune God, not an afterthought or consequence of sin entering into the world. God's plan has always entailed the Son ruling over a glorified creation. The incarnation, then, is not logically a consequence of the fall of humanity (though it is the means to rectify it). Rather, it is the fulfillment of God's first order of decree. When Christ returns at the eschaton, we see sin being forever vanquished, but we see more than that. We see the glorified Son bringing creation to God who reigns forever and ever (thus reflective of his chief purpose). Thus, we conclude that the incarnation precedes the decree to permit the fall.

By decreeing to permit the fall and knowing humanity's plight, however, God decreed to appoint Jesus as the Savior for the elect. We find it difficult to conceive how election could precede his will to create humanity with them existing as mere hypotheticals or possibilities (and not actuals). We also find it difficult to place election prior to his decree to provide salvation. God does have a sovereign decree for the election of certain people to salvation. We believe, however, that this decree necessitates a decree to provide Christ as atoning sacrifice. As only the foreordained elect will believe (as a consequence, not condition, of their election status), we believe the decree to elect some people and leave the rest to their own demise follows his decree to send Jesus to save. The end result is to have the first order of the decree actualized, namely the incarnation of the Son who serves as mediator between God and creation.

Summary

Christians recognize that God has plans that he determined would occur. We also recognize that God, being outside time, has an eternal will. We further know that God's will prevails and (as far as the Reformed believe) that his decree is not contingent upon human beings. How then does God's decree relate to people's salvation?

In this section, we have explored three major views that all reference God's intentions in salvation related to the fall (or *lapse*) of humanity. Supralapsarianism is the belief that election came before God's decree to create and permit the fall. Infralapsarianism is the belief that God decreed to create people, then decreed to permit the fall, then out of fallen humanity he elected some people to salvation. Sublapsarianism is the belief that God decreed first to create, then to permit the fall, then to provide salvation sufficient for everyone, then to elect. We find these views each to have some merit and that there is room for differences of opinion.

REFLECTION QUESTIONS

1. What is at stake with the ordering of divine decrees?
2. Which view of the decrees do you hold to, and why?
3. Did God ordain the fall of humanity?
4. Was the incarnation a response to sin entering the world?
5. Do our views of ordering divine decrees merit dissention in the church?

QUESTION 24

What Is the Relation Between Election and the Church?

Often when Christians speak of the church today, they are referring to a building they go to on Sundays or a denomination with which they align. People say, "It's time to go to church," or, "I belong to the Baptist church in town," or "I go to the church on the corner of Second Street." During times of capital improvements, we speak of needing to remodel the church, and through mission trips we help build a church in a new area through skilled labor and tools. Referring to the church in such a way can often leave us with the impression that the church is something we ourselves construct, attend, and then leave until next time. However, the New Testament never refers to the church in terms of a building (outside of 1 Cor. 3:9 and Eph. 2:20–22, which do not refer to literal buildings). The earliest Christians met in the houses of faithful members, not ornate buildings that they called "the church." For these Christians, they *were* the church. More than that, they viewed the church as ultimately a divine (not human) institution formed, led, and sustained by God.

As we root our doctrine of the church in the doctrine of election, we too will view the church as a divine construction built for God's glory rather than a human construction for the religious. The apostles did not disassociate the church from divine election, often calling churches the chosen of God (Col. 3:12; 2 Thess. 2:13; Titus 1:1; 1 Peter 1:1; 2:9; 2 John 1:1). By being known as God's elect, these churches were reminded that not only their individual salvation but also their very existence as the people of God was grounded in divine choice. The church is Christ's body on earth, rooted in his gracious will to have a collected people as his own treasured possession. It exists because God chose for it to exist both in its design and membership. It is not a building made with human hands or a collective hub created by Christians who want to hear sermons preached, worship songs sung, or mission efforts centralized. It is the people of God, created and sustained by God's grace. As Carl Trueman rightly said, "The church is not our human response to grace but is itself an act of God's grace."[1] Thus, because the church is a divine construct centered around the work of Christ, it cannot be understood (either in terms of its identity or function) apart from divine election.

A short survey of the major Protestant creeds and confessions shows how Christians, at least theologically, have understood the church in terms of divine election. When the Heidelberg Catechism asks what its confessors believe about the Holy Catholic Church, it states: "That out of the whole human race, from the beginning to the end of the world, the Son of God, by His Spirit and Word, gathers, defends, and preserves for himself unto everlasting life, a chosen community in the unity of the true faith."[2] Article 16 of the Scots Confession of Faith (1560) views the church as the multitude of people chosen of God through faith in Christ, elect of all ages. The Westminster Confession, chapter 25, says that the church consists of the whole number of the elect, gathered together under the headship of Christ.

As Scripture and church tradition have long held together divine election and the church, we must seek to understand this relationship better. Below we will analyze the relationship between the church and election in terms of its membership, its mission, and its marks.

The Church Local and Universal, Visible and Invisible

Defining the term *church* is no simple task, for as many Christian confessions and creeds have found (including the ones mentioned above), Scripture refers to the church (*ekklēsia*) in more than one way. Broadly speaking, we define *church* as God's chosen people who have been saved by grace through repentance and faith in Jesus Christ and are baptized and indwelt by the Holy Spirit for the purpose of glorifying God. Sometimes Scripture refers to local Christian congregations in specific geographical areas as churches, something we can call the *local church* (1 Cor. 1:2; 2 Cor. 1:1; 1 Thess. 1:1; 2 Thess. 1:1; Philem. 1:2). At other times Scripture uses the term *church* in a way we define as the *universal church*, namely the whole company of regenerate believers in Christ from all ages and all spaces, whether on earth or in heaven (Eph. 1:22; 5:23–32; Col. 1:18). There are a variety of metaphors used to describe the church, such as the body, temple, bride, and light.

The church, historically, has also been defined in terms of its visibility and invisibility, and while it relates to the local and universal church distinction, it ultimately addresses a different issue. When theologians speak of the visible

---

1. Carl R. Trueman, *Grace Alone: Salvation as a Gift of God, What the Reformers Taught . . . and Why It Still Matters*, Five Solas (Grand Rapids: Zondervan Academic, 2017), 164.
2. Philip Schaff, ed., *The Creeds of Christendom*, 6th ed., 3 vols. (Grand Rapids: Baker, 1998), 3:324–25.

and invisible church, they are referring to the church as God sees it where he alone can distinguish between true and false converts. When speaking of the *visible church*, we mean the community of individuals who profess faith in Christ and belong to various local congregations. Thus, the visible church is synonymous with the local church. However, the local, visible church is comprised of people who profess faith in Christ, which may or may not include false converts (1 John 2:19). The *invisible church*, on the other hand, is the true body of regenerate believers chosen by God for salvation. Only God can see into human hearts and know who is truly saved (2 Tim. 2:19). More than that, God knows the ones whom he has chosen. The invisible church, thus, is the elect and are de facto members of the universal church. Ideally, they should also be members of the local church.

As mentioned above, someone may be part of the local church without being a member of the universal, invisible church. Membership requirements into the local, visible church varies , with some churches requiring baptism, profession of faith, and/or catechism, and it is based upon the choices of people. Membership into the universal, invisible church, on the other hand, is by sovereign grace through faith based upon the choice of God alone.[3]

The Elected Mission of the Church

In divine election, God chooses not only the church's members but its mission. Churches who seek to be obedient to the will of God are not at liberty to determine their own purposes but instead must derive it from God, who gives his people their assignment. While churches, under the leadership of the Holy Spirit, should seek to accomplish that mission within their own unique contexts (something called *strategy*), the mission of God for the people of God has been and always will be the same. We believe the mission of the church is to glorify God through faithful worship, edification of believers, and evangelism to the lost.[4]

The primary focus of all ministry for the church is the glory of God, because that is why the community was designed (see Question 16). The glory of God is the fundamental purpose of all creation (Pss. 19:1; 147:1), and it was the chief mission of Jesus while on earth (John 12:27–28, 17:1, 4); however, because of the fall, creation does not glorify God as it should. Through the redemption found in Christ, the church can glorify its God who is, to this community of grace, not only Creator but Savior (Rom. 15:5–6; Eph. 1:5–6, 11–14; 1 Peter 2:9). They are able to sing a song no angel could sing, for they

---

3. See Gregg R. Allison, *The Church: An Introduction*, Short Studies in Systematic Theology (Wheaton, IL: Crossway, 2021), 43–50.
4. Mark Dever, "The Church," in *A Theology for the Church*, rev. ed., eds. Daniel L. Akin, Bruce Riley Ashford, and Kenneth Keathley (Nashville: B&H Academic, 2014), 634–39; Stanley J. Grenz, *Theology for the Community of God* (Grand Rapids: Eerdmans, 2000), 486–510.

sing of their redemption (Rev. 14:3). And while the non-elect will glorify God as objects of wrath and just judgment, the elect church will glorify God as objects of mercy forever and ever (Rom. 9:22–23).

While the glory of God through the church will endure forever, there is work to do in the here and now until the second coming of the Lord. This work includes both vertical and horizontal ministry. Vertically, the church is commissioned to worship its triune God. This worship entails weekly gathering in the name of Christ (Heb. 10:25). Gathering as the church is not optional or an individual exercise. To fulfill its first objective of worship, it must gather, though it still exists while separated (Acts 15:30; 20:7–8). While assembling, the church glorifies God through various acts of worship that include music (Eph. 5:19; Col. 3:16), giving (Matt. 6:2–3; Acts 4:35; 1 Tim. 6:17–19), and prayer (Eph. 6:18–19; 1 Thess. 5:17; 2 Thess. 3:1; James 5:13, 17).[5] Horizontally, the church also has a ministry to fellow people, whether saved or unsaved. To the saved, the church must edify believers in their faith. Activities under this category include preaching the Word (Col. 1:25–26; 1 Tim. 6:2; 2 Tim 4:2), fellowship (Acts 2:42; Rom. 12:13–15; 1 John 1:7), and teaching, training, and rebuking (1 Cor. 12:7–31; 14:26; Col. 1:28; 1 Tim. 5:20; 2 Tim. 4:2). Also horizontally, the church has a ministry to evangelize the lost with the gospel (Matt. 28:19–20; Acts 1:8; Rom. 15:20).

All three of these purposes must be rooted firmly in our doctrine of election, for God has elected its mission just as much as he has its members. We who have been chosen to this community must faithfully carry out these mandates; however, the good news is that the mission of the church is ultimately the mission of God. These tasks that he has called his chosen body to do are tasks he has equipped his body for. Because God has elected the people and purpose of his church, its ministry and activity are ultimately empowered and accomplished by God.

The Marks of the Church

As we said in the beginning, many people today associate the church with a building. They know a church when they see it because there is a building with a steeple, stained glass windows, and religious images on the walls. However, the creeds and confessions of the church show that for most of its history, the church has been primarily identified through faithful preaching of the Word and proper administration of the sacraments (ordinances).[6] These two marks are not exhaustive, and many churches and traditions have

5. Strictly speaking, edifying believers and evangelism are also acts of worship and should not be separated from it.
6. Belgic Confession, 29; Westminster Confession, 25.3; Augsburg Confession, 7; Thirty-Nine Articles, 19; Genevan Confession, 18.

included other marks, such as discipline, leadership, discipleship, and more (some of which include the three purposes of the church mentioned above). Rather than defining all the marks of a true church, our purpose is to show how these marks draw significance from divine election.

Divine election ensures that the church will be recognized for the work of God rather than the work of people. Consider the ministry of preaching. Is preaching merely the human act of a person speaking about God to the church, or is it a divine act of God speaking through a person to the church? We will answer this question largely in how we view God's choice in salvation. Church practice sadly reflects a philosophy of preaching that believes that people will be saved and saints discipled when preachers are compelling, entertaining, and culturally relevant. While there is nothing wrong with being any of these things, we may succumb to the temptation of believing preaching is ultimately a human activity and that the church is built and matured through preachers rather than the Word preached. If, however, we see preaching as it relates to divine election, we will proclaim the Word of God (Scripture) to the people of God (the elect) through the power of God (the Holy Spirit). In so doing, through faithful proclamation, God speaks through the preacher and effectually calls the elect into fellowship with himself. Thus, it is not ultimately the preacher who is speaking to the congregation but God. Many of the earliest Reformers believed preaching to be God's word and grace to the people. It is not that preachers were merely preaching about grace. The very act of preaching was God's grace, for by preaching God is speaking to the hearts of his people.[7] Preachers (who themselves were called both into salvation and into gospel ministry through no innate goodness of their own but solely to fulfill the electing purposes of God) are conduits through whom God speaks to his elect for the building of the church, thus ensuring that the Word will never return void and that the purposes of God will certainly prevail.

We may also consider ordinances such as baptism and the Lord's Supper. God—not the church—chose these ordinances. Baptism has been understood in many ways, as has the Lord's Supper. Regardless of these (important) differences, we must view these ordinances as God's graces to the elect church. Both baptism and the Lord's Supper are powerful displays of God doing for the elect what they never could do for themselves. Through baptism, we see that God has put to death our old, sinful selves and raised them anew in his Son. Through the Lord's Supper, we see through faith the brokenness of the Savior and his poured-out blood. These sacraments were chosen by God for the church and cannot be understood apart from divine election. Additionally, they remind us that salvation is all of grace and not of our own doing.

7. Trueman, *Grace Alone*, 174–75.

Summary

Through this question we have attempted to show the relation between divine election and the church in terms of its membership, mission, and marks. We found that it is because of divine election that the church itself exists, both locally and universally as well as visibly and invisibly. Moreover, we found that the threefold ministry of the church and its various marks should be grounded in a firm belief of election, for in so doing we ensure our beliefs and practices as a church are, like election, rooted in divine grace.

REFLECTION QUESTIONS

1. What is the difference between the local and universal church?

2. How does divine election determine the difference between the visible and invisible church?

3. What are the purposes of the church, and how do they each relate to divine election?

4. What are the marks of a true church?

5. Are the ordinances a response to God's grace or an act of God's grace?

PART 3

Ethical Considerations of Election

SECTION A

Election and the Divine Will

QUESTION 25

Does God Love All People If Only Some People Are Elect?

Thus far in our study, we have argued that divine election in salvation is single, unconditional, and individual from eternity past and effectual in its outworking, all for the glory of God. In this third part of the book, we seek to draw out ethical considerations related to these positions. Specifically, here we are trying to understand why God would elect people in the way he does (or at least in the way we *think* he does). We confess that explaining the infinite mind of God on these matters is beyond our capacity, yet we want to understand election from God's mind as best and faithfully as we can. Among the more significant questions is whether God truly loves all people if only some of them are elect.

We have to uphold that God is loving and that some people are unsaved if we are to be faithful to Scripture. Love is an innate characteristic of God, a trait that has been shown from all eternity between members of the Trinity (John 17:23–26; 2 Cor. 13:11; 1 John 4:8). God's love has extended to his creation and, specifically, to human beings. Passages like John 3:16 and 1 John 4:9–11 show that God truly loves the people of the world, a love that explains why the Lamb of God takes away the sin of the world (John 1:29) and is not willing that anyone perishes but that all people come to repentance (2 Peter 3:9). Even still, we affirm that not everyone is saved, and the unsaved were also not elected. If God chose before the foundations of the world not to elect some people to salvation, does he truly love them? This question has been a significant reason the non-Reformed tradition believes God elects only conditionally. For them, God does love everyone and gives everybody the opportunity to become elect. For those of us who ascribe to unconditional election, the answer to this question is more complex. It is not, however, novel, as many theologians have addressed the issue of how election relates to God's love.

Overview of God's Love and Election

Theologians as early as Augustine have tried to reconcile God's individual election with his love for all humanity. Tackling the problem in his commentary on John 17:21–23, Augustine affirmed that God does love everything he created, especially human beings (whether elect or not). God would not create something he innately hated, and as he did not create the evil that he hates, he thus loves humanity. Despite this love for people, there is a special love he has for the elect (what Augustine calls the "members of His Only-begotten"), a love surpassed only by the love that God has for the Only-Begotten himself, Christ the Lord.[1]

Thomas Aquinas also addressed this problem (citing Augustine), and he observed that, in a sense, God may love some things (namely people) more than others. That is to say, while he loves all his creation, he wills a greater good for some people (namely the elect) who are the recipients of his extraordinary goodness. At the same time, while he loves sinners as members of his creation, he justly hates them as ones who fall short of their true existence. Christ, on the other hand, is loved more than the whole human race, for God wills the greatest good for Christ, who has been given the name above all names.[2]

John Calvin did not hesitate to affirm that God loves all people. Commenting on John 3:16, he said, "Both points are distinctly stated to us: namely, that faith in Christ brings life to all, and that Christ brought life, because the Heavenly Father loves the human race, and wishes that they should not perish."[3]

In more recent years, D. A. Carson wrote on the subject by mentioning five specific ways God loves. The first of these loves is the love that the Father and Son have shared among themselves from all eternity. The second is God's providential love that extends over everything that he created. The third love is shown in God's salvific position toward the fallen world. Specifically, this type of love is shown to the whole world and not just to the elect. The love that God has toward the elect is the fourth love mentioned, a salvific love that is particular in nature and has been experienced by Israel and the church. Fifth, and finally, is a provisional love expressed to the elect contingent upon obedience. While the fourth love remains on the elect, Christians must abide in such love and will experience it more through obedience.[4] What is more,

---

1. Augustine of Hippo, *Homilies on the Gospel of John* in *Nicene and Post-Nicene Fathers*, ed. Philip Schaff, 14 vols. (Peabody, MA: Hendrickson, 2012), tractate 110.6, 7:411.
2. Thomas Aquinas, *Summa Theologica*, 1.20.2–4.
3. John Calvin, *Commentary on the Gospel of Jesus Christ According to John*, trans. William Pringle, 22 vols. (Grand Rapids: Baker, 1993), 1:123. See also Calvin's sermon on Deuteronomy 4:36–38 entitled "On Wednesday, the 5th of June 1555, the twenty eighth Sermon, which is the tenth upon the fourth Chapter."
4. D. A. Carson, *The Difficult Doctrine of the Love of God* (Wheaton, IL: Crossway, 2000), 16–24.

Carson convincingly wrote how necessary it is to uphold each of these loves if we are to remain biblical and true to the nature of God.

Thus, we can say that there is a strong tradition, as represented by these select examples, that affirms God's love to all people along with a specific and unique love for the elect. Nevertheless, some critics still find unconditional individual election (often labeled as just *Calvinism*) incompatible with God's love for all humanity. The basis for such a claim is that the non-elect cannot help but remain in their depraved state and persevere in sin, thus accumulating for themselves more condemnation when they face the Lord in judgment. What is more, there is no logical basis for ordaining such an end to the non-elect other than God's mysterious will or good pleasure. Finally, critics point to the often-held view within the Reformed tradition of limited atonement. If God sent his Son to die only for the elect, and Christ himself died only for the elect and not everyone, neither the Father nor Son can be said to love everybody. As it pertains to the Holy Spirit, he only opens the spiritual eyes of the elect and enables them alone to respond with faith, thereby implying that no member of the Trinity truly loves every human being under an unconditional, individual election view.[5]

These critiques of unconditional, individual election will be the focus of our attention for the next several questions. However, as the overall critique is that our view of election portrays God as unloving, we will here address that issue of God's love for all people and his special love for the elect.

God's General and Special Love

Like Augustine, Aquinas, Calvin, and Carson, we do not believe we have to choose between God's love for all humanity and his specific love for a select few, for Scripture teaches both.[6] God loves everything that he has created, and out of all creation we find he has special love for human beings, who are made in his image (Ps. 136). From the Old Testament, we see God having love for many nations (Isa. 42:6–7; Jonah) yet special love for Israel (Hos. 3:1; Mal. 1:2). Generally, God shows his love to all human beings by meeting their daily needs (Matt. 5:44–46), yet he shows special love to the poor and hurting (Matt. 7:8–11; 20:34; Mark 1:41). There is a love that God has for the whole world (John 17:23–26; 2 Cor. 13:11; 1 John 4:8) yet also a special love for the elect (Eph. 1:4–5).[7]

5. Jerry L. Walls, *Does God Love Everyone? The Heart of What's Wrong with Calvinism* (Eugene, OR: Cascade, 2016), 15–21.
6. We agree with many scholars today that divine love is best understood by looking at God's actions toward humanity; thus, the approach used in this section will explore God's love toward humanity even if the term is not expressly stated.
7. See Geoffrey Grogan, "A Biblical Theology of the Love of God," in *Nothing Greater, Nothing Better: Theological Essays on the Love of God*, ed. Kevin J. Vanhoozer (Grand Rapids: Eerdmans, 2001), 51–63.

In many ways, God may be said to love all people yet demonstrate a special love to select individuals whom he chooses. We find that loving people are often selective in their love. Consider an upright man who, in a way, loves all children. Many examples can be given throughout his life of how he has cared for them, even ones he has never met personally. However, this man may have a unique love for his own children. The love he has for his own children does not negate or even lessen the love for children who are not his, yet it says that there is something special both about the love itself and the ones he loves when it is targeted at his own children. This analogy is imperfect, for oftentimes people would love children who are not their own more if they had limitless resources (as God does), yet it hopefully reflects how we can have general love for all people yet special love for a few. So too we believe that God loves everyone yet shows unique love to the elect.

Although critics of unconditional, individual election would likely agree that God can show general and special love, they find that any such special love that results in the denial of any hope of salvation to the non-elect is incompatible with general love. To be clear, such critics do not deny that God would be just in denying salvation to the non-elect (for God would be right to condemn them for their sins). Rather, they would say it would be unloving of God if he provided salvation to some people to the rejection of others when it was just as possible for him to give it to everyone. One such critic, Jerry Walls, ultimately concludes that God would be unloving to all people if such a view of election were upheld. We quote his basic logical flow of the matter below:

1. God truly loves all persons.
2. Not all persons will be saved.
3. To truly love someone is to desire their well-being and to promote their true flourishing as much as you properly can.
4. The well-being and true flourishing of all persons is to be found in a right relationship with God, a saving relationship in which we love and obey him.
5. God could give all persons "irresistible grace" and thereby determine all persons to freely accept a right relationship with himself and be saved.
6. Therefore, all persons will be saved.[8]

Walls claims that because of the contradiction that exists between points 2 and 6, one or more of the points must be rejected. Arminians, says Walls, reject number 5, for they do not believe grace is irresistible. Calvinists, says Walls, must ultimately reject point 1 because, in their view,

8. Walls, *Does God Love Everyone?*, 30.

God could give irresistible grace to everyone and enable them to believe in Christ for salvation, yet he chooses instead for some people to be condemned to hell when it was within his power to save them. Thus, God must not love everyone.[9]

In response, we can say that adherents of unconditional, individual election can, at least in theory, agree with points 1–6. Points 1–4 are not in much dispute. The bigger areas of contestation would be in points 5–6. We can agree with Walls, as he has written it here, that God *could* give everyone irresistible grace and determine all people to be saved. Further, we can agree that, should point 5 be true, point 6 would also be true. However, we would then have to add the following points to his logical flow:

7. Because point 6 is unbiblical and contradictory to point 2, we must reject point 6 and affirm the scriptural and historical teaching that God has not given all persons "irresistible grace" or determined that all persons freely accept a right relationship with himself and be saved.
8. God has given only the elect "irresistible grace" and determined that they alone freely accept a right relationship with himself and be saved.
9. God has permitted the non-elect to stay in a willful state of rebellion and disbelief whereby they freely reject a right relationship with himself and salvation in his name.
10. Therefore, only the elect are saved.

There is a good deal more explaining that must be done (which will be done in subsequent questions). Nevertheless, God's love for all people need not be denied. God does truly love all his creation. Giving special love to the elect does not negate his love for the non-elect. It is merely a different type of love.

Summary

We acknowledge that there is difficulty in reconciling God's love for all humanity and his special love for those whom he has chosen for salvation. We have come to conclude, like many theologians of the past, that God does love all people as demonstrated by his word and actions, yet he has extended a special love to his elect whom he has chosen unconditionally and individually. We affirm what we have written elsewhere in this book that the purest unconditional love is expressed through unconditional election. Not from anything that we have done, but solely by his grace, are the elect brought into salvation in Christ.

---

9. Walls, *Does God Love Everyone?*, 33–35.

REFLECTION QUESTIONS

1. How would someone with a conditional view of election address God's love (both for the elect and non-elect) differently than someone who holds to an unconditional view of election?

2. Is it illogical or inconsistent to hold to divine universal love and unconditional election?

3. How does God show his love for all humanity?

4. Is that love distinct from the love he shows to the elect?

5. After reviewing Walls's logical flow, how would you adjust it to fit your view of divine love and election?

QUESTION 26

Does God Want All People to Be Saved If Only Some People Are Elect?

As we consider further implications of an unconditional, individual election view, we come to another question that closely relates to our preceding question about God's love for people. Here, we must ask if God truly desires everyone to be saved if he only elects some of them to salvation. It would seem on the surface that he would not if he eternally and unconditionally elected only a portion of them to salvation. But if this is true, it would present two considerable problems. First, it would seem to go against the clear teaching of Scripture that God does not want anyone to perish but for everyone to be saved. Second, it would seem to imply that God does not truly love everyone (discussed in the preceding question). Given our claim that God does love everyone, yet we say election is unconditional and individual from eternity past, is our view of election a logical and biblical contradiction? Some scholars suggest so.[1] According to them, only a conditional election view matched with universal atonement makes God truly loving of everyone, for it allows anyone the opportunity to be saved. Below, we will explore the extent of God's saving desire.

Affirming Universal Saving Desire

While we do not deny that some Calvinists believe God does not desire the salvation of everyone,[2] we find that many adherents of unconditional,

1. See J. Matthew Pinson, *40 Questions About Arminianism* (Grand Rapids: Kregel Academic, 2022), 114–15; Fritz Guy, "The Universality of God's Love," in *The Grace of God and the Will of Man*, ed. Clark H. Pinnock (Minneapolis: Bethany House, 1989), 36–39; Jerry L. Walls, *Does God Love Everyone? The Heart of What's Wrong with Calvinism* (Eugene, OR: Cascade, 2016), 39–43.
2. For example, see David Engelsma, *Hyper-Calvinism and the Call of the Gospel: An Examination of the Well-Meant Offer of the Gospel*, 2nd ed. (Jenison, MI: Reformed Free, 1994), 58.

individual election affirm God's earnest desire for all people to be saved. We will make this point biblically below, but let us first appreciate how Reformed theologians have affirmed God's universal saving desire.

John Calvin, commenting on John 3:16, said,

> And [Jesus] has employed the universal term *whosoever*, both to invite all indiscriminately to partake of life, and to cut off every excuse from unbelievers. Such is also the import of the term *World*, which he formerly used; for though nothing will be found in *the world* that is worthy of the favour of God, yet he shows himself to be reconciled to the whole world, when he invites all men without exception to the faith of Christ, which is nothing else than an entrance into life.[3]

Martin Luther also affirmed that God does not desire the wicked to die but rather that everyone be saved through the word of salvation preached to all people.[4] In more recent times, R. C. Sproul and John Piper have both affirmed that God does not want anyone to perish in hell but that everyone be saved.[5]

These theologians address many of Scripture's texts that reveal God's displeasure in the death of sinners and his desire for everyone's salvation. Consider Ezekiel 18. The Lord, speaking to Ezekiel, affirmed that he would rather see wicked people turn from evil and live than die for their sins (vv. 23, 32). We see later in Ezekiel 33:11 the Lord pleading for Israel to repent, for he takes no pleasure in the death of the wicked. Similarly, we see Jesus lamenting over Jerusalem, wanting to gather its children together as a hen gathers her chicks (Matt. 23:37). Regrettably, the people were unwilling. According to his disposition as reflected in these passages, we conclude that God takes no pleasure in disbelief and should never be thought of as a cruel tyrant who derives pleasure from people's condemnation.

We agree with Calvin and others that John 3:16–17 affirms the mission of God to be for the whole world—everyone indiscriminately. Evangelists are to call all people to believe in Christ, and everyone who believes will be saved. This view finds alignment with Paul in 1 Timothy 2:4, which expresses God's universal desire for all people to be saved. God does not want any to perish, says Peter, but all (meaning every person) to come to repentance (2 Peter 3:9).

---

3. John Calvin, *Commentary on the Gospel of Jesus Christ According to John*, trans. William Pringle, 22 vols. (Grand Rapids: Baker, 1993), 1:125 (italics original).
4. Martin Luther, *On the Bondage of the Will* in *Luther and Erasmus: Free Will and Salvation*, eds. E. Gordon Rupp and Philip S. Watson (Louisville: Westminster John Knox, 2006), 200–202. Note the important qualification to this statement mentioned below.
5. R. C. Sproul, *Chosen by God* (Wheaton, IL: Tyndale House, 1986), 195–97. John Piper, *Does God Desire All to Be Saved?* (Wheaton, IL: Crossway, 2013).

The Complexity of God's Will

How then do we and the theologians above reconcile God's universal desire for everyone to be saved with unconditional, individual election? The answer lies in what we call the complexity of God's will. By complexity, we are not meaning that God's will is confusing, conflicting, or complicated within himself. Rather, we acknowledge (as does Calvin, Luther, Sproul, and Piper) that God can both will and desire more than one thing.[6]

Calvin, for example, referred to God's love that he has for all people and the love he has for the elect (discussed in Question 25). In the same way, he can desire everyone to be saved but have a special desire to accomplish that salvation by enabling faith in the lives of the elect.[7] For Luther, there is a difference between the word preached whereby God desires everyone everywhere to repent and believe for salvation and the hidden will of God that desires only the elect to be saved. The elect hear this message, repent, and believe it, while the non-elect reject it to their own deserved peril.[8] Why does God work in the lives of the elect to embrace the gospel and not others if he desires everyone to be saved? Luther appeals to God's hidden will, which is mysterious and beyond humans' ability or right to inquire. Sproul rightly notes that Scripture speaks of the will of God in various ways, two of which are particularly helpful in understanding his desires in election and salvation. One way is what Sproul calls God's *efficacious will*, that is, God's sovereign will that is certain to be accomplished. This efficacious will is directed solely to the elect, for it is what brings about the certainty of their salvation. It is not directed to the non-elect, for then God's will that none perish but that all people be saved would be efficacious and lead to universalism. Sproul then speaks of God's *dispositional will*, referring to what pleases him.[9] By disposition, he desires all people to be saved and that no one perishes. As judge, however, he must uphold justice and sentence people to hell as consequence for their willful rebellion. This verdict is nothing that brings God innate pleasure. He would rather they never have sinned. Piper, in a similar way, acknowledges that to will the salvation of everyone and to unconditionally elect only some people implies that God has two wills or ways of willing. Citing many biblical examples, Piper shows how God wills things of which he disapproves (like the death of Christ by sinners, Pharaoh's hardened heart, and Judas's betrayal). In the same way, God truly desires all people to be saved, but he wills something more than that. Piper concludes that God's

6. Arminians, too, address this dilemma by appealing to similar categories (framed differently), such as God's antecedent will, which desires everyone's salvation, and his consequent will, which desires to judge persons who reject grace. See Pinson, *40 Questions About Arminianism*, 111.
7. Calvin, *Gospel According to John*, 1:125.
8. Luther, *Bondage of the Will*, 200–02.
9. Sproul, *Chosen by God*, 195–96.

glory in wrath and mercy (Rom. 9:22–23) is why God might desire everyone to be saved yet effectually will the salvation of the elect alone.[10]

Our own view on this matter is similar. God has a dispositional will that takes no delight in the demise of the wicked. His true desire is that no one sins but has close fellowship with him (Gen. 1–2). As it is, humanity has sinned and is deserving of God's wrath and judgment. Although God, in his disposition, wills for the non-elect's salvation, it will never come, for they willfully and defiantly refuse to repent and believe. Is God to be blamed because only his dispositional will desired their salvation but not his efficacious will? Absolutely not. The non-elect are responsible for their response to the gospel just as much as they are for their sin.

Still, someone may question whether God truly desires everyone's salvation if he only effectually calls and regenerates the elect while leaving the non-elect in their miserable state. Perhaps God does love all people and desires their salvation, as we have discussed here and in the preceding question, but it apparently must be significantly less than what he expresses toward the elect. If God truly loves everyone and desires all people to be saved, would not he give everyone the ability to believe? In response, we say that the non-Reformed notion of prevenient grace, which in their view gives everyone the ability to believe, has significant deficiencies (discussed in Question 12). We find it more problematic that God would elect because of humans meeting conditions rather than from unconditioned grace. Moreover, we find there to be no contradiction between God's desire for everyone to be saved and his saving of the elect alone. Our view of conversion, discussed in Question 19, entails a general call of salvation that is for all people. God desires the gospel to be preached to everyone because, out of love for all humanity, he desires them all to be saved. Regrettably, all humanity by nature rejects this gospel. Human rejection does not nullify God's universal love and saving intent. Even still, God effectually calls and regenerates the hearts of the elect alone. Why would he do such a thing if he desires everyone's salvation? Perhaps the better question is why he would effectually call anyone, knowing humanity's wickedness. To either question, we cannot give an answer, for then we are prying into hidden wisdom that does not belong to us. His Word clearly states he desires everyone to be saved, yet not everyone is saved. He has chosen some people to be saved because of grace, not human works or achievement. He may leave some persons in their own willful state of rebellion while transforming the hearts of the elect. Anything more pries into hidden knowledge, which (as Luther mentioned) exceeds our ability or right.

We might further add that it is not difficult to imagine a hypothetical world where God created human beings as good, permitted them to fall, desired them to be right with him, yet provided no remedy for their plight. He would find

10. Piper, *Does God Desire All to Be Saved?*, 38–39.

no pleasure in their condemnation but would carry out judgment nonetheless. In such a world, however, God would not get to display his glory in salvation. Desiring to glorify himself as redeemer while maintaining his justice over sin, he accomplishes salvation for those whom he has chosen for reasons known only to him. Thus, he can desire salvation for all humanity but uphold his attributes of justice and mercy for all eternity to the praise of his glory.

It may be helpful for some people who struggle with this issue to frame it in light of God's broader permissive will regarding sin. God is not willing that anyone sins, for sin displeases and dishonors him. He desires that people be holy and worship him as their God which, regrettably, many people refuse to do. God permits such disobedience despite it not pleasing him. In a similar way, he desires all people everywhere to believe in the Son for their salvation. He permits many people to follow their own desires of disbelief, just like he permits them to follow their own sinful passions, but he is not the cause of either their disbelief or sin. Even still, for the non-elect as well as the elect, he desires them all to be saved, though his permissive will allows the non-elect to stay in their unbelief while his efficacious will allows the elect to turn to belief.

Summary

In this question we have explored historically and biblically how to address the issue of God's desire for all people to be saved given unconditional, individual election. Our conclusion is that God does truly desire every single person to be saved. Building upon what was said in Question 25, we believe that God genuinely loves every person, whether elect or non-elect. Relatedly, we believe he desires all people to be saved. However, for reasons known only to God, he chooses to let some people remain in their willful rebellion, leading ultimately to a just and eternal condemnation. For other reasons known only to God, he chooses to effectually call and regenerate others so that they become saved. Is God being arbitrary in whom he chooses? We will discuss that in the next question. For now, we simply affirm that God does love all people and sincerely desires everyone's salvation, yet for reasons known only to him he unconditionally and individually elects some people for salvation while leaving others in their willful rebellion, all to his own glory.

REFLECTION QUESTIONS

1. Does God desire everyone to be saved, in your view?

2. Does a contradiction exist between God desiring everyone's salvation and unconditional, individual election?

3. Are there various wills within God at play when it comes to desiring everyone's salvation and saving the elect only?

4. How does your view of the atonement relate to God's saving intentions?

5. At what point do we need to appeal to mystery and God's hidden will when discussing his saving intentions and election?

QUESTION 27

Does God Choose People Arbitrarily?

As we consider further ethical implications of unconditional, individual election, we come to another dilemma related to the divine will, namely that of arbitrariness. Critics of our view of election claim that if God does love all human beings (discussed in Question 25) and desires everyone to be saved (Question 26) yet only effectually calls and saves the elect (Question 19), then there is no particular reason why God acts as he does. He simply saves or condemns people arbitrarily. The non-Reformed tradition, on the other hand, claims that a conditional view of election resolves the dilemma of arbitrariness, for God elects and saves people who freely choose to believe in Christ. God makes the playing field of salvation equal, giving everyone fair opportunity through prevenient grace to be saved, and it is up to a person to respond to that grace in faith. Upon so doing, the loving God who desires their salvation will save them (thus dispelling accusations of arbitrariness).

While the non-Reformed view has its own set of difficult implications, we recognize that the problem of arbitrariness is more difficult for those of us who hold to an unconditional election view. This dilemma, however, is not new, and Reformed theologians have addressed it time and again. Below we will explore the problem of arbitrariness and argue that God is not, in fact, arbitrary in divine election.

Of Purpose and Arbitrariness

When people accuse advocates of unconditional election of being *arbitrary*, they essentially mean that such a view shows God as having no rationale or purpose for choosing or rejecting people for salvation. He simply does as he pleases with the eternal destinies of his (supposedly) beloved creatures. By implication, critics say God would be unfair, unjust, unloving, and insincere in saving intention (which leads to further negative implications upon the divine nature).[1] Consider this statement from I. Howard Marshall:

> The Calvinist position also has serious consequences for the doctrine of God, for it considers the individual's conversion purely an arbitrary act of God. The convert had been a sinner because sin had taken control of him—he had been dead in trespasses and sins from the time of his conception. But God acted to take control of his life and to deliver him from sin. However, no reason can be assigned as to why God chooses some individuals and rejects others (or, if you prefer, passes them by). Thus the problem is that God appears to be capricious in granting his love. He may be steadfast in his love to the elect, but his choice of the elect is arbitrary. Of course, one may reply that God is free to show or to withhold mercy as he chooses, and so he is. But is it just to show mercy only to some? Shall not the judge of all the earth do right?[2]

Marshall's language must be considered carefully, for it is representative of many people who find unconditional election arbitrary. According to this criticism, unconditional election means that God's choice in salvation is "purely an arbitrary act," to which "no reason can be assigned," and it is "capricious."

This criticism, however, is unfounded. By saying divine election is unconditional, we are not saying there is no reason why God chooses certain sinners for salvation and not others. Rather, we are saying that such reason is not found in us. The reason belongs to God alone according to the intentions of his will. Similarly, when advocates of unconditional election appeal to divine mystery and hidden knowledge when explaining why God elects one person and not another, we are not saying there is no reason for God's choice. Rather, we are saying that we do not know the reason for God's choice. There is a significant difference between saying someone has no reason for doing something and not being able to explain that reason. Adherents of unconditional election do the latter, not the former.[3] R. C. Sproul rightly said, "To be arbitrary is to do something for no reason. Now, it is clear that there is no

---

1. Jack W. Cottrell, "Conditional Election," in *Grace for All: The Arminian Dynamics of Salvation*, eds. Clark H. Pinnock and John D. Wagner (Eugene, OR: Resource, 2015), 88. J. Matthew Pinson, *40 Questions About Arminianism* (Grand Rapids: Kregel Academic, 2022), 117, 269.
2. I. Howard Marshall, *Jesus the Saviour: Studies in New Testament Theology* (Downers Grove, IL: InterVarsity Press, 1990), 309–10.
3. Augustus H. Strong, *Systematic Theology* (Philadelphia: Judson, 1954), 787.

reason found *in us* for God to choose us. But that is not the same as saying that God has no reason in himself. God doesn't do anything without a reason. He is not capricious or whimsical."[4]

John Calvin, in a similar way, affirmed that the reason for election cannot be found inside the sinner. Rather, it must be found in God alone. Calvin admitted he did not know why God elected some people and not others, and he was more than willing to admit ignorance in these matters given that such answers belong to God's wisdom alone. That does not mean, for Calvin, that such answers do not exist.[5] It simply means that neither the answers nor the cause for God's choice in election are owed to the sinner.

One rationale our tradition gives for why God elects some people and passes by others is the glory of God. John Piper finds that when pressed for a reason why God unconditionally elects some people to salvation and not others, the best response is to appeal to God's glory.[6] Although Piper does not appeal to the divine glory as an argument against arbitrariness, divine glory nonetheless serves that purpose as rationale for why God might choose someone over and against another for salvation. Simply put, according to Piper, God would be more glorified by electing person A more so than person B, or (viewing the matter negatively) God would be more glorified in choosing person A to be an object of his mercy and person B to be an object of justice than for the circumstances to be otherwise. Piper's beliefs have been sharply criticized by those who hold to a conditional election view. That tradition sees no way in which God would be more glorified in condemning someone to hell unconditionally. Rather, God would be more glorified to have saved them on the basis of faith.[7]

In response, our own view on the matter is that God's ultimate glory is a revealed purpose as to why God elects certain people for salvation (Rom. 8:29–30; 9:11, 17; Eph. 1:5–6, 11–14; Heb. 13:20–21; 1 Peter 2:9; Rev. 21:1–7, 24–26). Thus, we can answer any query as to why God elected someone for salvation with an appeal to God's glory, thereby dismissing any accusations or concerns of arbitrariness. God has his reason for electing; in fact, he may have many reasons for electing someone over and against another. The only clear answers that we can make based upon the revealed will of God through Scripture is that God elected some people to salvation to bring him glory and, secondly, that this election was not of their own doing so that it could all be based upon grace.

---

4. R. C. Sproul, *Chosen by God* (Wheaton, IL: Tyndale House, 1986), 156 (italics original).
5. John Calvin, *Institutes of the Christian Religion*, 3.23.2–5, 3.24.14.
6. John Piper, *Does God Desire All to Be Saved?* (Wheaton, IL: Crossway, 2013), 53–54. See also Question 16.
7. Jerry L. Walls, *Does God Love Everyone? The Heart of What's Wrong with Calvinism* (Eugene, OR: Cascade, 2016), 43–51.

We might anticipate an additional question at this juncture. While a critic might accept that God's glory might serve as justification for God's electing activity (thereby dispelling immediate accusations of arbitrariness), would not God be arbitrary in picking which persons would glorify him more as objects of grace and justice if neither sin or human merit (faith) is considered in election? We will make two responses. First, we will engage in circular argumentation if critics appeal to arbitrariness and advocates to glory for every reply. At some point, we can only go so far in such circular argumentation before we must confront ourselves with this issue—is the problem that there is no reason or that we find such a reason unacceptable? While we would reject any and all forms of arbitrariness in God's electing activity, we must examine ourselves if we will accept what God determines as right and most pleasing in his sight or if we find any such determinations as purely arbitrary. Second, if trying to seek explanation beyond God's glory as to why God would elect some persons and not others, we step into hidden mystery (a matter which we will now explore).

Appealing to Hidden Wisdom and Divine Mystery

In light of God's transcendence, we should not think that God and his ways can be fully grasped by mere mortals. Humans lack both the capacity and right to know things God refuses to reveal to us, and prying into such hidden knowledge amounts to divination, which is expressly forbidden (Lev. 19:26; Deut. 18:10). Theologians must appeal to mystery when we have gone beyond what we can confidently say God has disclosed.

With that said, there are some basic rules of engagement that we should abide by when delving into deep matters that edge on the borders of divine mystery. First, we should appeal to divine mystery only when revelation has not removed the mystery. When God's Word has addressed the issue, we must accept it and can no longer appeal to unknowability. Second, we should speak logically and coherently and not appeal to divine mystery in order to escape every difficulty or apparent contradiction. Third, we should appeal to divine mystery when we know that something is rooted in the divine will or nature, is presented as true, yet is beyond anyone's ability to explain. That is to say, there are things that may exist but are not revealed. At such a juncture, it is appropriate to appeal to divine mystery. Within this framework, we argue that Scripture presents divine election as rooted in the divine will, has its reason and basis within the divine will, and yet is not revealed as to why that divine will is as it is regarding election, thereby justifying an appeal to hidden wisdom and divine mystery.

One of the classical texts used by advocates of our view of election in appealing to divine mystery is Romans 9:14–24. When pressed for rationale of God's sovereign election, even the apostle Paul did not know. God has mercy on whom he will have mercy—that much Paul knew. Yet he also knew it does not depend upon the man who wills or runs (vv. 15–16), a reference to human volition.[8] God had a purpose in the hardening of Pharaoh's heart, one rooted within the will of God (vv. 17–18). Thus, God is not arbitrary. As it is, that purpose was to demonstrate God's power and to proclaim his name among the whole earth (similar to our appeal to God's glory). Yet Paul's point was that God may do that very thing still in accordance with what he desires. Why does he do such a thing? Paul said we have no right to know the reason, not that there is no reason (vv. 19–22).[9] What we can and should know is that God's right as potter over clay (as Lord over all creation) is grounded in his mercy, rooted in his purpose, and not in the slightest bit capricious.[10] With the apostle Paul in Romans 11:33–35, the Reformed viewpoint affirms that the riches of God's wisdom and knowledge are infinitely deep, and his judgments are unsearchable and unfathomable to us. The wisdom and knowledge are indeed there but beyond our grasp; his judgments are searchable and fathomable only by God alone. Thus, God's election of persons is not arbitrary even if the reasons are unknowable to us.

What we can know are the truths that are revealed to us. First, God is free and sovereign. Because no person deserves mercy, yet God is Lord over all creation, he can extend mercy to whoever he pleases or (to use another attribute) extend special love to persons he chooses (as mentioned in Question 25), like a husband to his bride. As Charles Spurgeon once said, "Some men cannot endure to hear the doctrine of election. I suppose they like to choose their own wives—but they are not willing that Christ should select His bride, the Church!"[11] He has freedom and sovereignty to choose certain people to the exclusion of others as he pleases. Second, God's election is based upon mercy and grace. We need not fear this doctrine, for it is rooted in God's matchless mercy (Rom. 9:15–16). Third, while there may be many hidden reasons why God chooses as he does, we may confidently say election culminates in God's glory.[12]

Summary

We have responded to the ethical implication of unconditional election as set forth by critics who accuse the view of being arbitrary. We have argued that unconditional election is not, itself, arbitrary given that God has reason within himself to do as he does. As it has been revealed to us by Scripture, we may

8. Leon Morris, *The Epistle to the Romans*, Pillar New Testament Commentary (Grand Rapids: Eerdmans, 1994), 359.
9. Morris, *Epistle to the Romans*, 364.
10. See Douglas J. Moo, *The Epistle to the Romans*, 2nd ed., New International Commentary on the New Testament (Grand Rapids: Eerdmans, 2018), 625–28.
11. Charles Spurgeon, "Hearing, Seeking, Finding," in *Metropolitan Tabernacle Pulpit*, 63 vols. (Pasadena, TX: Pilgrim, 2006), 44:479.
12. See G. C. Berkouwer, *Divine Election* (Grand Rapids: Eerdmans, 1960), 66–88.

confidently affirm that because of God's glory, there is no arbitrariness in God's election. Because of divine mystery, we may say there may be other reasons of which we are ignorant. However, if God is not arbitrary in his choosing, and the choice is based upon his will alone without consideration of the person's will, is he thereby being unjust? We will explore that question next.

REFLECTION QUESTIONS

1. How do Calvinist and Arminian traditions resolve the problem of arbitrariness differently?
2. What ethical problems would arise if God were arbitrary in election?
3. When should Christians appeal to divine mystery?
4. How does God's glory address the problem of arbitrariness?
5. In your view, is God arbitrary in choosing the elect? Explain.

QUESTION 28

Is God Unjust to Predetermine the Salvation of the Elect Only?

In the preceding question, we argued that God is not arbitrary in selecting whom he does for salvation, for there are reasons known to God for why he chooses as he does (one of which we can confidently say is his glory). If, then, God chooses some people and not others, and those reasons are based upon God's will alone, without consideration of people's foreseen faith or goodness, is his choice just and right?[1] The issue of injustice within God may be more severe than arbitrariness, for though God may have his own sovereign reasons for choosing as he does, might his actual choices not be good or right?

Critics of unconditional election believe our view not only makes God unloving, insincere in saving intentions, and arbitrary (as discussed in the previous questions) but makes him unjust. One of those critics is Steve Lemke. Lemke states that because God's nature is that of love and holiness, and his will is that everyone be saved, he would not predetermine the salvation of just a few people. He illustrates this point through an analogy of a fireman who goes into a burning orphanage to save children. Being the only one able to save them, he brings out just three of the thirty children. Rather than going back into the burning building to rescue more of them, which was within his ability to do, the fireman goes to the media to proclaim how good and praiseworthy he is for saving the three children. Lemke argues that such a fireman (while doing a good thing in rescuing the three) is not morally praiseworthy, for he had the means to help more children but chose not to do so.[2] Even in

---

1. As it relates to justice, we look both to and beyond the legal motif of justice and consider that which is morally right and good.
2. Steve W. Lemke, "A Biblical and Theological Critique of Irresistible Grace," in *Whosoever Will: A Biblical-Theological Critique of Five-Point Calvinism*, eds. David L. Allen and Steve W. Lemke (Nashville: B&H Academic, 2010), 149.

our human courts, such an action would be found unconscionable and condemnable and would lead to serious ramifications. If unconditional election were true, would God, in a similar way, be unjust and morally culpable?

God's Justice in Condemnation

Our answer to the question of God's goodness and justice in condemning the non-elect is largely determined by how we view humanity's nature and position. If human beings were, as in the analogy above, innocent and helpless orphans desperately seeking to be saved from a destruction they did not cause or deserve, and a savior could have helped but willingly chose to leave them to a horrific fate when it was his obligated duty to save them, then we would certainly cry, "Injustice!" However, is that the nature and position of human beings and God?[3]

Far from viewing people as victims of an undeserved demise, Scripture portrays humanity as hostile enemies of God deserving death. In Romans 1:18–32, Paul portrayed humans as being cognizant and intentional in their sin against God; as a result, they are without excuse and deserving of death.[4] Calling us God's enemies in Romans 5:10, Paul affirmed there is no one righteous before God (Rom. 3:9–10; see also Pss. 14:3; 53:1–3). This plight, according to Scripture, is universal (Rom. 3:23; 5:12) and merits God's retribution (Rom. 1:32; 2:5–9; 6:23; Eph. 5:5–6; Col. 3:6; Rev. 14:10, 19). Thus, humans are not innocent victims.

Perhaps, therefore, a better analogy than a burning orphanage would be vassals who were graciously given use of their lord's land and its goodness, and in return they would render him homage. Suppose that rather than giving their lord glory, they rebelled, committed the highest treason, profaned the good things given to them, and set themselves up as their own lords. In addition, suppose they murdered their sovereign lord's only son. Would the lord be unjust in enacting punishment for such egregious evil? Would he be under any obligation to spare any of them?[5] We answer, "No."

God's Justice in Election

We believe that God's judgment over all sinners is justified because of their willful rejection of divine authority and rebellion against his commands as affirmed by the texts above as well as by historical witness.[6] Further, we

3. In no way are we accusing Lemke of Pelagianism. Rather, we are stating that the issue of God's salvation and treatment of sinners must account for humanity's willful rebellion and the freedom of God.
4. Leon Morris, *The Epistle to the Romans*, Pillar New Testament Commentary (Grand Rapids: Eerdmans, 1994), 83, 99–100.
5. This analogy reflects Jesus's parable of the wicked tenants in Matt. 21:33–41 and parallels.
6. Augustine, "On the Gift of Perseverance," ch. 16, in *Anti-Pelagian Writings*, in *Nicene and Post-Nicene Fathers*, ed. Philip Schaff, 14 vols. (Peabody, MA: Hendrickson, 2012), 5:531; John Calvin, *Institutes of the Christian Religion*, 3.23.3; 3.24.14; article 1 of the Canons of Dort.

believe God is under no obligation to pardon anybody. Infractions against God's law mandate justice, not mercy. What is more, almost all critics of unconditional election agree with these very things. All non-Pelagians recognize inherited sin and lack of personal merit before God. That is why such critics of unconditional election typically find no injustice on God's part for having the right to condemn all sinners. Rather, the injustice they find is over God selecting certain sinners for salvation while assigning (or passing by) others to condemnation without any consideration of faith.[7] It would seem that some people are saved and others condemned for infractions against the same laws without any consideration of how they might respond to the gospel. Perhaps someone assigned to death and destruction might genuinely want to be saved, but no opportunity was even afforded to that person while others were saved without any consideration as to whether they would freely believe the gospel in light of prevenient grace.[8] Would such actions truly be good and just?

As we consider this matter of goodness and justice, we must consider what standard defines goodness and justice. Typically, all Christians believe God himself defines what is good and just, and any action of God must meet that criterion. Advocates of conditional election believe that because God loves all his creation and desires their salvation (discussed in Questions 25–26), he cannot be a respecter of persons, be arbitrary, or ignore the free will of people. God obligates himself by his nature to showcase his love by making all people savable, and if they will freely believe (possible by prevenient grace) in Christ, they will be saved and be among the foreknown elect.

Scriptural proof that God must make all people savable is difficult to find, so the non-Reformed tradition typically argues that, by implication, God must provide salvation equally for all people if he loves them and desires their salvation. This implication, however, is certainly not the case, for God is not obligated to save everyone or make everyone savable even if he loves his enemies and desires that they do not fall into judgment. God is obligated by his moral nature (aseity) to enact justice upon wickedness. He is not obligated, however, to provide salvation. He may love those who rebelled against him, he may desire that they be saved, but like any good earthly judge, he is not obligated to do anything in himself other than condemn wickedness. Returning to the analogy of the vassals above, God would be just to condemn each person to death, and no one could question his goodness. This condemnation does not mean he did not love them or that he wanted to destroy them.

---

7. See I. Howard Marshall, *Jesus the Saviour: Studies in New Testament Theology* (Downers Grove, IL: InterVarsity Press, 1990), 309–10.
8. Braxton Hunter, "Commentary on Article 8: The Free Will of Man," in *Anyone Can Be Saved: A Defense of "Traditional" Southern Baptist Soteriology*, ed. David L. Allen, Eric Hankins, and Adam Harwood (Eugene, OR: Wipf & Stock, 2016), 120–25; Norman Geisler, *Chosen but Free*, 2nd ed. (Minneapolis: Bethany House, 2001), 47; see also Question 30.

He desired them to love and honor him instead. As it is, God must punish all wickedness, and he is not obligated in himself to save anyone. Again, on this matter, Reformed and non-Reformed traditions are mostly agreed.

What is not agreed upon is what God is obligated to do further. God's choice in sparing some undeserving sinners does not obligate him to spare (or even offer the opportunity to spare) others. While critics of unconditional election may say there is injustice, we must remember both that justice only requires condemnation (not mercy) and that obligation itself nullifies grace. Grace is a free gift that is undeserved. Should God have been required to save (or avail the opportunity for everyone to meet a certain condition in order that they might receive saving grace), then we cannot say grace was the motivating factor behind election. God is the potter, and humans are but clay (Rom. 9:21–24). Although debate on these verses typically revolves around the outcomes of the vessels (people), Paul's point was God's sovereign right to do as he pleases (v. 21).[9] Because he has sovereign right over creation to assign everyone to be vessels of dishonor, we should marvel that anyone would be assigned as a vessel of honor.[10] While some people wonder why God would offer grace to just a few people, we wonder why God would offer grace to anyone at all.

Consider further the demons. Does God owe fallen angels—who were once made sinless and pure but sinned against their Creator whom they were to love, serve, and glorify—fair opportunity for salvation? Is God unjust because he does not make these moral beings savable? Is it unfair that the cross did not atone for demonic sin? Apparently not, according to 2 Peter 2:4, Jude 6, and Revelation 20:10, and hardly anyone would argue otherwise.[11] Why? Because they deserve condemnation, and God is free. Cannot the same be said about other free creatures God made (namely people)?

What about foreseen faith? Would it not be unjust of God to ignore how people would freely respond to the gospel, and would it not be unjust for God to refuse salvation to people who might have otherwise truly desired it? These questions, although deserving of response, are based upon false assumptions. We have already argued in Question 12 that this non-Reformed

---

9. Douglas J. Moo, *The Epistle to the Romans,* 2nd ed., New International Commentary on the New Testament (Grand Rapids: Eerdmans, 2018), 622–23; Thomas R. Schreiner, *Romans* 2nd ed., Baker Exegetical Commentary on the New Testament (Grand Rapids: Baker Academic, 2018), 503.
10. Our exegetical perspective aligns with Matthew Barrett, *40 Questions About Salvation* (Grand Rapids: Kregel Academic, 2018), 100–03.
11. This point is acknowledged by an advocate of conditional election, namely Kenneth Keathley, "The Work of God: Salvation" in *A Theology for the Church*, rev. ed., eds. Daniel L. Akin, Bruce Riley Ashford, and Kenneth Keathley (Nashville: B&H Academic, 2014), 544. He states, however, that the qualifying difference is that humans are made in the image of God. While true, that fails to explain why God owes humanity equal opportunity to be saved.

notion of prevenient grace is flawed. Scripture affirms that for the sinful effects of the fall to be overcome, God must redeem and regenerate a person (see Question 31). The non-Reformed notion of prevenient grace falls short of redemption and regeneration. Moreover, Scripture nowhere indicates that people are brought to a state of neutrality, being somewhere in between dead in trespasses and sin and alive in Christ, just waiting to make a self-determined decision because of prevenient grace. People do not need to be brought to a crossroads; they need to be brought to the cross. Further, we also affirmed in Question 14 that there are significant problems with making election dependent upon any human activity. Our synergistic cooperation that causes the outcome of our election may very well undermine the very grace on which election is based.

Even still, let us consider one further point. If God were to see from eternity past how we would freely respond to the gospel in light of prevenient grace, would he actually see anyone willingly trust Christ as Savior and Lord? Would God see people (albeit with a prevenient grace they never actually consented to) desire his rule over their lives for his glory alone? Would God see that no further supernatural, regenerating work or special gifting of faith would be needed other than prevenient grace for people to die to themselves and approach the almighty God of this universe (1 Tim. 6:16) for undeserved salvation and eternal life? We hardly think so. When faced with the option of self-denial through the taking up of a cross (Matt. 16:24) or indulging in the virtually limitless temptations of the world, we human beings would most certainly choose the latter. It is not that people desire to go to hell. No reasonable person would desire that. It is that we do not want to live for God's glory alone. Even if the sinful effects of the fall were undone we would, like Adam and Eve in the garden, find ourselves wanting to be gods over our own lives. Thus, we find that God would not foresee faith on our part.

Therefore, as it relates to God's justice, God owes humanity nothing because of some supposed foresight of their meeting a condition like faith. Most likely, that foresight of faith would never be seen. Even if faith was foreseen, if that activity (work?) obligated God to give humanity their due, grace is nullified. Election is God's gift to humanity. It is undeserved favor. God is free to give his good gifts to whoever and to whatever extent he pleases without being unjust.

Summary

We have here defended unconditional election against accusations of injustice. We base this defense on the facts that God is not obligated to offer mercy to anyone, that choosing to save some people over and against others is within his sovereign rights, that he has no obligation to make everyone savable, and that humanity does nothing that obligates God to intervene on their behalf. We thus conclude that God loves everyone, desires that everyone be saved, is not arbitrary in his choosing, and is completely just in electing activity. If that is the case, then why would not God elect everyone? We will explore that question next.

REFLECTION QUESTIONS

1. What is God intrinsically obligated to do toward sinners?

2. What analogy might you give to illustrate a biblical portrayal of the human condition that reflects God's treatment of sinners?

3. Is God unjust to select certain people for salvation?

4. Does God's justice require that everyone be savable?

5. Do you believe God foresees people's faith from eternity past and considers it in his determination of election?

QUESTION 29

Why Does God Not Elect Everyone?

As we close this part on election and the divine will, let us do a quick recap of what we have affirmed thus far. God genuinely loves all people and desires their salvation. Out of his perfect will, he chooses people (not arbitrarily) to be saved by grace. In his act of choosing, he is free and just to choose whoever and however many people he desires. If these points uphold, we come to one more significant question: Why then does he not elect everyone for salvation? Does it not stand to reason that if God did love everyone and desired everyone to be saved, and he is completely free and just to elect whoever he wants to that salvation, that he would want to elect everyone?

As we will find below, there are three primary responses to this question. Universalists would challenge the very premise of the question and argue that God does, in fact, elect everyone to salvation. Non-Reformed evangelicals, on the other hand, would say God does not elect everyone because of reasons within people. Finally, the Reformed tradition believes God does not elect everyone because of reasons within himself. Below, we will explore these viewpoints and conclude (with appreciation for hidden knowledge and divine mystery) that God has reasons within himself for not electing everyone.

Universalism

Universalists are found in many religions, each with their own unique traditions and perspectives. For our purposes, we will focus on Chrisitan universalism. John Hick serves as a notable example. Hick finds that all religions have some awareness of the Ultimate Being, though Christianity reveals him fully. As it relates to salvation, Hick believes we should not frame it as forgiveness of one's sins through faith in Christ. Rather, it should be thought of as human change, a moving away from self-centeredness to God-centeredness whereby we live moral lives.[1] Christianity does not own the monopoly on morality, claims Hick, and people from other religions are able to live good and moral lives, expressing the attributes of God while being liberated (the true meaning of salvation) from self-centeredness. For Hick, Jesus was not divine but was simply someone who revealed God to humanity and showed them how to live morally. All people and faiths that follow that pathway experience salvation (not in terms of heaven or hell but in an experience of the Ultimate Being). As it relates to morality and the Divine Being, Hick claims that such a good and loving God would not consign someone to eternal torment in hell.[2]

Another type of Christian universalism, called *evangelical universalism*, affirms many points of traditional orthodoxy (like the Trinity, sin, atonement, the return of Christ, and salvation by faith in Christ alone) while holding to universal salvation. In this view, it is not that all religions lead to salvation, for salvation is possible only in the person and work of Christ. Rather, it is the view that everyone will ultimately be saved in Christ. Interestingly, adherents of this form of Christian universalism affirm a notion of hell for sinners; however, that destiny is not eternally fixed. People in hell can (and do) repent and call upon the merciful God to save them in Christ. What is more, God will certainly save them upon such an appeal, and everyone in hell will, given enough time, come to this response.[3]

Immediately, critics of universalism will think of the many passages of Scripture that indicate that there are sinners in eternal hell. In response, scholars such as Hick say that such notions of hell are contrary to the divine nature.[4] If someone (like Hick) is prepared to reject Scripture's teaching on the divinity of Jesus, it is not difficult to reject its teaching on hell. Evangelical universalists, however, acknowledge that Scripture teaches that certain sinners are in hell but deny eternal retribution. Scripture that speaks of eternal judgment should be understood metaphorically, in this view, as hell is not an eternal torture chamber but more of a temporary school to show the consequences of sin and the need for mercy.[5] Both responses, we find, appear to be ultimately concerned about the good nature of God and the well-being of people, and both views appear to make biblical/exegetical leniencies to accommodate their view of universalism.[6]

---

1. John Hick, "A Pluralist View," in *Four Views on Salvation in a Pluralistic World*, eds. Dennis L. Okholm and Timothy R. Phillips, Counterpoints: Bible and Theology (Grand Rapids: Zondervan Academic, 1996), 37–43.
2. Hick, "A Pluralist View," 45, 52.
3. Gregory MacDonald, *The Evangelical Universalist* (Eugene, OR: Cascade, 2006), 6.
4. Hick, "A Pluralist View," 31; and *An Interpretation of Religion: Human Responses to the Transcendent* (New Haven, CT: Yale University Press, 1989), 68.
5. MacDonald, *The Evangelical Universalist*, 136–55.
6. MacDonald acknowledges Jesus spoke frequently on hell and eternal fire but that these statements are references to being rejected from God's kingdom and that hell is to be

Scripture is clear that hell is an eternal reality for sinners not redeemed in Christ (e.g., Matt. 3:12; 8:12; 10:28; 13:50; 25:41, 46; Luke 16:23; John 3:36; 2 Thess. 1:9; Rev. 14:11; 20:15). Jesus said in Matthew 25:46, "these will go away into eternal punishment, but the righteous into eternal life." Eternal punishment and eternal life are clearly juxtaposed, showing that our lives after death are eternal. There is no exegetical allowance either for annihilation or second chances at salvation.[7] Thus, we have to uphold the premise that God does not elect everyone for salvation. If that is the case, is that reason because of people or God?

Hypothetical Universal Election

Non-Reformed evangelicals expressly reject universalism because salvation is only possible through faith in Jesus Christ and there are people suffering eternally in hell for their sins.[8] Thus, they affirm that God does not elect everyone. Uniquely, their rationale for why God does not elect everyone is for reasons within people, not within God. All people are electable, in this view, and God would have been pleased to elect everyone should he have foreseen their faith in Christ from eternity past. As God did not foresee faith in them but saw, instead, their unbelief, he did not elect them.[9]

We call this view *hypothetical universal election* given that universal election was a possibility though not a reality. Everyone everywhere has been given the capability of believing in Christ for salvation (and thus is able to become elect) because of God's universal prevenient grace (discussed in Question 5). The only person standing in the way of someone becoming elect is oneself. Jerry Walls compares it to a train bound for heaven. Everyone is free to get on the train and make it to that foreordained destination. Each person, however, must choose to board and remain on the train. Christ has purchased the ticket and provided everyone the ability to come aboard that vessel for eternal life, yet respects each person's choice not to board or to exit the train early. That is to say, everyone has been given the opportunity to become among the elect if they will but meet that one condition of faith. As many people regrettably do not meet that condition, God did not elect them. However, God remains

---

avoided, not that it is eternal retribution (*The Evangelical Universalist*, 142–44). We do not find this argument convincing.

7. David L. Turner, *Matthew*, Baker Exegetical Commentary on the New Testament (Grand Rapids: Baker Academic, 2008), 610.
8. Roger E. Olson, *Arminian Theology: Myths and Realities* (Downers Grove, IL: IVP Academic, 2006), 222. This statement is true for other non-Arminian evangelicals who reject unconditional election.
9. Norman Geisler, *Chosen but Free: A Balanced View of Divine Election*, 2nd ed. (Minneapolis: Bethany House, 2001), 97; Thomas C. Oden, *The Transforming Power of Grace* (Nashville: Abingdon), 135.

truly loving and desiring that everyone be saved because he gave everyone the same opportunity.[10]

In response, we have already affirmed that an unconditional election view affirms God's universal love and desire for all people to be saved, and we have also found many issues with the conditional election viewpoint. We will not reiterate those points here. Instead, we will evaluate what is, to some people, the underlying necessity of making the human (not divine) will the reason not everyone is elect: namely, the goodness of God. For some people, it is unconscionable to think that God would create someone who would have no opportunity to become elect and saved.[11] How a good, loving God would create someone who had no hope of salvation is unthinkable.

In response, we find that non-Reformed evangelicals are confronted with the very dilemma they seek to avoid. In their view, God foresees people's response to the gospel before anyone is ever born. He knows that, should he create them, certain people will never accept Christ as Savior. He creates them anyway, fully knowing there is no chance whatsoever that they will come to faith.[12] It was within his power not to create them, yet he created them for reasons known only to him. Thus, he created people who would not be elect for reasons within himself. We find, then, that non-Reformed evangelicals do not get out of the same difficulty as Reformed evangelicals simply by appealing to human free will (which is never actually denied by the Reformed tradition). Rather, we find that we must consider a third possibility regarding why God would not elect everyone, namely for reasons within himself.

Particular Election

Our view, articulated in Question 9, is that election is rooted in the divine will. If God has chosen to elect some people for reasons within his own will, we likewise affirm that he has chosen not to elect some people for reasons within his own will. Why would he choose to do so if he loves everyone and desires that they be saved? Our broad answer is so that he might be glorified as a God of justice.

As discussed in Question 16, the ultimate purpose of election is not found in sinners but in God. His glory is the final reason why he elects. We should not minimize this ultimate purpose, for it gives the basis for all secondary purposes to transpire—like saving sinners. That is, God elects sinners because he will ultimately see himself glorified by them. The same principle applies for

---

10. Jerry L. Walls, *Does God Love Everyone? The Heart of What's Wrong with Calvinism* (Eugene, OR: Cascade, 2016), 63–67.
11. John Wesley, *Calvinism Calmly Considered* (1752; repr., Salem, OH: Schmul, 2001), 43–47.
12. Greg Welty, "Election and Calling: A Biblical Theological Study," in *Calvinism: A Southern Baptist Dialogue*, eds. E. Ray Clendenen and Brad J. Waggoner (Nashville: B&H Academic, 2008), 230.

why he does not elect everyone, namely to see himself glorified as a righteous judge over sinners.

We should not assume that just because God is loving, he must choose anyone or everyone for salvation. We can all imagine a judge who loves a friend who committed a heinous offense yet, by nature of his position, must condemn him. Still, someone may object that God *could* have shown that person mercy in Christ and was not obligated to condemn him. That is true, yet he has chosen not to condemn some people. Why? We argue that God is glorified in showing justice as he also is in showing grace.[13]

With modern notions of God being only kind and loving, it is difficult for some of us to picture God getting glory and pleasure out of condemning certain sinners. The Scriptures, however, attest to this very thing. In the Old Testament, Moses gathered the elders of Israel and charged them to be faithful to the Lord lest God be delighted in seeing Israel perish and destroyed just as much as he delighted to prosper them (Deut. 28:63). In the New Testament, Paul spoke of the riches of God's glory toward vessels of wrath and mercy in Romans 9:22–23.[14] We do not mean that God derives sadistic pleasure from people being tormented in hell. Rather, just as people today can be pleased when justice is served upon a wicked criminal, God can be pleased when he serves judgment to people who deserve it.

One more point must be observed, and it is particularly targeted at anyone who might assume that people in hell deserve another opportunity to be saved. The assumption is that, upon death and entry into hell, an unregenerate person immediately feels a sense of regret, remorse, repentance, and belief in God. The thought is that if they knew when they were alive what they know in the afterlife, they would have immediately repented and believed in the gospel. Some people believe temporary sin on earth does not merit eternal retribution and that God's loving nature compels him to extend additional saving opportunities. We find, however, all these presuppositions to be based upon unbiblical assumptions.

We should be mindful that souls in hell are still unredeemed and unregenerate. They are still dead in trespasses and sins and not alive in Christ, still bound to their carnal nature. While they have perhaps a greater awareness of God (though Rom. 1 tells us they already had awareness), there is no reason to assume they now desire to give God glory. No one can call Jesus "Lord" except by the Holy Spirit (1 Cor. 12:3), and there is no reason to suppose, just because of their position in hell, that they are able to call upon the Lord to be saved. What is more, there is every reason to believe that sinners in hell are still sinning. Revelation 21:8 affirms that they will be consigned to hell for

13. For helpful elaboration, see Sam Storms, *Chosen for Life: The Case for Divine Election* (Wheaton, IL: Crossway, 2007), 183–87.
14. John Piper, *Does God Desire All to Be Saved?* (Wheaton, IL: Crossway, 2013), 39, 46.

their sin, yet no indication is made that they have any change of heart. The reason their punishment is everlasting and their banishment permanent before the Lord (2 Thess. 1:9) is likely because they continue in their sin. Thus, God is justified and glorified in punishing eternally those who are eternally rebellious to him.

Summary

Would God elect everyone to salvation? Universalists, for different reasons, say yes. We find this view to be contrary to Scripture and the heart of the gospel message. Non-Reformed evangelicals, say, "No, because those whom God did not elect did not meet the condition of faith." We find this response to have significant flaws. The Reformed tradition, says, "No, because God (for reasons known only to him) chose not to elect everyone so that he might be glorified as a God of justice as well as mercy."

REFLECTION QUESTIONS

1. How do universalists attempt to answer the question as to the extent of whom God elects?
2. How should evangelicals respond to universalists who claim everyone is elect?
3. How do non-Reformed and Reformed evangelicals answer similarly and differently as to why God does not elect everyone?
4. Do unredeemed people in hell deserve and/or receive another opportunity to respond to the gospel in the afterlife?
5. Do the elect have grounds for pride and superiority over the non-elect because they were chosen for salvation?

SECTION B

Election and the Human Will

QUESTION 30

Are the Non-Elect Responsible for Their Sin and Disbelief?

We have made the case throughout this book that election is ultimately rooted in the divine (not human) will, but as we found in Question 12 the human will is also intricately involved and impacted. How election relates to the human will regarding specific ethical issues will be the focus of the next section of this book, recognizing that it cannot be truly separated from the previous section on the divine will.

We will begin by considering further how divine election relates to human responsibility, particularly regarding what responsibility the non-elect have regarding their sin and disbelief. If, as we have affirmed already, humans are born into a state of sin and are not able to come to saving faith on their own initiative, yet only the elect are effectually called and gifted with faith, how can the non-elect who were not effectually called or given faith justly be held responsible for their sin and disbelief? Would not supralapsarianism be the inevitable conclusion we must reach if God does not extend saving grace toward the non-elect, and if not, how can we say they deserve to be in hell if they were denied even the opportunity to believe? We will tackle this issue below while also addressing a related concern of whether God is the author of unbelief and evil.

Who Is Culpable?

Evangelical Christians are not so much disagreed among themselves as to who is responsible for sin and unbelief as they are as to which system best accounts for human responsibility. Given that the strongly Reformed hold to eternal, unconditional election of individuals, they are often criticized for removing human responsibility altogether (something they expressly deny). As one author, critical of our view, states:

> We must conclude that to say man is free to do what he wants, but not free to want what he wants, is to say that man is not genuinely free to make undetermined choices. . . . God is found punishing, and in some cases angry with, individuals for choosing wrongly among a set of all wrong options.[1]

Other scholars, like Roger Olson, believe that anyone who holds to God foreordaining and rendering certain circumstances to be as they are makes God the ultimate author of sin, evil, and innocent human suffering (thus implicating God with evil).[2] These criticisms do not even address their concerns about supralapsarianism.[3]

What makes greater sense and best accounts for human freedom and divine innocence, in their view, is to root election and condemnation (predestination) in God's foreknowledge of human free agency. Whether through libertarian freedom or moral self-determinism, whether through Molinism or Arminianism, many non-Reformed evangelicals argue that divine election and divine condemnation are based in what God foresees from eternity past in people. In the Arminian system, God foreknows how each person would respond to the gospel in light of prevenient grace. As in the case of Molinism, God has infinite knowledge of an infinite number of possible worlds, knowing how each free agent would act in any possible situation at any possible time. Although these two systems are unique, they believe in common that God foreknows how creatures will freely choose, and he bases his decision on humanity's decision. To the point at hand, the non-elect are responsible for their sin and unbelief because they were not divinely determined (only foreknown) to sin and disbelieve, and their choices originated within themselves, whereby they could have chosen otherwise. God, then, would not be the author of evil as its origins and actions reside in human free agency.

The Reformed tradition likewise affirms that humans are responsible for their sin and disbelief even if they hold to eternal foreordination in election.[4] Although there have been hyper-Calvinists who hold to equal ultimacy double predestination (discussed in Question 13), the more common views are

1. Braxton Hunter, "Commentary on Article 8: The Free Will of Man." in *Anyone Can Be Saved: A Defense of "Traditional" Southern Baptist Soteriology*, eds. David L. Allen, Eric Hankins, and Adam Harwood (Eugene, OR: Wipf & Stock, 2016), 121.
2. Roger Olson, *Against Calvinism: Rescuing God's Reputation from Radical Reformed Theology* (Grand Rapids: Zondervan Academic, 2011), 84.
3. See "On Predestination," in *The Works of James Arminius*, trans. James Nichols and W. R. Bagnall, 3 vols. (Spring Valley, CA: Lamp Post, 2009), 1:165–66; and Kenneth Keathley, *Salvation and Sovereignty: A Molinist Approach* (Nashville: B&H Academic, 2010), 143–44. See also Question 23. We reject supralapsarianism.
4. See, for example, article 3.1 of both the Westminster Confession and the 1689 London Baptist Confession, which together affirm that God is not the author of sin, nor is violence done to the will of creatures by God. See also article 5 of the Canons of the Synod of Dort.

unequal ultimacy double predestination and single predestination. In other words, it is a hyper-Calvinistic view (rejected by most Reformed evangelicals) that suggests predestination is symmetrical in nature with God working both salvation for the elect and condemnation for the reprobate. We hold to an asymmetrical view of predestination where God merely works positively in the hearts of the elect to bring them to salvation while leaving the non-elect to their own willful sin and disbelief. Election is unconditional because it is not based upon what people do. Condemnation, on the other hand, is conditional because it absolutely is based upon what people do. God is free to save whoever he chooses, yet remains just in condemning guilty sinners who reject his mercies in Christ.[5]

As such, the heart of this matter is not whether the non-elect sin, disbelieve the gospel, and deserve condemnation. Both traditions affirm as much. The bigger issue is whether God's act of predestination in salvation is a cause for the non-elect's sin and unbelief. By way of an analogy, suppose someone was to commit the illegal offense of robbing a bank and was captured by the police. The perpetrator is culpable for the offense. However, suppose that person was coerced to commit that crime by someone else. In that case, the person who solicited the crime would also be culpable, for he made a person do something that person may not have wanted to do. Applied to salvation, the non-elect may be culpable for sinning and disbelieving, but were they forced (perhaps against their will) to do such things?

The Cause of Sin and Unbelief

We believe the non-elect were not forced to sin or disbelieve in the gospel and that both offenses originate deliberately within each non-elect person. We will make that case below through five broad and interrelating points.

First, Scripture affirms that sin originates in people, not God. God tempts no one to sin and evil (James 1:13), and as a God of sinless perfection, there is no evil or corruptible action done by him (1 John 1:5). Sin came into the world through Adam (Rom. 5:12), not God, and each person sins by indulging in his own lusts (James 1:14–15). Disbelief, likewise, originates within the unrighteousness of people who suppress the truth (Rom. 1:18–20). The Reformed tradition has never claimed that God creates sin and unbelief in the hearts of sinners. Sinners come by those traits inherently.[6]

Second, election is a determination to change the nature of the elect, not the nature of the non-elect. God would only be responsible of coercing the non-elect if he were to change a believing and obedient person into a sinful and disbelieving person. However, we should remember that the elect and

5. See Matthew Barrett, *40 Questions About Salvation* (Grand Rapids: Kregel Academic, 2018), 108.
6. Michael Horton, *For Calvinism* (Grand Rapids: Zondervan Academic, 2011), 41–59.

non-elect are born into the same depraved spiritual condition as one another. Both elect and non-elect alike are incapable of going to God for salvation by their own will and accord. God determines to effect change in the lives of only the elect by changing their nature. He does not, however, change the nature of the non-elect but merely leaves them to it.[7] We here reiterate what was mentioned in Questions 12, 21, and 22: Such sin and disbelief are the expressed desires of the non-elect. God does not work sin and disbelief into the non-elect's hearts both because such actions would be immoral and because sin and disbelief are already there.

Third, God's predestination is not solely causative but also permissive in nature. God permits free agents like humans and demons to exercise their own free will. However, rather than being an aloof spectator who observes but does not control his creatures, God sovereignly decrees (permissively) for certain things to be as they are while directing them according to his eternal purpose.[8] Thus, he permits (not causes) the non-elect's sin and disbelief, making them responsible for their actions and eternal destinies. As Louis Berkhof said well, God's permissive decree "is a decree which renders the future sinful acts absolutely certain, but in which God determines (a) not to hinder the sinful self-determination of the finite will; and (b) to regulate and control the result of this sinful self-determination."[9]

Fourth, it is a logical contradiction to assume that an act of giving good things to some people implies giving bad things to others. While it is true that God regenerates, effectually calls, and gifts faith to the elect, that does not mean he gives disobedience and disbelief to the non-elect. There is nothing in either eternally decreeing or effectually saving the elect that constitutes the impartation of sin and disbelief into the non-elect. The non-elect remain fully responsible for their actions and were neither coerced nor programmed by God toward sin and disbelief.

Finally, given that sin and unbelief dishonors God, we find it inconceivable that he would create the non-elect for the purpose of sinning, disbelieving, and dishonoring him. It seems more plausible, in our view, that God created all things for his glory and pleasure while permitting the sin and unbelief of the non-elect so that he might be glorified as judge (see Questions 16 and 29). Thus, sin and disbelief are not things God desires to reside within any of his creatures. He created them good (Gen. 1:31) and even revealed himself to them all (Rom. 1:19–20). However, humanity sinned and dishonored him, yet that sin was a consequence, not a purpose, of creation.

---

7. R. C. Sproul, *Chosen by God* (Wheaton, IL: Tyndale House, 1986), 144–45.
8. Michael Horton, *The Christian Faith: A Systematic Theology for Pilgrims on the Way* (Grand Rapids: Zondervan Academic, 2011), 310–13.
9. Louis Berkhof, *Systematic Theology*, 4th ed. (Grand Rapids: Eerdmans, 1976), 105.

A Matter of Fairness

We have affirmed thus far that Reformed and non-Reformed evangelicals believe the non-elect are responsible for their sin and disbelief and that unconditional election does not suggest that God is culpable for the sin, disbelief, or retribution of the non-elect. We anticipate one further concern related to this matter, namely that of fairness. Is it fair that God would gift salvation to some of his creatures and not to others, even if neither are deserving of such glorious gifts? A non-Reformed person might illustrate this matter of fairness as two children who were equally naughty and undeserving of Christmas presents. Whenever it came to Christmas Day, the father gave gifts to one child and not the other. The one who did not receive presents truly did not deserve them, yet neither did the other child. If, all things being equal, the father showed favoritism toward one child yet showed deserved justice toward another child, is the father being fair? In the same way, wouldn't God be unfair in showing mercy to the elect and judgment to the non-elect when both are equally guilty?

In response, we will make two points. First, if asked if election to salvation is fair, we respond, "Certainly not." Only Jesus Christ deserves to be the chosen of God. Only he gets by right what he deserves. The elect, on the other hand, do not get what they deserve (which is nothing short of death, per Rom. 6:23). The beauty of grace is that it is all a gift freely given. The fact that anyone receives it is truly a miraculous and undeserved gift. God does not give us what we deserve but what we do not deserve. This unconditional election is actually great news for us, for if God were to give us what he foresees in us, we would only get his judgment.

Second, we must understand the difference between mercy, justice, and injustice in relation to fairness. Suppose persons A and B both broke the law. Suppose further that a judge were to pardon person A while holding person B to justice. Person A received mercy, which was not receiving what was deserved, while person B received justice, which was deserved. However, neither person received injustice, receiving punishment that was undeserved. By comparison, God, again, would not be culpable of injustice in this model. Now, as it relates to the matter of fairness, someone may well ask, "But why did God not show mercy to all people like he did to the elect?" We cannot answer that question, for we must appeal to divine mystery and hidden wisdom. We can say, however, that God is not unjust in his treatment toward sinners. Neither person A nor person B received injustice, and as authority belongs to God to judge, he has freedom to issue mercy or justice as he sees fit without being subject to human charges of (un)fairness. Scripture never places blame upon God for why he brings some people to faith and leaves the rest to their own sin and disbelief. Rather, Scripture affirms (as shown above) that the fault lies with humanity alone.

Summary

We have developed our position that the non-elect are solely responsible for their actions and that God is in no way culpable of forcing the non-elect into sin or disbelief. We have also addressed the matter of fairness and affirmed that election is not based upon what we deserve but on the graciousness of God. Even still, God does no injustice to people when he leaves them in their natural state. If, however, the non-elect are left to their natural state and incapable of believing in Christ for salvation, might they actually want to be saved but merely lack the capacity? We will explore that very issue next.

REFLECTION QUESTIONS

1. How do adherents of conditional election attempt to place responsibility upon the non-elect differently than those who hold to unconditional election?
2. Does unconditional election excuse the non-elect of their sin, in your view?
3. Is viewing predestination in light of God's causative and permissive will particularly helpful, in your view, in addressing the issue of human responsibility?
4. Is election fair?
5. Does God incur guilt, in your view, if he does not enable faith for everyone?

QUESTION 31

Do the Non-Elect Desire to Be Saved but Merely Lack the Capacity?

We have argued that the non-elect are responsible for their sins and disbelief in the preceding question. Put simply, God permits the non-elect to do exactly what they want, namely, sin and reject the gospel. However, the matter of the human will does not settle the issue. When we speak about divine election and human agency, we must consider not only desire but ability. Jerry Walls and Joseph Dongell (critics of unconditional individual election) provide a helpful illustration of will and ability as it relates to election, which we will summarize.

Suppose there is a basketball game coming up that a group of friends wants to attend. However, tickets to the game are expensive. One friend may desire to go to the game but cannot afford it. In such a case, the will is present but the ability is absent. Contrastively, consider that the friends pay for the ticket and invite their friend to come along at their expense. However, the friend does not want to go. In such a case, the ability was there but the will was not. For actions to be truly free and people held responsible for their actions, there must be both will and ability to do otherwise, according to Walls and Dongell. As it relates to election, they raise this question: Can the non-elect actually go to Christ but do not desire to do so, or has God withheld from them the ability to desire to be saved (denying them an effectual calling)?[1] Walls and Dongell accuse the Reformed tradition of holding to the latter while their view is the former. Notice that the notion of ability changes the cause of the non-elect's condemnation from their unwillingness to their inability (something God could have remedied). While the non-elect do not desire to

1. Jerry L. Walls and Joseph R. Dongell, *Why I Am Not a Calvinist* (Downers Grove, IL: InterVarsity Press, 2004), 166–68.

be saved, are they able to do otherwise? Not according to the Reformed view, say Walls and Dongell.

The non-Reformed tradition believes God gives everyone the ability (through prevenient grace) to be saved. He does not coerce people's will so that they are made (or forced) to believe. Rather, the focus of God's work is enablement. Consider article 4 of the Articles of the Remonstrants: "Man himself, without prevenient or assisting, awakening, following and co-operative grace, *can* neither think, *will*, nor do good."[2] That is, without grace, humanity lacks the "can" (or ability) as well as the "will" in salvation. As it is, because of these graces, humanity is *able* to exercise the will freely, and God elects those persons who *desire* to believe in Christ. Jacobus Arminius's sentiment on this issue is also worth quoting:

> This decree [to save and damn certain particular persons] has its foundation in the foreknowledge of God, by which he knew from all eternity those individuals who would, through his preventing grace, believe, and, through his subsequent grace would persevere, according to the before described administration of those means which are suitable and proper for conversion and faith; and, by which foreknowledge, he likewise knew those who would not believe and persevere.[3]

Notice the emphasis Arminius places on both ability and will. God does not merely foreknow and consider the human will concerning the gospel when he elects, for if that were the only consideration, he would not see faith. As it is, God foreknows how humanity would willingly respond to the gospel in light of his enabling grace. Thus, election is synergistic in that God provides the enablement and humans provide the will.

Given that the Reformed tradition believes that God does not enable the non-elect (through regeneration and effectual calling) to believe freely in the gospel, might there actually be non-elect persons who would desire to be saved if they were afforded the ability?[4] In line with what we have affirmed thus far throughout this book, we answer this question negatively.

Lack of Will as Well as Capacity

Before we delve too much into the matter of will and ability, we should first affirm that the non-elect's inability to believe is owed to themselves, not God.

---

2. Article 4 of "The Five Arminian Articles," *The Creeds of Christendom*, ed. Philip Schaff, 6th ed., 3 vols. (Grand Rapids: Baker, 1998), 3:547 (emphasis added).
3. "My Own Sentiments on Predestination," in *The Works of James Arminius*, trans. James Nichols and W. R. Bagnall, 3 vols. (Spring Valley, CA: Lamp Post, 2009), 1:185.
4. See Question 28 for how this issue was addressed from another angle.

More specifically, we should affirm that their desires led to their incapacity. God does not impose the inability to believe upon anyone (see Question 13). Rather, that effect is attributed to the willful actions of sinful people. A common analogy used to express this point is a man who has squandered all his income away on things he wants. When it comes time to pay his taxes, he cannot afford them. His own actions led to his inability to render what he should, and he did so fully knowing the expectations and consequences. However, his inability to pay his taxes does not excuse him from having to pay them, leading to his just condemnation. Applied to salvation, God chose to let people do exactly what they want to do, namely sin. Their willful sin led to voluntary inability. God is not to be blamed for requiring what is owed to him.

Consider what the apostle Paul said in Romans 6:16: "Do you not know that if you present yourselves to anyone as obedient slaves, you are slaves of the one whom you obey, either of sin, which leads to death, or of obedience, which leads to righteousness?" He went on to say in verse 19, "you once presented your members as slaves to impurity and to lawlessness leading to more lawlessness." It was the act of willingly presenting oneself to sin that led to forced slavery, a slavery that sinners willingly obey.[5] Because sinners pursued their will, it led to voluntary bondage, which results in the depraving effect of spiritual inability. Desire both precedes and inevitably leads to inability. Like the Israelites after their exodus from Egypt, who would rather return to servitude under their wicked masters' tyranny in exchange for lesser things than what God promised (Num. 14), so sinners by nature desire that which is contrary to God even if it leads to spiritual enslavement. A lack of will led to a lack of capacity, not a lack of capacity leading to a lack of will.

Second Peter 2:10–22 speaks of false teachers who lead the masses to indulge their lust and insatiable appetites for sin.[6] While they promise their hearers freedom in sin, that sin makes them slaves of corruption (v. 19). Left to our own devices, our hearts will seek sin, even if it means spiritual bondage, rather than faith and obedience in Christ that leads to freedom. Thus, even if non-elect people were brought to a spiritual crossroads, they would choose sin leading to slavery.

Now, when we ask if the non-elect would desire to be saved if they were enabled, we must ask what is meant by "want to be saved." If we mean, Do the non-elect want to be spared from God's wrath, or have the negative, controlling consequences of sin removed?, we might rightly think, "Yes, the non-elect would want that." However, when Scripture speaks of salvation, it is not simply referring to having the consequences of sin removed; it refers to being

5. Thomas R. Schreiner, *Romans*, Baker Exegetical Commentary on the New Testament, 2nd ed. (Grand Rapids: Baker Academic, 2018), 336.
6. Gene L. Green, *Jude and 2 Peter*, Baker Exegetical Commentary on the New Testament (Grand Rapids: Baker Academic, 2008), 291–300.

in Christ. If people in their natural, unregenerate state were asked to choose between lordship over their own lives or Christ's lordship over their lives, they all would always choose the former, for no one can call Christ their Lord except by the regenerating work of the Holy Spirit (1 Cor. 12:3). This is why the Holy Spirit applies not only redemption (freedom of ability) in Christ upon the elect but also regeneration (freedom of the will), leading to a new nature.

Regeneration Precedes Faith

The non-Reformed tradition believes that if God merely gives people the ability (through prevenient grace) to believe, some people will desire to believe accordingly. Robert Picirilli says, "By this gracious, pre-regenerating work, the Spirit enables the otherwise unable person to receive Christ by faith."[7] However, if God only gives people the ability to believe but not a regenerate heart to believe, will they believe? This view assumes people need redemption from sin (ability) but not full regeneration (a new will) in order to believe, and it is predicated upon the non-Reformed belief that faith precedes regeneration.

While we cannot develop this issue of the priority of either regeneration or faith exhaustively here, we find that scriptural support for faith preceding regeneration is notably weak and that the biblical and theological support for regeneration preceding faith is considerably stronger.[8] In all soteriological usages of the Greek terms for regeneration, God is always the subject of the verb and humans are the passive recipients of it. Consider John 3:5, Ephesians 2:4–5, Colossians 2:13, and Titus 3:5. These verses affirm that humanity must be born again by God, for naturally they are spiritually dead and incapable of doing anything (like believing) to enter the kingdom of God. The non-Reformed tradition, at this juncture, says that to be spiritually dead does not mean that people lack ability or will toward God. They can still call out to God and accept his grace (prior to regeneration) because of universal prevenient grace.[9] All that is lacking is the expression of that ability by faith. However, Scripture is clear that God must give us both the ability and the will to believe, and the ability (regeneration) must precede the act of the will (belief). God alone brings people to a point of regeneration (John 3:3–5; Titus 3:5; 1 Peter 1:3, 23), not God and a person's faith. To be regenerated is to pass from death into life, which is why the New Testament authors often spoke of regeneration

---

7. Robert E. Picirilli, *Grace, Faith, and Free Will* (Nashville: Randall House, 2002), 155.
8. See Daniel Kirkpatrick, "An Exegetical and Theological Argument for the Priority of Regeneration in Conversion," *Mid-America Journal of Theology* 31 (2020): 89–101.
9. Paige Patterson, "Total Depravity," in *Whosoever Will: A Biblical-Theological Critique of Five-Point Calvinism*, eds. David L. Allen and Steve W. Lemke (Nashville: B&H Academic, 2010), 39, 43; Vernon C. Grounds, "God's Universal Salvific Grace," in *Grace for All: The Arminian Dynamics of Salvation*, eds. Clark H. Pinnock and John D. Wagner (Eugene, OR: Resource, 2015), 18–28.

in relation to spiritual death and natural inability (Eph. 2:5–8; Col. 2:11–13). In John 5 Jesus said the Father raises the dead and gives life (regeneration), leading to belief and eternal life (vv. 21, 24).[10] If we merely had ability without a regenerate heart, we would return to our depravity (2 Peter 2:10–22). The solution God gives, however, is not just freedom from bondage but a renewal of our nature that leads to a new desire (faith), resulting in spiritual freedom.

Adam and Eve: A Case Study

We will make one final argument about whether having the ability to believe would result in a will to believe through a case study of Adam and Eve in Genesis 1–2. There in the garden, humanity was truly free. Adam and Eve had the ability to know and follow God in faith and obedience without any restraints. Aside from Satan (who, granted, is a formidable foe), there were no external tempters to provoke disobedience, yet what was Adam and Eve's response? It was nothing less than sin and disobedience. If we take a federal headship view of Adam from Romans 5, we would find that Adam acts as a representative of what every single human on earth would choose to do. If prevenient grace gives every person the ability to believe but does not regenerate the heart to be willing to believe, then like our first parents we will always choose sin and disobedience. We agree wholeheartedly with E. Earle Ellis, who said:

> Some suppose that if our will is "free" to accept or reject Christ, many will accept him. But is that true? If our first parents (Gen 1–3), whose wills were truly free, chose against God, do we suppose that any of their children, sullied by sin from earliest experiences, would make a godlier choice than they? Would we, who were at enmity with God, controlled by ego, surrounded by a thousand temptations (Adam and Eve faced one), make a better choice than they? Hardly. . . . "Free will" is precisely what God permits to the terminally unrepentant, and it is a one-way ticket to destruction in Hell. If salvation came through our free choice, we would all be lost. No one would be saved except Jesus Christ.[11]

Summary

We have here explored the matter of human ability as it pertains to salvation, arguing that the non-elect's inability is due to their own choices, that a universal prevenient grace as articulated by the non-Reformed tradition is

10. See Leon Morris, *The Gospel According to John*, New International Commentary on the New Testament (Grand Rapids: Eerdmans, 1981), 101.
11. E. Earle Ellis, *The Sovereignty of God in Salvation: Biblical Essays*, T&T Clark Biblical Studies (New York: T&T Clark, 2009), 5.

not enough to bring someone to faith, and that God must accomplish regeneration in addition to redemption in order for someone to believe. Still, there is a greater point we wish to make. We should not have a view of election where some people desperately seek to be saved in Christ but God denies them the ability. All who call upon the name of the Lord will be saved (Rom. 10:13), and if anyone truly desires to be saved, God will save that person. The non-elect, however, choose not to believe, and their choices (their will) lead to an inability of their own choosing. An unconditional, individual election of God does not mean God is a moral monster who binds people into spiritual incapacitation and unbelief. Those conditions are attributed to sin, and the non-elect would not have it any other way.

REFLECTION QUESTIONS

1. Why should we distinguish between will and ability regarding salvation?
2. Do the non-elect lack the will to be saved, the ability to be saved, or both?
3. Do people just need the ability to believe or also a new will to believe the gospel?
4. Does an unconditional, individual election view make God responsible for a person's inability to believe the gospel?
5. Which precedes the other in your view—regeneration or faith? Why does it matter?

QUESTION 32

How Does Election Relate to the Soul Competency of Infants and Children?

The topic at hand is, without question, the most difficult issue to write about in this book. This difficulty is due not only to the complex theological issues at stake but the deep and painful emotions it raises. As Christian parents, we long for our children to hear and embrace the good news of Jesus Christ. Although we discussed in the preceding question that people need both the will and ability to repent and believe the gospel, we also realize that infants and small children lack the will and ability to make a conscious decision to embrace Christ as Savior and Lord.[1] When we couple that claim with what we have already said about humanity's inherited sin from Adam, we naturally become concerned about the eternal spiritual welfare of our children who may not yet be aware of their sin and need of a savior.

Although this issue is far too complex to exhaust here, and there is great need to be both pastorally as well as theologically precise, we will still attempt to summarize the major viewpoints on this issue while also exploring how a robust doctrine of divine election informs our theology and strengthens our confidence concerning God's sovereign salvation over infants and small children.

Inherited Sin and Infant Baptism

Augustine (considering Rom. 5:12 and 1 Cor. 15:21) developed a systematic understanding of infants and inherited sin that largely informed the theology and practice of the early church. Consistent with his anti-Pelagian views, Augustine believed original sin passes to all people, infants and children included, because of Adam's natural headship over humanity. Although

1. This issue is just as relevant for people who have mental disabilities from birth or early childhood, to the extent that they are incapable of understanding their sin or the gospel message. We believe the same principles will apply.

infants are not guilty of having committed sins personally, they are still reckoned as sinners and guilty before God by virtue of their descent from Adam. An infant's guilt of original sin can be pardoned, however, through the mode of baptism, and the faith and repentance of the parents are considered to belong to the child.[2] Thus, Augustine upheld all notions of sin and guilt as well as repentance and faith. Additionally, he articulated a system of thought that affirmed both ability and will. Although infants lack both ability and will to respond, God gives grace through the laver of baptism while also accepting the repentance and faith of the parents. If, however, an infant was not baptized by believing parents, Augustine believed that such a child would be "damned, but most lightly."[3]

Ambrose, on the other hand, believed that corruption transmits to infants, but the guilt of original sin belongs to Adam alone. For Ambrose, people inherit sin from infancy (which most likely refers to an inclination to sin), and this sin increases as sinners grow older. Guilt, however, belongs only to the offender. People are only punished for personal sins, not inherited sins. Infant baptism is certainly necessary, for it avails that child to salvation. Even still, inheriting a sinful nature that is inclined toward sin does not bring condemnation in his view, and infants (and their parents) can be assured of their place in heaven.[4]

We see from these two examples that from the earliest of times, the Christian church has debated whether original sin entails inheriting sin and guilt, or just sin without guilt. This debate continues to this day, and discussion on the matter still often entails infant baptism. Currently, the Roman Catholic Church affirms that humans, from infancy, are born with a fallen human nature and have original sin. People need regeneration, which comes through baptism (prescribed from birth), which assures them of heaven.[5]

Numerous Protestant traditions likewise practice infant baptism (though it is theologically construed differently).[6] Among Anglicans, infants who cannot repent of sin and believe in Christ are baptized by promise of their sureties.[7] Article 7 of the Methodist Articles of Religion affirms original corruption and inclination toward evil from all offspring of Adam, who are far

---

2. Augustine, "On Forgiveness of Sins, and Baptism," in *Anti-Pelagian Writings*, in *Nicene and Post-Nicene Fathers*, ed. Philip Schaff, 14 vols. (Peabody, MA: Hendrickson, 2012), 1.20–26.
3. Augustine, "On Forgiveness of Sins, and Baptism," 1.21, 22.
4. Ambrose, "On the Mysteries," in *Ambrose: Select Works and Letters*, in *Nicene and Post-Nicene Fathers*, 6.32. See J. N. D. Kelly, *Early Christian Doctrines*, rev. ed. (New York: HarperCollins, 1978), 354–55.
5. *Catechism of the Catholic Church*, §1250–1252, 1262–1263.
6. See Carl R. Trueman, *Grace Alone: Salvation as a Gift of God, What the Reformers Taught . . . and Why It Still Matters*, Five Solas (Grand Rapids: Zondervan Academic, 2017), 196–207.
7. "The Anglican Catechism, 1549," in *The Creeds of Christendom*, ed. Philip Schaff, 6th ed., 3 vols. (Grand Rapids: Baker, 1998), 3:517.

from original righteousness. However, article 17 affirms the practice of baptism for young children, which is a sign of regeneration, or new birth, that they then possess. Scriptural support for these views often includes Acts 2 and the numerous references throughout the New Testament where whole households were baptized.

Age of Accountability

Other Protestant traditions view the matter of soul competency in light of an *age of accountability*, a time when persons become morally responsible for their sin and are subject to guilt and condemnation. This view holds that all people were involved in Adam's sin and are corrupt by nature, yet God does not condemn someone until he or she can make moral decisions.[8] This view argues for symmetry between personally ratifying the work of Christ on the cross to be true for oneself along with personally ratifying the disobedient work of Adam in the garden, per Romans 5. Just as a person cannot automatically be saved without personal consent, so a person cannot be personally guilty without personal consent. Infants and small children are secure until they reach that age of accountability, and should they tragically die before that age is reached, they will be with God in heaven.[9] Additional scriptural support for this view includes Deuteronomy 1:39, 2 Samuel 12:23, Isaiah 7:15–16, and Matthew 19:14.

Election and Soul Competency

While matters of inherited sin and guilt, baptism, and personal responsibility are insightful and worthy of every consideration, we find that the doctrine of election (which is often overlooked in the discussion) can and should inform our theology of the eternal welfare of infants and children. In particular, we believe that our view of unconditional, individual, eternal election gives the best assurance (over and against other views of election) that infants and small children will be safe in the arms of the heavenly Father should they leave this life.

---

8. Millard Erickson, *Christian Theology*, 2nd ed. (Grand Rapids: Baker Academic, 2003), 654–56. Erickson believes people inherit sin and guilt, yet God does not hold someone accountable for that guilt until the age of accountability is reached. Other scholars believe only sin (read: inclination to sin) is inherited, not guilt. See Adam Harwood, "Commentary on Article 2: The Sinfulness of Man," in *Anyone Can Be Saved: A Defense of "Traditional" Southern Baptist Soteriology*, eds. David L. Allen, Eric Hankins, and Adam Harwood (Eugene, OR: Wipf & Stock, 2016), 37–51.
9. See John MacArthur, *Safe in the Arms of God: Truth from Heaven About the Death of a Child* (Nashville: Thomas Nelson, 2003) for an excellent pastoral and theological treatise on the issue of infant mortality and assurance of heaven. He also admits there is no age of accountability clearly taught in Scripture, though there are biblical reasons to support his view that infants are sinful but may be treated as innocent and thereby enter into heaven.

Let us consider again Romans 9. Paul said that the true people of God are not of physical descent but those of God's promise, a promise made "though [Rebekah's children] were not yet born and had done nothing either good or bad—in order that God's purpose of election might continue, not because of works but because of him who calls" (Rom. 9:11). God has purposes in election, and his purposes prevail (according to Paul). From this passage, we are reminded that divine election is not dependent upon the chosen people but upon the choosing God, "not because of [human] works but because of him who calls." If someone is incapable of personally repenting and believing in the gospel, it will not stop that person from being among the elect (much like Jacob), for election is not conditioned upon a person choosing but upon God and his eternal purposes. Paul was clear that God's choice in election long preceded humanity's choice of him (Question 10), for we were chosen before we were born (Rom. 9:11; see also Matt. 25:34; Eph. 1:4–5; Rev. 13:8, 17:8).[10] To be chosen before our birth means that infants and small children can be among the elect in Christ. Their merits (belief) or demerits (inherited sin) were not considered when God elected (Question 11), for his election is unconditional. This unconditional election is of tremendous encouragement to us as it relates to the possibility of childhood mortality, for just as Jacob was elect before he was born apart from having done good or bad, so too can young children be elect apart from meeting any condition.

If our election was based upon God foreseeing from eternity past whether we would choose to believe in Christ for salvation, we might have grave concern for children who are unable to believe. If, however, our election is rooted solely in the divine will (which never changes and certainly prevails), we can have utmost confidence that God will do what is right based upon his mercy and not upon human will or exertion (Rom. 9:14–16).

Let us return to our wider discussion over ability and will. We made the case in Questions 30–31 that God must grant both the will and ability to believe the gospel in order for people to be saved. What is to be said of those people who lack ability and will, in light of what we have said about unconditional, individual, eternal election? Our view aligns with the Westminster Confession of Faith, one of the few great confessions that rightly frames infant mortality in light of divine election. It states: "Elect infants, dying in infancy, are regenerated and saved by Christ through the Spirit, who worketh when, and where, and how he pleaseth."[11] That is, the infants that God elects (which we believe is all of them) are saved efficiently, materially, and instrumentally by God alone (just like all the rest of the elect). Though they lack the will and ability, they are not saved because of their will and ability.

---

10. Douglas J. Moo, *The Epistle to the Romans*, 2nd ed., New International Commentary on the New Testament (Grand Rapids: Eerdmans, 2018), 600–02.
11. Westminster Confession of Faith, 10.3. See also London Baptist Confession 1689, 10.3.

They are saved by grace. As such, God may provide other means to work his salvation into their lives.

Someone may contest how the inability and lack of will from the non-elect (for whom God does not intervene) is so radically different than the inability and lack of will from infants (for whom we argue he does intervene). The difference, however, is great in every way. The view we have articulated in this book is that the inability of the non-elect is owed to their own sinful desires. That is, there is a willful defiance and rejection of the gospel that has caused their inability. Infants and young children who are incapable of understanding and actively resisting the gospel do not fit into this category. There is a clear distinction between people whose inability is due to immaturity and underdevelopment and those whose inability is due to willful defiance and rejection. Additionally, there is a difference between people who corrupted their will and ability to the point of incapacitation and those who never had them. Infants and small children do not have soul competency to either embrace or reject the gospel or exercise their wills toward sin; the non-elect do. Paul said in Romans 1 that the ones who incur guilt and are without excuse are those to whom divine revelation was made "plain to them," having "been clearly perceived," and to those who "knew God" but "did not honor him as God" (Rom. 1:19–21). Such things cannot be said of infants and small children. Thus, we believe God saves these precious souls should they perish prematurely; and, like the Westminster Confession says about infant mortality, he saves them when, where, and how he pleases (an appeal to divine mystery) as an act of divine mercy.

Summary

The issue of inherited sin, guilt, and salvation concerning infants and small children has been a difficult dilemma from the earliest periods of church history. To address the issue, many theologians have affirmed inherited guilt and/or sin and proposed baptism into grace as the cure. Other traditions believe there is an age of accountability (or period of responsibility) until which God graciously accepts infants and small children who lack soul competency into heaven.

Our approach to this matter is from an unconditional, individual, eternal election perspective. Because election is unconditional, it does not depend upon someone's good deeds (like faith) or bad deeds (like sin). It is fully dependent upon the merciful will of God. Because it is individual and not solely corporate, we can be assured that God personally chooses whomever he desires and does not merely set a criterion for a group of people to meet (something infants could never do). Finally, it is eternal, meaning that God, from all eternity, has chosen his elect for salvation, and nothing can prevail against that. As such, we can trust not only that God loves his creatures better than any other person on earth, but that he can and will do only that which is right.

REFLECTION QUESTIONS

1. Do infants inherit Adam's guilt as well as sin (or sinful tendencies), in your view?

2. What role, if any, does baptism have regarding the salvation of infants, in your view?

3. Is there such a thing as an age of accountability?

4. How does divine election give unique insight into the difficult issue of childhood mortality?

5. What is the difference between infants and small children who lack the will and ability to respond to the gospel and the non-elect who also lack that will and ability?

QUESTION 33

Can We Have Assurance That We Are Elect?

If the view of election we have presented in this book holds, then the joys of being among the elect are without measure. To be adopted as God's children, to be loved with the same love that the Father naturally has for the Son, to be the objects of God's mercy rather than objects of his justice are all blessings too glorious for words. However, it raises one further question: How do we know if we truly belong to the elect? How do we know we are not deceiving ourselves into thinking we are among the elect when in reality we are not? Peter, after all, warned us to be diligent in making our calling and election sure (2 Peter 1:10), for he knew of the reality of false converts, much like other apostles (2 Cor. 13:5; 1 John 2:19). Similarly, Jesus spoke of people who had assurance of their salvation but were, tragically, self-deceived (Matt. 7:22–23) and not among the elect. Is there any way to know, this side of eternity, if we are truly among the elect?

This present question is more than asking who comprises the elect (namely the church or people who have put their faith in Christ for salvation). It is also more than the eternal security of salvation (covered in Question 20), though it is intricately related to it. Here we are dealing with the matter of *assurance*, or knowing for certain that we belong to the elect of God. This doctrine of assurance is a historic one, and many Christians have had differing views on whether we can be confident that we belong to the elect. As we will develop below, our position on the matter is that Christians may, indeed, have assurance of their election. Such assurance, however, must be put in the right place. Below we will explore various viewpoints on assurance in order to make our theological conclusions.

Secured but Not Assured

Augustine considered the matter of assurance deeply in light of perseverance and unconditional, eternal election. In his view, the elect are absolutely *secured* in their salvation, for God bestows the gift of perseverance on their behalf. However, the elect are not *assured* of their salvation. He wrote, "For who of the multitude of believers can presume, so long as he is living in this mortal state, that he is in the number of the predestinated? Because it is necessary that in this condition that should be kept hidden; since here we have to beware so much pride."[1] Augustine's concern was that assurance of salvation would lead to hubris and the sin of presumption. Contrastively, the bishop believed there is healthy fear in being ignorant of one's predestination and salvation, for it leads to pious living. Unlike theologians of the Reformation, Augustine believed predestination is the consummation of God's work, not its starting point. Said another way, God predestines people so that they would be people of faith and holiness. To give the elect assurance of their salvation is to hinder that greater purpose (in his view), and although God knows the predestined elect and secures them in that salvation, he keeps that knowledge to himself in order that the elect grow in their sanctification.[2]

Assured but Not Secured

The Arminian tradition, on the other hand, holds that believers may not have security in their salvation, for the possibility of falling away from the faith always remains up to the point of death (see Question 20). Nevertheless, believers may have assurance as long as they hold on to Christ by faith. Classical Arminians like F. Leroy Forlines, for example, believe that apostasy is possible as believers fall into such things as heresy, habitual and unrepentant sin, or a change in their belief system; however, Christians may still have assurance of salvation, for God is patient, loving, and gracious in dealing with his people. As long as believers abide in the faith, they can have assurance of their salvation, for God is faithful.[3] J. Matthew Pinson, a Reformed Arminian, believes that apostasy is possible (albeit differently from classical Arminians); however, believers may still have assurance because of the active and passive obedience of Christ imputed to believers by faith. As such, the sinful lapses of believers will not separate them from Christ. Only a blatant resistance of grace and a renouncement of the faith can lead to apostasy. Therefore, believers may have great assurance of their salvation this side of eternity.[4]

---

1. Augustine, "On Rebuke of Grace," in *Anti-Pelagian Writings*, in *Nicene and Post-Nicene Fathers*, ed. Philip Schaff, 14 vols. (Peabody, MA: Hendrickson, 2012), ch. 40, 488.
2. Philip Schaff, *History of the Christian Church*, 8 vols. (Grand Rapids: Eerdmans, 1987), 3:855–56.
3. F. Leroy Forlines, *Classical Arminianism: A Theology of Salvation*, ed. J. Matthew Pinson (Nashville: Randall House, 2011), 346–53. See also I. Howard Marshall, *Jesus the Saviour: Studies in New Testament Theology* (Downers Grove, IL: InterVarsity, 1990), 322.
4. J. Matthew Pinson, *40 Questions About Arminianism* (Grand Rapids: Kregel Academic, 2022), 106.

Assured and Secured

A final view we will explore, found broadly across Reformed circles, is that the elect are both assured and secured in their election status. Because election is rooted in the eternal will of God and not the will of people who are prone to sin and folly, election is as secure as the promises of God, who never changes his mind or shifts like shadows. His love will never depart from them due to what they have done, for the verdict of "justified" has already been pronounced and their adoption as God's children has been finalized. As a result, Christians are assured because God has secured them.

Luther and Calvin are both particularly insightful on this point, approaching the problem as much pastorally as theologically. In their view, Satan has every desire to destroy a Christian's assurance and lead that person to doubt the saving promises of God. However, God's love precedes our actions and is rooted in himself rather than in the sinner. Even more, God's love is not far away or separate from the sinner (as though it was merely some promise made long ago). Rather, God gives us his Son in the here and now, along with all his benefits, so that he is ours and we are his. Thus, Christians are secured in God's love and salvation and assured by God's very presence that they belong to him. If believers need assurance of their election and salvation, they need only to look away from themselves and to their precious Savior.[5]

Objective and Subjective Assurance

Like Luther and Calvin realized, this issue is as much pastoral as it is theological. Many devout Christians struggle, at times, to fully embrace God's love and saving intentions in their lives. They wonder how a truly saved Christian could act the way they do and why God would really love them. For other people, assurance is difficult to accept under an unconditional election model because there is nothing that anyone can do to become elect. Election is simply a sovereign act of God, and they may feel that they were somehow left out. What are these people to do (if anything) to gain assurance of their election?

We should be mindful that the matter of assurance is a matter of perspective for the believer, not God. God already knows those who are his (2 Tim. 2:19), and we have already affirmed that he has secured them in their salvation. Thus, we are ultimately addressing how people may find peace of mind knowing they are among the elect, not whether or not they are elect. Our view is that the best way to determine if someone is elect is to ask, Did you repent of your sins and believe in the gospel of the Lord Jesus Christ? If the person has done so, then that person is elect because conversion is something God only brings about in the elect. The decision to repent and believe in Christ is not something people cleverly do on their own. It happens only because God

---

5. See Martin Luther's sermon, "Christ's Holy Sufferings," 3.15; and John Calvin, *Institutes of the Christian Religion*, 3.2.24.

chooses them from eternity past and effectually calls them in a moment in time.[6] What is more, if such conversion took place, there are signs that will be sure to follow. Thus, we can have assurance of our election status by looking both to the event of conversion (what we call here our *objective assurance*) as well as by signs of conversion (which we call *subjective assurance*).

The elect's most firm assurance comes from the foundation of one's belief (namely Christ himself) rather than the signs of faith. That is, there is subjective assurance as evidenced by external signs of faith (things such as good works, repentance of sin, and godly fruit), yet the objective grounds for assurance is the presence of the Holy Spirit (Rom. 8:16; Eph. 1:13), the person and work of Christ (2 Cor. 3:4), and God's eternal will expressed through the gospel (2 Tim. 1:12; Heb 10:22; 1 John 3:18–22; 5:13). As D. A. Carson rightly said, "Although works cannot save and cannot be the primary ground of one's assurance (that, surely, is Christ and his work and promises), they may serve as corroborating evidence."[7] If someone has experienced conversion and has embraced Christ as the object of his or her faith and there are subjective signs that follow, there is no reason a person should doubt his or her election. God has every desire to assure the Christian of his love, for it leads to holiness. He knows that a lack of assurance will hinder that person's spiritual growth.[8]

Moreover, the view of election we have put forth here gives us great assurance. If our election and salvation were dependent upon the strength of our faith, the quality of our fruit, or the amount of works we muster, we would rightly have reason to fear. Likewise, if our election was dependent upon our continuous ability to meet the condition of faith, or if it were sourced in our will rather than God's will, or if it is merely in accordance with what God foreknows we will do but not God's relational knowledge of what he will do for us, then we would have no firm assurance. As it is, if we look away from ourselves and to the finished work of Christ that was brought to us from a divine determination before the foundations of the world and applied directly through the work of the Spirit, we can rest assured we are his and he is ours.[9] As we have said before, faith itself is the sign of our election, not the cause of it. If we believe, it shows we are elect. Relatedly, if we do not believe, or if our faith is spurious, we are not elect.

---

6. Bruce Ware, "Divine Election to Salvation," in *Perspectives on Election*, ed. Chad Owen Brand, Five Views (Nashville: B&H Academic, 2006), 17–18; and R. C. Sproul, *Chosen by God* (Wheaton, IL: Tyndale, 1986), 168.
7. D. A. Carson, "Reflections on Assurance," in *Still Sovereign: Contemporary Perspectives on Election, Foreknowledge, and Grace*, eds. Thomas R. Schreiner and Bruce A. Ware (Grand Rapids: Baker Academic, 2000), 274. Consider John 15. Belonging to the vine is the objective grounds for assurance, and the accompanied fruit would be subjective grounds.
8. Sproul, *Chosen by God*, 168.
9. Calvin, *Institutes*, 3.2.24, 3.24.5.

Moreover, while there is great difficulty in not having assurance of salvation, there is arguably greater danger of having it in the wrong place. Scripture speaks of people who believed in Jesus (John 2:23–25), belonged to a church (1 John 2:19), and did great religious signs (Matt. 7:21–23) but did not belong to Christ. They had the subjective grounds of assurance without the objective grounds of Christ himself. Other people tragically thought they had objective assurance because of their belief in Christ but lacked any signs of the subjective grounds (James 2:14). It ultimately comes down to what our assurance is founded in. If a person's faith is in the gospel of Jesus Christ, and he as the figurative vine (John 15) is producing spiritual fruit by the Spirit that no one could do on his or her own, then there is no reason to lack assurance. If, however, a person's assurance is found in his or her own moral striving to be good or do religious works, or if that person's faith is spurious, then that person has assurance in the wrong things, which will neither save nor last.[10] The point is that our assurance must be first and foremost in Christ and confirmed by external signs. Peter, who knew of the reality of false converts but already believed his audience to be believers and brothers (2 Peter 1:1, 10), called us to make our calling and election sure by looking at the qualities of a changed life (vv. 5–7). These signs help give his spiritual brothers and sisters assurance of their calling and election until their entry into the eternal kingdom of Christ (v. 11).[11]

Summary

Because our faith is weak and our obedience imperfect, we may understandably struggle with assurance that we are one of God's own. What are we to do through those struggles? The first view we observed says to struggle all the more because it will make you more sanctified in the end, despite your already being secured in salvation. The second view calls us to be assured of our salvation but to keep doing the right things in order to be secured in your salvation. The final view, which we believe gives us the most assurance, calls us not to look to what we have done but to what Christ has done for us to secure us in the salvation he has predestined from all eternity, and upon so doing he will bring about a transformation in our lives that is nothing short of supernatural. This final view is built upon an unconditional, individual, eternal election rooted fully in the will of God. Thus, because our election is secured in that way, we have every reason for assurance and no reason to doubt.

---

10. Carson, "Reflections on Assurance," 264.
11. See Sinclair B. Ferguson, *The Whole Christ: Legalism, Antinomianism, and Gospel Assurance—Why the Marrow Controversy Still Matters* (Wheaton, IL: Crossway, 2016), 201–4.

REFLECTION QUESTIONS

1. What is assurance, and how is it related to and different from security of salvation?
2. Would God want to give us assurance that we are saved in your view, or would he want to keep that a mystery?
3. Can a person have assurance of salvation without having security of salvation?
4. What are objective assurance and subjective assurance, and what are their purposes?
5. How does someone's view of election affect their view of assurance?

PART 4

Practical Considerations of Election

QUESTION 34

How Does Election Affect a Christian's Identity?

When the New Testament authors wrote about divine election, they did not write of it as some abstract academic concept to be debated by elite academics. Rather, they wrote to normal Christians who were trying to live out their new identities in a lost and broken world. These early saints needed to have their affections stirred for Jesus, their lifestyles motivated to holiness, and their hope strengthened through life's trials, which is why the apostles regularly tied these very things to divine election. We see this in Paul's letter to Titus, where he wrote "for the sake of the faith of God's elect and their knowledge of the truth, which accords with godliness" (Titus 1:1). Peter, writing to the elect exiles in what is modern-day Turkey, said their election is for obedience to Jesus Christ (1 Peter 1:1–2). The apostle John wrote his second epistle to the elect lady (the church) in order that they might love one another, abide in Christ and his teachings, and not take part in wicked works. At no time did the New Testament authors divorce divine election from the Christian life, and thus neither should we.

In the final part of this book, we will look at how divine election practically relates to the Christian life, and we will begin by exploring its impact upon a believer's identity. When we speak of a Christian's *identity*, we are referring to the elect's sense of self in light of their newly redeemed life in Christ, and while divine election radically changes every aspect of a believer's identity, we will limit our focus to three specific markers.

Humility and the Error of the Romans

We have already found Romans 9–11 to be a hallmark passage on divine election, but what is often overlooked is Paul's argument on how divine election affects a Christian's identity. In this passage, the apostle anticipated a question that would have been on the minds of his readers: Have God's promises to Israel, whom he had chosen, failed, given that most Jews had rejected the promised Messiah (9:6)? This question would have been of utmost importance to his Gentile audience, for if God's promises to Israel failed, why should they hold for Gentiles? Paul's answer was that the promises of God have not failed, for his saving plans include the salvation of Israel. In Romans 9:30–10:21, Paul affirmed two important truths about Israel: Their rejection is due to their unbelief in and rejection of Jesus as the Messiah (9:30–10:13), and they are therefore responsible for their situation (10:14–21). Because they pursued their own righteousness through the law rather than through Christ (10:1–4), a hardening has come upon them. However, this hardening was temporary, and its purpose was constructive. God had, indeed, preserved a remnant from Israel, chosen by grace (11:5), but God is going to use the Jews' rejection as a way to bless the Gentiles. The conversion of the Gentiles would ultimately lead to Israel becoming jealous, spurring the Jews to faith in the gospel they once rejected (11:11–12). Thus, this rejection (or hardening) was only temporary, and God's promises have not failed.[1]

What does this line of thought have to do with the identity of the elect? For Paul and his Roman audience, the answer was, "Everything." Apparently, there were some Gentile Christians in Rome who became arrogant and boastful in their new status as the chosen people of God. Thinking they somehow replaced Israel in God's saving plan, they believed they had a superior status than the Jews. To rebuke this pride and boasting, Paul used a metaphor of an olive tree (11:17–24). There is one tree (the people of God), but there were natural branches (ethnic Israel) who were cut off due to unbelief so that believing Gentiles could be grafted in. These Gentile believers have no reason to feel superior, for their election and salvation were by grace, and God's plans are to bring ethnic Israel into the elect community as they embrace Christ by faith.

Paul's words to the Romans remind us that a Christian's election status is no grounds for feeling superior or accomplished. While it is right and good for Christians to feel inexpressible joy in their salvation, they should never lose their humility or sense of wonder. Any evidence of self-exaltation, pride, self-election, and self-justification is nothing more than a perversion of grace and amounts, ultimately, to Pharisaism.[2] There is no reason any person

---

1. In terms of Paul's overall argument as developed here, there is a strong consensus between Reformed and non-Reformed scholars. See I. Howard Marshall, *New Testament Theology: Many Witnesses, One Gospel* (Downers Grove, IL: IVP Academic, 2004), 323–26; Douglas J. Moo, *The Epistle to the Romans*, 2nd ed., New International Commentary on the New Testament (Grand Rapids: Eerdmans, 2018), 728–32.
2. G. C. Berkouwer, *Divine Election* (Grand Rapids: Eerdmans, 1960), 319. Tragically, there are egregious and especially deplorable extremes of such superiority, such as the "Christian Identity" movement (an anti-Semitic supremacist sect found in North America), which encourages violence and abuse to people who do not fit their mold.

should be chosen for God's favor other than Jesus Christ himself. It is this unconditional nature of divine election, then, that makes the Christian truly humble. If a person had a right to salvation, if God were indebted to provide his blessing, then a person might have grounds for pride. As it is, the elect are chosen by grace, and that is the very reason their posture must be one of humility and gratitude.

What is more, a true sense of divine election will lead to a burden to reach the lost, not a complacency toward the lost. Paul never separated divine election (Rom. 9) from the importance of evangelism (Rom. 10:13–17), and neither should we. If modern estimates are correct, somewhere between 62 to 78 percent of Christians have not shared their faith with anyone over the past six months.[3] If we remember, however, that we are no more deserving than anyone else for salvation and that God's desire is to graft more people into the olive tree of his people, then we will embrace the identity God has given to us in humility matched with compassion for the lost.

Holiness and the Error of the Antinomians

God has not only elected for his people to be humble; he has chosen for them to be holy. We have said throughout this book that to be elect is to be in Christ. Just as Christ is holy, and we are in Christ by faith, so too are we conformed to his likeness. If our view of election is so narrow that it is only concerned about going to heaven when we die, we will have little concern for personal holiness in the here and now. On the other hand, if we see election as being in Christ, we will be holy as he is holy.

One of the great misunderstandings of the earliest Christians was between law and gospel. Salvation was not by works, but it was not without works either. *Antinomianism* refers to a view whereby Christians are free from works-based righteousness and the penalty of the law to the extent that personal holiness is diminished or altogether lacking. It supposes that because we are saved and secured by grace, any pursuit of personal holiness is unnecessary at best and legalistic at worst. However, to be God's chosen people is to be a holy people (Col. 3:12; 1 Peter 2:9). Indeed, personal holiness is confirmation that someone belongs to the elect just as disobedience is a sign of non-election.[4]

---

3. Lifeway Research, "Evangelism Explosion Study of American Christians' Openness to Talking about Faith," August 4, 2022 https://www.google.com/url?sa=t&source=web&rct=j&opi=89978449&url=https://research.lifeway.com/wp-content/uploads/2022/08/Evangelism-Explosion-Survey-of-American-Christians-Report-8_4_22.pdf&ved=2ahUKEwiQ6aunnemKAxXyDkQIHSr9KI0QFnoECCEQAQ&usg=AOvVaw2K2acw9d3Ffky1Jqw5p1u1; Lifeway Research, "Study: Churchgoers Believe in Sharing Faith, Most Never Do," January 2, 2014. https://research.lifeway.com/2012/08/13/churchgoers-believe-in-sharing-faith-most-never-do/
4. Benjamin B. Warfield, *Biblical and Theological Studies* (Philadelphia: P&R, 1968), 305. See also Michael Horton, *For Calvinism* (Grand Rapids: Zondervan Academic, 2011), 124–26, 132–33.

The beauty of divine election is that God has eternally purposed to bring holiness about inside the unholy people of the world. Thus, we should not think that holiness is solely a human endeavor (as if someone is saved by grace and then lives out a holy life by works). Scripture never depicts God as a hands-off observer watching to see if the elect grow in holiness. Rather, his purposes in election are to make his chosen people holy as he is holy.

Commenting on Philippians 2:13, Augustine affirmed that even the sins of Christians fall under the sovereign plan of God to bring about good to the elect. God has purposed from all eternity to work all things together for the good of the elect so that not even their sin will prevail.[5] Believers, then, can have the strongest hope that, though they feel weary from the battle, sin will never have the victory, for God has eternally promised to bring about holiness in his elect. Thus, a strong view of divine election does not lead to moral lackadaisical-ness. Rather, it is the beginning point of personal holiness. The people God chooses for salvation are the people he chooses to be in Christ, who is holy, and that holiness will not occur apart from God foreordaining from eternity past to overcome people's depravity, regenerate their dead hearts, and bring about a life of faith and godliness in the Son of God.

Freedom and the Error of the Judaizers

We will explore one more facet of the elect's identity, namely that they are a redeemed and free people. According to Scripture, sinners are enslaved to sin, death, and the devil (John 8:34; Rom. 6:9–22; Titus 3:3; Heb. 2:14–15; 2 Peter 2:19), and as we lack the means necessary to set ourselves free, we are ever tied to our life of bondage.[6] We are self-destructive people, willingly returning time and again to sin and its tyranny. We think we can be in control over our sin, but our sin is in control of us. We foolishly think sinning means freedom to do what we want, but as we engage in it we find no freedom at all. This is our hopeless estate.

However, there is a Redeemer in Christ the Lord who, through the blood of his cross, sets free the elect so they are slaves no more. Paul told us that Christ was put forth to redeem specific sinners through his blood (Rom. 3:23–25), to redeem the elect from every lawless deed (Titus 2:14), and to purchase believers in whom the Holy Spirit of God dwells (1 Cor. 6:20). In Christ, we are set free from a futile way of life (1 Peter 1:18), having been cleansed from dead works and transgressions (Heb. 9:12–15). This redemption and freedom

5. Augustine, "On Rebuke of Grace," in *Anti-Pelagian Writings*, in *Nicene and Post-Nicene Fathers*, ed. Philip Schaff, 14 vols. (Peabody, MA: Hendrickson, 2012), XXIV, 481.
6. See Daniel Kirkpatrick, "What Is Redeemed in Redemption? An Argument for Unconditional Redemption," *Evangelical Review of Theology* 47, no. 2 (2023): 177–88. Here, the argument is made that redemption, like election, is unconditional because it is not dependent upon the actions of the enslaved but the actions of the redeemer, thus affirming that redemption is owed all to grace through God's monergistic work.

from slavery were the predestined plans of God that give us a new identity as adopted sons and daughters who walk in freedom (Eph. 1:4–7).[7]

The implications of redemption for a Christian's identity are numerous. Through Christ our redeemer, our debt to God has been paid. We no longer have to succumb to tyranny nor try to pay for our sins through works-based righteousness. In Paul's day, the Judaizers were a sect of Christian Jews who tried to impose Jewish law upon Gentile Christians (Gal. 2:14–16). As Paul's opponents apparently failed to realize that Christ had fulfilled the law, he argued that to subject oneself to the law for righteousness is to consign oneself to slavery. The law cannot change someone's spiritual condition, but Christ the redeemer can. As such, Christians enjoy freedom *from* sin, though not freedom *to* sin (Gal. 5:13, 1 Peter 2:16).[8]

Practically, this means that in Christ the elect are free, never to be slaves to sin again. We serve a greater master, a loving redeemer, who has changed our identity from slaves to sons and daughters of the most high King (Rom. 6:16–18, 22; Gal. 5:1, 13). Christians should never view themselves as defeated, because they are one with the risen, conquering King. Some Christians view God as being constantly frustrated with them, merely tolerating them because they are not good enough. Such a distorted view of God leads people back mentally (though not spiritually) to the very slavery that God graciously redeemed them from. However, God's chosen children are infinitely accepted, beloved, and (very importantly) free, both now in this earthly existence and on to all eternity.

Summary

The three identity markers we give here (humility, holiness, and freedom) do not exhaust all that the elect are in their new identity in Christ. Rather, they are examples of how the apostles appealed to divine election to refute heresies that would try to distort who a Christian truly is in Christ. While we may not encounter many Roman elitists, Greek Antinomians, or Judaizers today, we will still be confronted with worldly messages on who we are supposed to be. In divine election, however, God has chosen for the elect to be in Christ, and it is therefore Christ who determines our sense of self. We are who we are because of whose we are, and with that comes a long list of identity markers that we share by grace.

---

7. For a thorough treatment on this, see Leon Morris, *The Apostolic Preaching of the Cross* (Grand Rapids: Eerdmans, 1965), 11–64.
8. Stephen Westerholm, *Perspectives Old and New on Paul: The "Lutheran" Paul and His Critics* (Grand Rapids: Eerdmans, 2004), 370–73.

REFLECTION QUESTIONS

1. Do Christians today struggle with knowing who they are in Christ, in your view?

2. How can divine election help address that struggle?

3. What could you say about divine election to a Christian who is constantly dwelling on his or her past sins and lifestyle?

4. Why is it important to focus on what election means for a Christian now rather than just from eternity past or eternity future?

5. What other identity markers can you think of that relate to divine election?

QUESTION 35

What Is the Role of Prayer in the Lives of the Elect?

We cannot discuss divine election for too long before someone, understandably, raises a question about how it relates to prayer. Why should anyone pray if God has foreordained whatever comes to pass from all eternity, even the salvation of particular people? Is praying for the lost to be saved or God's will to be done on earth as it is in heaven (Matt. 6:10) necessary, given his eternal, immutable, and infallible will? Moreover, if God has already willed good things for the elect while simultaneously willing for the non-elect to remain in their deserved state of judgment, why should anyone pray for their situation in life to improve? Granted, the New Testament commands Christians to pray (Matt. 6:9; Col. 4:2–3; 1 Thess. 5:17, 25; Jude 20), but if our view of prayer is that our petitions are coerced and all things are inevitable, would not such commands be exercises in futility?

These questions show just how difficult it is to reconcile prayer with God's sovereignty. However, because prayer is our means of communicating with the triune God and the medium through which we experience personally what he has promised generally through his word, there must be authenticity in the act of prayer that somehow reconciles itself with the sovereignty of God. Below we will show that prayer is indeed authentic, and plays a vital role in the lives of the elect.[1]

1. For other authors within this 40 Questions series who have addressed prayer and divine sovereignty, see Joseph C. Harrod, *40 Questions About Prayer* (Grand Rapids: Kregel Academic, 2022), 79–84; and Shawn D. Wright, *40 Questions About Calvinism* (Grand Rapids: Kregel Academic, 2019), 261–66.

Both/and, Not Either/or

When it comes to reconciling God's sovereignty over all things with the meaningfulness of prayer, let us not think that we must sacrifice one for the other. It is a gross misrepresentation of Scripture and the natures of both God and human beings either to make God dependent upon people or to view ourselves as puppets under a fatalistic God. Scripture affirms both that God is sovereign and that prayer is authentic. Reconciling these two truths is something almost all people at some point in their lives have had to do, and that is no less true for the apostles and their first-century audiences. The apostle Paul, who wrote of God's divine election from the foundations of the world in Ephesians 1:4, told us to be praying always in the spirit in Ephesians 6:18. The two are not mutually exclusive. Again, we can look at Romans 10:1. There we see Paul praying for the Jews' salvation despite just earlier affirming God's sovereignty in electing Gentiles and breaking off ethnic Israel for unbelief. We may look to Peter, whose audience was the elect of God (1 Peter 1:1), and yet he called them to live lives of godliness so their prayers would not be hindered (1 Peter 3:7; 4:7). We do not see the apostles going to great lengths to explain the mechanics of how divine sovereignty in election relates to human prayer, only that both are true. For the biblical writers, divine sovereignty does not preempt prayer, nor does prayer place God at humanity's beck and call. Rather, the two are both biblical truths. How can such a thing be?

Back in Question 12, we affirmed a view called *compatibilism*, the belief that people act in accordance with their own desires, and those desires and actions are not forced extraneously by God. God does not cause people to act contrary to their own will, and this particularly is important when discussing the matter of prayer. In prayer, a Christian is acting as the *proposer*, and those requests are real and sincere. God, in prayer, acts as the *disposer* who responds to those requests in accordance with his perfect plan. When Christians pray, they ask for God to intervene in some particular way yet ultimately submit their will to God's will and plan.[2] Here we see God's sovereignty, for he is under no obligation to answer according to the petitioner's desires. Still, we see his real and sincere love for the elect as he relates to them by listening and caring for the longings of their souls. Our prayers are real and authentic, and the Lord hears them and acts according to his good pleasure.

Means and End

Once we understand the first premise, that authentic human will is compatible with the divine will, we may better understand the second premise, that God appoints not only the ends but the means of carrying out his purposes.

---

2. Donald J. Westblade, "Divine Election in the Pauline Literature," in *Still Sovereign: Contemporary Perspectives on Election, Foreknowledge, and Grace*, eds. Thomas R. Schreiner and Bruce A. Ware (Grand Rapids: Baker Academic, 2000), 74–75.

Said another way, God has appointed prayer as the medium through which he bestows blessings upon the elect, apart from which such blessings will not be received. A. A. Hodge developed this point masterfully:

> If a man who prays for a crop neglects to sow the seed; or if a man who prays for learning neglects to study; or if a man who prays for the cure of disease neglects to take the appointed remedies; or if a man who prays for sanctification neglects to use the means of grace; or if a man who prays for the conversion of sinners neglects to work for it as far as his power or opportunity goes—then, in every case, he disobeys and insults God. . . . Means in relation to ends, and ends in dependence upon means, are as much an ordinance of God and as obligatory on us as prayer itself.[3]

Without prayer, the elect should not expect to receive good things from God, for prayer is the medium through which he accomplishes his ends of bestowing his mercy and goodness. Jonathan Edwards gave two primary reasons why prayer is essential in order to receive God's benefits. First, God is glorified when his creatures humbly petition their Lord for mercy in their need. As all things are made for his glory, and he is glorified by caring for his children, he thus requires his people to pray in order to receive what he freely desires them to have. Second, God bestows mercy only after his people approach him in prayer because such petitions prepare the heart to see it, rejoice in it, and thank God for it, which ultimately result in God being glorified.[4] God desires more than just giving his children good things. He desires a relationship with them, and prayer is the means by which we partake of his mercies in authentic relationship. Thus, apart from God's sovereignly appointed means of prayer, we will not receive the end for which we seek.

Let us explore the relationship between prayer and salvation with a hypothetical scenario concerning the salvation of a friend.[5] If God unconditionally elects whomever he wills toward salvation, what is the need to pray for that friend to be saved? The answer lies in the fact that God ordained not only your friend's salvation but your prayers as well. That is, God ordained that you would

---

3. A. A. Hodge, *Evangelical Theology: Lectures on Doctrine* (Carlisle, PA: Banner of Truth, 1990), 90. As Hodge rightly notes, this same principle applies to evangelism, where the will of God resolves to save a person sovereignly and unconditionally while simultaneously using the divinely appointed means of evangelism to accomplish that end apart from which the end will not be achieved.
4. "The Most High a Prayer-Hearing God," in *The Works of Jonathan Edwards*, 2 vols. (Carlisle, PA: Banner of Truth Trust, 1979), 2.115–16.
5. This illustration and resulting conclusions originate from Sam Storms, *Chosen for Life: The Case for Divine Election* (Wheaton, IL: Crossway, 2007), 172–78.

have a real love and compassion for your friend, and he is pleased to hear your prayers for salvation, leading to God's glory and your friend's good. Granted, because God is sovereign, he is under no obligation to save your friend just because you ask. Even still, he lovingly hears your prayers while staying true to his eternal will. Now, suppose that God does desire to save your friend, but you failed to pray for that person's salvation. Would God save your friend anyway? We believe he would not, but not for the reason many people think. We would not want to say that God will only save someone if we desire it in our prayers, for salvation is rooted in the divine will rather than the human will. Moreover, we would not want to restrict God by limiting him to the realm of our prayers. Rather, we would say that if you failed to pray for your friend's salvation that day, God did not intend to save that person on that day. The end that God has determined (your friend's salvation) also entails the means that God has determined (your prayers and the faithful proclamation of the gospel). If God ordains to save your friend, he will also ordain your fervent prayers.

We see throughout Scripture that God ordains not only the end of people's salvation but the means of prayer to accomplish those ends. The Colossian church, called "chosen ones" by Paul (Col. 3:12), were asked to pray that God might open a door for the word of the gospel to go forth (4:3). Again, Paul knew God was sovereign in choosing whoever he chose, but he also knew that God ordained prayer to be the means by which opportunities for the gospel come. Likewise, in 2 Thessalonians 3:1–2, Paul beseeched his brothers to pray for him so that the word of the Lord would go forth. Why is such prayer necessary? It is necessary because God purposes not only to spread the gospel but to use prayer as what moves the gospel with power and efficacy according to the will of God.[6] Consider also physical healing. James called the elders of the church to pray over the sick in order to receive healing from the Lord (James 5:13–16). Regarding our need for food, we know that God knows our needs and will supply them (Matt. 6:26–33), yet he still requires that we ask him for our daily bread (Matt. 6:11).[7] All this is to say that we should not think that a high view of God's sovereignty precludes a need to pray, for God has not predestined the end apart from the means of accomplishing that end.

The Role of Prayer

If prayer is indeed real and authentic, as we have said, we must now consider its function in the lives of the elect. Rather than exploring the various

---

6. See John Piper, *The Pleasures of God: Meditations on God's Delight in Being God* (Colorado Springs: Multnomah, 2000), 205–14.
7. See John Calvin, *Commentary on a Harmony of the Evangelists, Matthew, Mark, and Luke*, trans. William Pringle, 22 vols. (Grand Rapids: Baker, 1993), 1.325. Calvin rightly observed that our bread will not be supplied apart from toiling the fields and harvesting the produce, further emphasizing that the divine end comes through divinely appointed means.

types of prayers we can pray (important as they are), we will focus our attention on what prayer does in us and for us.

We must first understand prayer in light of covenant.[8] In our carnal condition, we have no means of communicating with God nor any basis by which to request his blessings. However, God himself overcame this communication barrier as he effectually called us out of our sinful state into the covenant of grace in Christ. This covenant means we do not merely approach God with requests; we approach him with relationship. Only the elect are brought into this type of fellowship in which they receive not only his blessings but God himself (Rom. 8:15; Gal. 4:6). Prayer is not a one-sided conversation, as if we are informing God of information he does not already know (Matt. 6:31). It is not speaking to God but rather speaking with God, as the elect reside in perpetual communion with him. Election ensures that fellowship between Christ and his church, expressed through prayer, was the plan of God from all eternity, and such fellowship is truly an act of grace.[9]

Because the elect are in covenant with God, they have an objective and external basis from which to pray. Election is in Christ, as we have said, and it is through intercession by Christ that the elect can pray (giving rise to the practice of praying "in Jesus's name"). Prayers are not heard because of the worth of the ones praying but because of the worth of the one interceding for them, namely Christ Jesus. Because of their election in Christ in this new covenant, the elect have absolute assurance their prayers are heard by God and are responded to in accordance with God's will, which entails his glory and their good (Matt. 7:7–11; Luke 11:13; John 17; Heb. 7:23–28). Christ is the sympathetic high priest who knows what it is like to be tempted and suffer (Heb. 2:17–18), and from that basis the elect have grounds to approach the throne of grace with confidence so they may receive grace in time of need (4:16).

Summary

At first glance, it may appear that prayer holds no place of importance under an all-sovereign God who elects and does as he pleases. However, we have argued here that human beings are not forced by abstract notions of fate whereby their desires and requests are disingenuous or altogether dismissed. Rather, prayer is authentic, and God is sovereign. We must uphold both truths. God has divinely decreed not only for there to be certain ends, but for there to be means by which those ends transpire. One of the chief means by which God communicates his grace is through prayer, for it is through prayer

8. Michael Horton, *The Christian Faith: A Systematic Theology for Pilgrims on the Way* (Grand Rapids: Zondervan Academic, 2011), 786.
9. See Carl R. Trueman, *Grace Alone: Salvation as a Gift of God, What the Reformers Taught . . . and Why It Still Matters*, Five Solas (Grand Rapids: Zondervan Academic, 2017), 217–29.

that the elect commune with God under the new covenant of grace and receive his mercies that lead to God's glory and their good.

REFLECTION QUESTIONS

1. Is prayer compatible with a sovereign God, in your view?
2. Considering the notion of means and ends, should we expect people to come to faith in Christ without our prayers?
3. How does election relate to intercession in prayer?
4. Is prayer a human response to grace or a means of God's grace?
5. Why do you think God would want people to pray for things, rather than just giving things to them?

QUESTION 36

How Does Election Relate to Personal Evangelism and Missions?

If God has sovereignly elected people from eternity past, what is the purpose of sharing the gospel locally and abroad? Why bother evangelizing if the elect's salvation is certain? Why do missions if the non-elect cannot be saved? These questions are common and expected when we advocate for a view of sovereign, unconditional election. In fact, these questions are found in the New Testament itself. Consider Paul's lengthy treatment on election in Romans 9, where he affirmed that God is sovereign in all aspects of salvation. He then anticipated a question on the part of his readers: If God is sovereign in salvation, why should anyone bother with evangelism? He providede his answer in Romans 10:14–17 and affirmed that the preaching of the gospel is absolutely essential for people to come to salvation. Clearly, reconciling divine election with evangelism and missions has been a challenge even from Paul's day.

In our own day, there are scholars who find our view of unconditional election to be quite irreconcilable with things like God's universal love for humanity and the need for evangelism. Jerry Walls and Joseph Dongell find it difficult to accept the command to love people God has eternally determined to damn. Relatedly, they argue that people who perish without ever hearing the gospel were those God determined not to elect anyway (thus implying the Reformed perspective has no rationale for evangelism).[1] Preston Nix states that a belief system that entails determined election diminishes and dismisses the Great Commission.[2] Frank Page goes so far as

1. Jerry L. Walls and Joseph R. Dongell, *Why I Am Not a Calvinist* (Downers Grove, IL: InterVarsity Press, 2004), 191, 197.
2. Preston Nix, "Commentary on Article 10: The Great Commission," in *Anyone Can Be Saved: A Defense of "Traditional" Southern Baptist Soteriology*, eds. David L. Allen, Eric Hankins, and Adam Harwood (Eugene, OR: Wipf & Stock, 2016), 154–55.

to say that such logic makes a missionary or evangelistic spirit unnecessary, leading ultimately to a lack of compassion for the lost and subsequent decline of Christian denominations.[3] Clearly, any discussion of divine election must entail its relation to personal evangelism and international missions. Below, we will explore the topic by looking at God's sovereignty over every aspect of evangelism.

Election, Evangelism, and Evangelists

God's electing plan is older than the foundations of the earth. Christians may (perhaps unconsciously) assume that God had to scramble to find a way to save sinners when his original plan failed at Eden, inevitably leading to the death, burial, and resurrection of Jesus as a figurative plan B. However, Christians' most cherished beliefs (such as the incarnation, the atonement, and justification by faith) are not mere afterthoughts in the mind of God after sin entered the world. Rather, glorifying the Son in procuring salvation for sinners was the foreordained plan of God before the foundations of the earth (Eph. 1:4–5, 11; 1 Peter 1:20–21).[4] This claim is not to suggest that God foreordained the fall or humanity's rebellion (see Question 23). Rather, it is to suggest that the incarnation of Christ ruling over the created order as the second and better Adam (fulfilling what the first Adam failed to do) was always God's plan. God's desire was to have a people saved through the person and work of Christ from the very beginning. This belief is the very heart of election. Thus, election begins and ends with the election of Christ, who was appointed to be the Savior and ruler of the world (Isa. 42:1–4; Matt. 12:18–21), and there would be no evangelism or gospel to proclaim without it.

Additionally, election ensures that evangelism and salvation are not human constructs. They exist by the sovereign will of the triune God. Evangelism is God's invention. As the one who elects not only people for salvation but people for service (see Question 1), the Lord raises up evangelists who are filled with his Spirit to carry out his elected saving agency. As such, evangelists (much like the Old Testament prophets) share God's message not because they are intrinsically worthy (or met some conditions), but because God sovereignly and unconditionally appointed them to that task. Paul clarified in Ephesians 4:11 that evangelists (like apostles, prophets, pastors, and teachers) are God's gifts to the church (v. 7). Paul pointed to his own evangelistic work as an act of God's divine choice earlier in Ephesians 1:1 (being "an apostle of Christ Jesus by the will of God") and later in 3:7–8. Just as sinners

---

3. Frank S. Page, *Trouble with the Tulip*, 2nd ed. (Canton, GA: Riverstone Group, 2000), 74–75.
4. See Michael Horton, *The Christian Faith: A Systematic Theology for Pilgrims on the Way* (Grand Rapids: Zondervan Academic, 2011), 446; and N. T. Wright, "Romans," in *New Interpreter's Bible Commentary*, 10 vols. (Nashville: Abingdon, 2002), 10:601–4.

owe all their salvation to the grace of God, so evangelists owe their ministry to the electing grace of God. Divine election ensures that gospel witness is not our work done for God, but God's work done through us. Without divine election, there would be no evangelists or evangelism.

Thus, it should be evident that God ordains not only the ends of salvation (*who* he will save) but the means of salvation (*how* he will save). Much like our discussion in the previous question on prayer, we affirm that God has sovereignly, unconditionally, and eternally appointed evangelism to be the means by which the end goal of salvation is achieved. He has eternally chosen for evangelists to be the agents who carry the gospel message that effectually calls the elect to salvation. Without God's sovereignly appointed means, the end goal of salvation will not be reached. This fact has every importance when it comes to the evangelists' power. Because God has chosen evangelists and evangelism as the catalyst to reconcile the world to himself in Christ, he has promised his power and presence for that very task. Christ promised the Holy Spirit would empower his elect for witness (Acts 1:2, 8), and as such, evangelists are divinely strengthened vessels through whom God saves. Thus, the elect, in their task of evangelism, rely upon the power of the Holy Spirit to reach the lost, not their own power or persuasion (1 Cor. 1:17–21). Evangelists may take no credit or blame for lives changed or unchanged when they faithfully proclaim the gospel, for their calling, content, and outcomes are all chosen by the Lord. While Christians should grieve that there are people who (of their own volition) reject the gospel, and that sadly these numbers are growing,[5] they can take great comfort in knowing the gates of hell will not prevail, for God's purposes in salvation remain his and will not fail, despite human rejection (Rom. 9:6).

Let us address one more issue that is undoubtedly a concern for many people. If God has predestined the elect unconditionally to salvation (the position stated here), should that limit evangelistic zeal or (as said at the beginning by Walls and Dongell) make it difficult to love the lost? May it never be. Rather, election justifies evangelistic zeal and love for the lost. What could motivate us more to boldly proclaim the gospel than an awareness that God saved us freely and unconditionally? When we realize our wretchedness in sin matched with the glorious splendor of our holy God, we know God's choice of us was nothing within ourselves. Compelled out of love for God and people who share our former desperate state, we proclaim the gospel to all people. Guilt, duty, and a sense of obligation make terrible motivators for evangelism. Knowing that we are unworthy but saved unconditionally compels us to proclaim such grace boldly and gratefully.

---

5. Ryan P. Burge, *The Nones: Where They Came From, Who They Are, and Where They Are Going* (Minneapolis: Fortress, 2021).

Evangelism to the Elect

Although God knows the people he has appointed to eternal life, Christians do not (and cannot). There are hidden matters known only to God (Deut. 29:29), and any attempt to divine such information will prove fruitless and sinful. However, evangelists/and missionaries do not need to know who the elect are. They need to know that no one will be saved without the preaching of the gospel (Rom. 10:14). As we have said, God's means of saving the elect through evangelism is just as eternally ordained as the outcome of the elect's salvation. Without faithful proclamation of the gospel, no one will be saved.

It is worth reiterating here that someone may absolutely be elect without being saved (Question 15). Election takes place from eternity past, but salvation occurs at the point faith is expressed. Someone may be elected for salvation but not be saved until later in life. When the elect hear the gospel, they will yield to their God in faith (even if initially resistant) (see Question 19). Faith does not make them elect; it makes them saved. The gospel is absolutely necessary to bring such salvation into reality, and there is no salvation apart from it. Thus, we should evangelize locally and abroad so that sinners may be saved in Christ as they hear the gospel, repent, and believe.[6]

In his excellent book *The Gospel of the Kingdom*, George Eldon Ladd wrote of the future return of Christ, the work of evangelism and missions, and the meaning of the gospel being preached to the whole world before the end will come (Matt. 24:14). He is worth quoting at length:

> Someone else will say, "How are we to know when the mission is completed? How close are we to the accomplishment of the task? Which countries have been evangelized and which have not? How close are we to the end?" . . . I answer, I do not know. God alone knows the definition of terms. I cannot precisely define who "all the nations" are. Only God knows exactly the meaning of "evangelize." He alone, who has told us that this gospel of the Kingdom shall be preached in the whole world for a testimony unto all the nations, will know when that objective has been accomplished. But I do not need to know. I know only one thing: Christ has not yet returned; therefore, the task is not yet done. When it is done, Christ will come. Our responsibility is not to insist on defining the terms of our task; our responsibility is to complete it. So long as Christ does not return, our work is undone. Let us get busy and complete our mission.[7]

---

6. For a through treatment on this topic, see J. I. Packer, *Evangelism and the Sovereignty of God* (Downers Grove, IL: InterVarsity Press, 2012), 91–122.
7. George Eldon Ladd, *The Gospel of the Kingdom: Scriptural Studies in the Kingdom of God* (Grand Rapids: Eerdmans, 1988), 136–37.

This quote has every significance for divine election. Christians do not know who the elect are. We cannot intricately reconcile God's sovereignty in salvation with the mandate for all persons to repent and believe the gospel. These things are not our responsibility. Our responsibility is to proclaim the gospel to the ends of the earth. As Ladd went on to say, "Do you love the Lord's appearing? Then you will bend every effort to take the Gospel into all the world."[8] Here, we might say, "Do you love God's choice to save sinners? Then you will bend every effort to take the gospel into all the world." People who are unamazed that God chose to save sinners will never become missionaries. However, people who are amazed that God chose to save the unworthy will be faithful to the missionary task set before the church.

Finally, knowing the great sacrifices and risks that international missionaries take on a regular basis, we may also say that divine election secures both their salvation and service in the sovereign plans of God. The psalmist reminded us that our days were ordained by God before any of them happened in real time (Ps. 139:16). This passage provides hope and confidence for all Christians to go boldly in the name of Jesus to proclaim the gospel, even in the most difficult and dangerous situations, knowing the saints of God will not arrive home in glory one moment before God sovereignly determines. This confidence is not a call to be reckless or presume upon God's grace by putting ourselves in danger. Relatedly, it is not to minimalize the horror and evil experienced by our brothers and sisters persecuted and martyred in faithful service to Christ. Rather, it is a call to confidence. There is nowhere the Christian can preach the gospel where God has not sovereignly determined the outcomes. Paul knew that his final trip to Jerusalem would entail his persecution, but he went ready to die for the name of the Lord Jesus if it was the will of the Lord (Acts 21:11–14). People with a high view of God's election will know that God's choices are right and good even if they entail suffering. We can be obedient to God's call in missions, knowing God will save whom he desires to save, use whom he desires to use, preserve whom he wants to preserve, and call to glory those saints whom he desires to come home. Until God so chooses, the Christian is preserved under God's providence and able to say with the psalmist, "The Lord is on my side; I will not fear. What can man do to me?" (Ps. 118:6).

Summary

When thinking of evangelism, missions, and divine election, it is natural to jump immediately to the issue of relevance. Many people have questioned whether evangelism and missions are necessary because of divine election. This question argues that divine election is what makes evangelism and missions possible. Without divine election, Christ would not be chosen to atone

8. Ladd, *Gospel of the Kingdom*, 139.

for human sin, evangelists would not be chosen and empowered to preach, and the lost would not be able to believe. As it is, God has chosen Christ to save, evangelists to preach, missionaries to go, and sinners to respond to the glorious gospel of Jesus Christ.

REFLECTION QUESTIONS

1. Must Christians choose between evangelistic and missionary zeal and sovereign divine election, or can both of these beliefs be held together?

2. How does divine election make evangelism and missions possible and pleasurable?

3. How can belief in divine election bring comfort to evangelists and missionaries who labor faithfully but struggle to see numerical growth?

4. Can divine election bring a sense of confidence to people who fear evangelizing or serving as international missionaries?

5. In your view, how did Paul reconcile God's sovereignty in election with his burden to see fellow Jews saved?

QUESTION 37

Is There Such a Thing as a Well-Meant Offer of the Gospel?

What we affirmed in Questions 35–36 is that God has ordained not only the end but the means of salvation. We affirmed that, for the elect to receive their salvation (the end), they must hear and respond to the gospel (the means). However, let us apply that concept of end and means to the non-elect. If God has ordained to leave the non-elect in their willful state of rebellion (the end), was the gospel (the means) truly offered to them? Naturally, this issue relates to questions we have already addressed as to whether or not God truly loves all people and desires their salvation (Questions 25–26); however, it is even more specific. When evangelists proclaim the gospel and say such things as, "Whosoever repents and believes this gospel will be saved," is such a thing true or even possible?

Before we develop a response, a few points of clarification are in order. First, the *well-meant offer of the gospel* (sometimes called the *free offer*) refers to the sincerity of the gospel message shared to all people. It asks, If God has ordained each person either to salvation or condemnation, is a gospel message that invites all people to come to faith in Christ sincere? Second, the matter of sincerity is twofold. In one sense, we must ask if the gospel offer is well-meant on the part of God who has already determined the end of each person, and, in another sense, we must ask if the gospel offer is well-meant on the part of the evangelist who proclaims God's universal love and desire that all people be saved. Our view is that any well-meant offer must be sincere both on the part of God and the evangelist. Finally, we must recognize that there are many perspectives on this issue. Arminians have no issue affirming that Christ has died for all people and freely offers salvation to anyone who believes. Because of their views on unlimited atonement and conditional election, they find no reason to hesitate in affirming that the gospel message is for all people.[1] Additionally, there are various Calvinistic traditions who deny the well-meant offer of the gospel.[2] As our view of election exists between these two perspectives, we must determine how sovereign, unconditional election for some people reconciles with a well-meant offer of the gospel.

Sincerity in God's Invitation

Let us begin our discussion on this topic by reaffirming our view that God truly loves all people everywhere and desires every single person on earth to believe in Jesus Christ for their salvation. God spoke through the prophet Isaiah that he was ready to be sought by people who never asked for him, ready to be found by people who did not seek him, and already spreading out his hands all day to people who rebel against him (Isa. 65:1–2). Similarly, we hear the heart cry of Jesus over Jerusalem as he longed to gather its people together as a hen gathers her chicks under her wings, but the people were unwilling to come to him (Matt. 23:37; Luke 13:34). In what is the most famous passage in all of Scripture, we see that God sent his only begotten Son, Jesus, into the world so that anyone who believes in him will not perish but have eternal life (John 3:16).[3] Our view is that God sincerely invites sinners to come to Christ.[4]

Thus, we conclude that God is sincere when it comes to the free offer of the gospel, for he does not desire anyone to perish but for everyone to reach repentance (2 Peter 3:9; see Acts 17:30).[5] Naturally, here we begin to wonder how God's sincerity in inviting all people to salvation reconciles with individual, unconditional election.

In response, let us consider these words found in the Westminster Confession (1644–46), the Savoy Declaration (1658), and the 1689 Baptist Confession: The Lord "freely offereth unto sinners life and salvation by Jesus Christ, requiring of them faith in him, that they may be saved; and promising to give unto all those

1. J. Matthew Pinson, *40 Questions About Arminianism* (Grand Rapids: Kregel Academic, 2022), 134.
2. See Herman Hanko and Mark H. Hoeksema, *Corrupting the Word of God: The History of the Well-Meant Offer* (Jenison, MI: Reformed Free, 2016), 173–242.
3. See Donald Macleod, *Compel Them to Come In: Calvinism and the Free Offer of the Gospel* (Tain, Scotland, UK: Christian Focus, 2020), 71–80.
4. As stated in Question 26, John Calvin (a strong advocate for unconditional election) believed the gospel is an invitation for all people to believe. John Calvin, *Commentary on the Gospel According to John*, trans. William Pringle (Grand Rapids: Baker, 1993), 125.
5. See John Piper who, reflecting our own position, affirms the scriptural testimony of unconditional election with God's universal love and saving desire through a bona fide offer of the gospel (*The Pleasures of God: Meditations on God's Delight in Being God* [Colorado Springs, CO: Multnomah, 2000], 130–33). We recognize that we are dealing with paradoxes that cannot be fully explained; however, our inability to explain exhaustively how these two truths reconcile with one another is no reason to forsake one truth for the other.

that are ordained unto life his Holy Spirit, to make them willing and able to believe." Note that adherents of these confessions hold to a free offer of the gospel; however, there is a qualification to God's desire: "requiring of them faith in him, that they may be saved."[6] God freely offers salvation unto sinners who believe in Christ. Where does such belief in Christ come from, and who can do it? Let us consider John Calvin's commentary on John 3:16:

> Let us remember, on the other hand, that while *life* is promised universally to *all who believe* in Christ, still faith is not common to all. For Christ is made known and held out to the view of all, but the elect alone are they whose eyes God opens, that they may seek him by faith. Here, too, is displayed a wonderful effect of faith; for by it we receive Christ such as he is given to us by the Father—that is, as having freed us from the condemnation of eternal death, and made us heirs of eternal life, because, by the sacrifice of his death, he has atoned for our sins, that nothing may prevent God from acknowledging us as his sons.[7]

Universal salvation is not God's desire, and orthodox Christianity must reject any notion that God unequivocally desires each and every person to be saved. God has sovereignly placed a qualifier upon who he desires to save, namely people who place their faith in Christ. The non-elect refuse to believe in Christ and are thus unsaved, while the elect believe in Christ and are subsequently saved due to the effectual calling of and regeneration by the Holy Spirit. Thus, God desires for everyone to be saved and freely offers salvation to anyone who believes, yet not all people believe, which results in their just condemnation.

Let us return to our discussion of means and ends. The end for the elect is salvation through means of the gospel in which they believe. The gospel message was sincere and effectual. The end for the non-elect, on the other hand, is just condemnation for their sins. This end does not negate the means, however, for God did not deny the non-elect the means. That is to say, the means of the gospel was still availed to them, and if they had embraced it they would have been saved too. However, they willfully rejected it in accordance with the appointed end. The judgment for the non-elect is not God denying them the message of the gospel. Rather, their judgment is that they would justly be left in their desires to resist the gospel. God, then, does not fail in his saving intentions, and he remains sovereign over all his creation because the end that he determined (for the elect as well as the non-elect) certainly comes to pass.

---

6. See Westminster Larger Catechism, 32.
7. Calvin *Commentary*, 125 (italics original).

We should also include in this discussion a caution against assigning human emotions to God when we speak of such things as "desire." When speaking of the divine, we should not perceive desire to be some sort of hopeful wish that may or may not come to pass (like wishing to win the lottery or hoping that we get a date with the person of our dreams). When we speak of divine desire, we are referring to God's character of what is right and good, matched with his pleasure when his creatures obey, rather than emotions.[8] God desires (as reflected by his character) people to be righteous. He would not desire people to hate and rebel against him. He has been pleased to accept anyone into eternal glory who has his or her righteousness in Christ by faith while simultaneously desiring to leave the rebellious in their state of sin. In such a way, the gospel is well-meant by God, who has his arms ready to receive anyone who repents and embraces the Son by faith.

Sincerity in Evangelists' Invitations

The Great Commission given by Christ to the church in Matthew 28:18–20 commands his disciples to make disciples of all nations. Peter exhorted Christians to make a defense to anyone who asks for a reason for the hope inside us (1 Peter 3:15). When we read the book of Acts, we nowhere find evangelists restraining their gospel message to a select few or qualifying that their message is only sincere for a small group of people. Rather, we see calls for everyone to repent, believe, and be baptized in the name of Jesus Christ for the forgiveness of sins (Acts 2:38–39). The clear teaching of Scripture is for the gospel to go forth to all people as an invitation (and command) to repent and believe in Christ for the forgiveness of sins. How can Christians who hold to unconditional, individual election proclaim such a message sincerely?[9]

The answer lies in the fact that God will never refuse to save anyone who repents and believes in Christ for salvation. Jesus said in John 6:35 that anyone who comes to him to satisfy his or her spiritual hunger will find life, joy, and salvation (see John 6:40). Evangelists do not know the end of any person's destiny, for such a thing is not for them to know. They merely know the means, the gospel of the Lord Jesus, and they are commanded to share it with everyone, everywhere. Granted, the non-elect will refuse it. What is more, the non-elect lack the ability to embrace it. Ability, however, should not be confused with willingness. It is not as though God makes the willing unwilling or the able unable. By the sinner's unwillingness, he is unable to do what God commands, including accepting the means of salvation.

---

8. This point, along with many other interesting insights, was a key issue in the Fifteenth (1948) General Assembly of the Orthodox Presbyterian Church. See Orthodox Presbyterian Church, "Report of the Committee on the Free Offer of the Gospel, Minority Report," 1948, https://opc.org/GA/free_offer.html/#Minority.
9. See the excellent work of Shawn D. Wright, *40 Questions About Calvinism* (Grand Rapids: Kregel Academic, 2019), 273–78.

Depending upon the evangelist's view on the extent of the atonement, popular evangelistic phrases like "Christ died for you" may need to be omitted in order for the gospel message to be sincere on their part. John Owen, a proponent of limited atonement, could not in good conscience call all people to believe that Christ died for them, for then he would be proclaiming something that he believed to be untrue. Nevertheless, his view of limited atonement did not stop him from boldly proclaiming the gospel to each and every person. Owen once said:

> The general publishing of the gospel unto "all nations," with the right that it hath to be preached to "every creature," Matt. xxviii.19; Mark xvi.15; because the way of salvation which it declares is wide enough for all to walk in. There is enough in the remedy it brings to light to heal all their diseases, to deliver them from all their evils. If there were a thousand worlds, the gospel of Christ might, upon this ground, be preached to them all, there being enough in Christ for the salvation of them all, if so be they will derive virtue from him by touching him in faith.[10]

Owen knew that no one can come to faith in Christ apart from the gospel, and he knew that evangelists cannot know who will believe it. For this Puritan, it was enough to know that everyone should hear the gospel and that God will accomplish his plans in salvation.

It is thus quite the misnomer to say that anyone who holds to unconditional election is insincere in inviting all people to come to Christ for salvation. We must persuade, petition, and plead for every person everywhere to repent and believe in the gospel, for this gospel is humanity's only hope. There is pardon available for anyone who will receive it, the well of grace is infinitely deep for anyone who drinks from it, and Christ will never reject anyone who falls into his arms of forgiveness.

Summary

It is natural to wonder if a well-meant offer of the gospel could reconcile with individual, unconditional election. In response to that question, we affirm that the gospel message is sincere on the part of God, who loves all people and earnestly desires their salvation as he provides to all people the means of salvation found in the gospel. What is more, we find that the gospel offer is also sincere from the evangelist, who can (and should) proclaim with

---

10. John Owen, *The Death of Death in the Death of Christ* (1852; repr. Carlisle, PA: Banner of Truth Trust, 2007), 185.

all confidence, humility, and persuasiveness that everyone, everywhere must turn from their wicked ways and embrace Jesus as their Savior and Lord.

REFLECTION QUESTIONS

1. What makes the issue of a bona fide offer of the gospel so difficult as it concerns divine election?
2. Is understanding the free offer of the gospel in light of means and ends helpful?
3. Should Christians qualify what they mean when they say that God wants everyone saved?
4. Where in the life and ministry of Jesus do you see him inviting all people to himself?
5. How could you articulate a well-meant offer of the gospel that aligns with your view of divine election?

QUESTION 38

How Does a Formulated Doctrine of Election Help Me in Personal Holiness?

Oftentimes, belief and debate about divine election revolve around where people will spend their eternity. Important as that is, Scripture does not divorce divine election from the Christian life. An election that only matters after death could hardly give Christian sojourners any real peace in their journey through this unholy world, nor would there be much of a rationale for holy living in the here and now. When the apostles spoke of divine election, they often tied this doctrine to how Christians are to live their daily lives, appealing to it to provide comfort through life's trials and motivation to become like the God who elected them. They knew that election is directed to a person (Jesus Christ) more so than to a place (like heaven), which means that election entails God's choice not only to bring a believer to the eschatological home but to bring that person into the likeness of Jesus Christ.

Tying divine election to the Christian life, while being the practice of the apostles, is sadly not always the practice for believers (and, ironically, Christian theologians). Election and sanctification are oftentimes separated from one another as if there were an infinite chasm between the beginning of salvation and the perfecting of salvation in the *ordo salutis*. As we will show more below, however, the Scriptures inseparably tie election and sanctification together, with the former making the latter possible. As we will find, God's plans in election entail his choice to make the elect into the likeness of Christ. Said another way, from all eternity past, God has sovereignly chosen a people for himself over whom sin will have no victory. He has foreordained not only that the penalty of sin will be removed through justification in the elect, but that the power of sin shall be abolished through sanctification. He has chosen that there will be a holy church, a cleansed bride without spot or wrinkle, presented unto himself with no spot or blemish (Eph. 5:25–27), and he will do this by his grace and for his glory. In this section, we hope to explore these truths more deeply, provoking not only our thoughts but our adoration for our God who has chosen to defeat the rule and reign of sin through the power of the cross for those whom he has predestined to save.

Chosen from Sin, Not Holiness

Before we delve too deeply into this subject, we must stress the proper ordering of election and holiness. To repeat our definition of divine election, mentioned in Question 1, election is God's gracious choice to save certain sinners through the person and work of Jesus Christ. It is critical that we keep with this type of definition, namely that God chooses to save certain *sinners*, people in their state of sin, and not certain people who achieve certain *holiness*. If such election were the case, no one would be elect except Jesus Christ.

Consider Paul's letter to Titus, written "for the sake of the faith of God's elect and their knowledge of the truth, which accords with godliness" (Titus 1:1). Here, we see that the purpose of Paul's apostleship was to bring the elect to saving faith and, upon so doing, for that faith to yield godliness.[1] Notice that such godliness does not yield election, but election brings about faith that in turn yields godliness. Thus, sanctification has its grounds in election, not election in sanctification. Paul went on to say that the elect's salvation was not because of works done by them in righteousness but according to God's own mercy, through regeneration and renewal by the Holy Spirit (Titus 3:4–5). Paul wanted to abolish legalism and self-righteousness, grounding people's godliness in God's gracious plans for the elect.[2] Commenting on this text, John Calvin believed it madness that people (called "foolish" and "disobedient" in Titus 3:3) would think their own preparations allow them to approach God for salvation. Rather, Calvin rightly believed that election, by free grace, is the foundation of good works, not good works the foundation for election.[3] We must not invert the order of election and sanctification.

Consider further Paul's words from 2 Thessalonians 2:13: "We ought always to give thanks to God for you, brothers beloved by the Lord, because God chose you as the firstfruits to be saved, through sanctification by the Spirit and belief in the truth." Paul gave God thanks not because his audience was chosen on account of their progress in sanctification, but because God would choose to save them as they believed the truth and were sanctified by

---

1. William D. Mounce, *Pastoral Epistles*, Word Biblical Commentary (Nashville: Thomas Nelson, 2000), 46:379, 382.
2. George W. Knight III, *The Pastoral Epistles*, New International Greek Testament Commentary (Grand Rapids: Eerdmans, 1992), 340–41.
3. John Calvin, "The Epistle to Titus," in *Calvin's Commentaries*, trans. John King, 22 vols. (Grand Rapids: Baker, 1989), 11:331–32.

the Spirit.[4] Their sanctification was evidence of their election, not the cause of it, which in turn championed the grace of God and removed any grounds for boasting in one's accomplishments.

Tragically, many Christians today, perhaps subconsciously, believe God only wants them or accepts them when they do their best. Though few believers would articulate it this way, some believe God is chronically frustrated with them, gazing down from heaven upon their lives with a constant look of frustration and disapproval. Perhaps if they could improve themselves in some way, then God might love them. If they could just get their lives together, then they would feel more confident about being a child of God. The underlying assumption is that God only chooses to save people who, by their good works and holy conduct, deserve it. Naturally, grace is nullified in such a view, and it promotes either self-righteousness or self-loathing, both of which are gross distortions of election and personal holiness.

However, when we realize that, from all eternity past, God knew just how sinful we would be, that we would never measure up to his holy standards on our own, and that we would never have anything of value to bring to him, yet he still cried over our lives, "Mine," we find the freedom he has always wanted his children to have. God's choice of whom he will save is rooted in his good, perfect, and gracious will, not our sinful and sullied wills. God wanted us despite us. When we had nothing good to offer, when we gave him every excuse not to want us, he still decreed that sin will not have the final word over our lives, and for that, our hearts can be at peace and rejoice in his goodness.

Chosen for Holiness, Not Sin

While sinners are not chosen *from* holiness, they are chosen *for* holiness. God's purposes in election include having a holy people as his own possession. However, when we look at our own lack of personal holiness, at times we may fear that we have not produced enough holiness (leading us to question whether we are truly elect). This problem, encountered by the apostles, led the New Testament writers to write of holiness in a twofold sense, namely, positional sanctification and progressive sanctification.

Positional sanctification refers to sinners being reckoned as holy by virtue of their union with Christ by faith. Christians are oftentimes called "saints" or "holy ones" (Rom. 8:27; 1 Cor. 6:2; Eph. 1:18) to reflect their undefiled status. Because their election was an election in the person of Christ, they are reckoned to have a position of holiness before God.[5] Paul called the elect "God's

4. Jeffrey A. D. Weima, *1–2 Thessalonians*, Baker Exegetical Commentary on the New Testament (Grand Rapids: Baker Academic, 2014), 549, 552.
5. Bruce Demarest, *The Cross and Salvation: The Doctrine of Salvation*, Foundations of Evangelical Theology (Wheaton, IL: Crossway, 2006), 407–11; Louis Berkhof, *Systematic Theology*, 4th ed. (Grand Rapids: Eerdmans, 1976), 532–38.

chosen ones, holy and beloved" (Col. 3:12) as a way to affirm believers' definitive state as chosen and holy in God's eyes. In this sense, a believer's holiness is complete in the eyes of God, for the work of Christ belongs to a believer by virtue of that union by faith (Rom. 6:2, 6, 11, 14, 17; 1 Cor. 1:2; 6:11).[6]

Progressive sanctification, on the other hand, refers to the lifelong pursuit of spiritual maturity (both in abstaining from sin and progressing in conformity to the likeness of Christ). Again, it is critical we understand this sense of sanctification in light of election. Paul said to the Colossians that, as God's chosen ones, they were to put on holiness (Col. 3:12), or to clothe themselves in light of their new identity in Christ, to reflect by their ethical life the God who chose them by grace.[7] Their election status, as chosen ones, was definite; however, their growth in holiness was progressive. Consider further 1 Thessalonians 1:4–7, where Paul told this church that God "has chosen you," and they, in turn, became imitators of Paul and of the Lord. Paul appealed to divine election both to comfort them as they experienced opposition and ostracism in their lives as well as to challenge them to live in a manner appropriate to their calling.[8] God has chosen them definitively, yet they were to progress in their holy conduct and be examples to all believers of the transforming work of God (v. 7). The apostle Peter also tied divine election to progressive sanctification. In his first epistle, he wrote "to those who are elect exiles . . . in the sanctification of the Spirit, for obedience to Jesus Christ" (1 Peter 1:1–2). The elect were chosen with a purpose: to grow in the Spirit's work of conforming to Christ.[9] The same points are reiterated in 1 Peter 2:9, where Peter referred to his audience as a chosen race, a holy nation, who were called out of darkness and into the light. Here, we see that Christians are positionally chosen and holy, yet as they are called out of darkness and into the light, they live out, progressively, their new identities in Christ. Finally, we will consider John's second epistle where he wrote to the "elect lady and her children," of whom some were found to be walking in the truth, and all were called to walk according to Christ's commandments (2 John 1:1–6). This church was to walk (or live) in an ongoing, progressive way, in obedience to Christ's commands. They were both chosen by grace and called to walk in that grace. Thus, to be elect of God is to be chosen for a life of holiness that in one sense is definite and positional and, in another sense, is ongoing and progressive.

It is therefore a comforting thought for Christian sojourners to know that God has chosen not only to predestine us for glory but to begin preparing and forming us for that glory in the here and now. Sanctification is God's work done in the lives of the elect (Eph. 5:26; 1 Thess. 5:23), which he graciously

6. Anthony A. Hoekema, *Saved by Grace* (Grand Rapids: Eerdmans, 1994), 202–6.
7. G. K. Beale, *Colossians and Philemon*, Baker Exegetical Commentary on the New Testament (Grand Rapids: Baker Academic, 2019), 294–95.
8. Weima, *1–2 Thessalonians*, 92.
9. Karen H. Jobes, *1 Peter*, Baker Exegetical Commentary on the New Testament (Grand Rapids: Baker Academic, 2005), 71.

accomplishes in us by the Holy Spirit. Even still, Christians are called to exert sincere effort to abandon their former way of life and grow into spiritual maturity (2 Cor. 7:1; Heb. 12:1). We work out our own salvation with fear and trembling (Phil. 2:12–13), despite being positionally sanctified, and must make every effort to add to our faith goodness and godliness (2 Peter 1:5–8).

Summary

Ephesians 1:4 states, "he chose us in him before the foundation of the world, that we should be holy and blameless before him." Election, ever tied to sanctification, is more than just going to heaven when we die. It is God's choice to defeat sin in the lives of his chosen people, to conform us to be like the Son in whom we were chosen, and to be guaranteed that, despite our weak and fickle wills, we will receive the victory over our sin. What is more, election ensures our personal holiness is evidence, not grounds, of our salvation.[10] The elect are chosen from sin, not holiness, for nothing of our intrinsic goodness would make us worthy of God's grace. Even still, the elect are chosen for holiness. Although, in a sense, the elect are as holy as we will ever be by virtue of our union with Christ, there is another sense where we must grow in our new identity in Christ through continual repentance and grace-filled obedience. This progressive sense of sanctification is itself a gift of God's grace, for Christians are never alone in our struggle against sin. God has chosen not only that his people would be holy but that he will make his people holy—and God, as in all things he chooses to do, never fails.

REFLECTION QUESTIONS

1. How does election ensure that sin will have no ultimate victory over Christians?

2. How can sinners be both a holy people and growing in holiness?

3. Why is it important for Christians to believe they were chosen in their state of sin, not their state of holiness?

4. Thinking of a sin that you have struggled with for some time, how can election help you find comfort in the midst of temptation and failure?

5. How could you use the doctrine of election to help a fellow believer that feels defeated by sin?

---

10. Charles Hodge, *Systematic Theology*, 3 vols. (Peabody, MA: Hendrickson, 2013), 2:341–42.

QUESTION 39

How Does a Formulated Doctrine of Election Help in Ministry?

If our study on divine election has shown us anything, it has revealed that our God is sovereign. He does what pleases him. God chooses (or elects) to do something, and it is so. His choices are rooted in his divine will, are not based upon human goodness or merit, and are sure to come to pass the way he intends. What is more, our God's nature is kind, so we do not need to fear these sovereign choices. By unmerited grace, he has chosen certain people for blessings too wonderful to be earned.

This electing grace entails God's choice to save certain sinners through Jesus Christ, and if God chose to do nothing else but this, he would be worthy of all praise and honor for all eternity. As it is, however, God's choices entail more than just election to salvation; they include God's election to service. Moreover, the way God elects people to service is very similar to how he elects people to salvation. He elects people to serve him out of his sovereign will, his choice is not based upon a person's innate goodness, and his nature is kind, so people do not need to fear what he has called them to do. Here we will explore God's choice of people to service and, hopefully, find how this glorious doctrine shapes our mindset and comforts our hearts as we serve the Lord in any area of ministry to which we are called.

Individual Election of Servants

Consider these words from the apostle Paul:

> He gave the apostles, the prophets, the evangelists, the shepherds and teachers, to equip the saints for the work of ministry, for building up the body of Christ, until we all attain to the unity of the faith and of the knowledge of the Son of God,

> to mature manhood, to the measure of the stature of the fullness of Christ. (Eph. 4:11–13)

These verses teach us many things, but included in Paul's meaning is that God chose to appoint servants to specific areas of service, be they apostles, prophets, evangelists, pastors, or teachers.[1] These offices, despite being distinct from each other, all share a common purpose: to equip the church for ministry, unity, and maturity. When we recognize that God has specifically chosen and called people individually to areas of ministry such as this, we are dealing with God's election to service, an election from eternity past that continues to this day as the Lord chooses and calls special servants into unique areas of Christian ministry.

What we should also see is that, much like God's election to salvation, God's election of service is individual in nature. Said another way, God has chosen specific individuals for specific roles at specific times in specific places. Granted, there are broad offices God chooses for service, namely apostles, prophets, pastors, missionaries, evangelists, and teachers; however, those elected groups are comprised of chosen and called individuals, for not everyone is called to each of those offices.

Consider the individual choice of Jesus, who called each of his disciples to follow and serve him. They were individually chosen and personally responded to that area of ministry. Consider Acts 1:2, which tells us Christ's disciples were chosen to be apostles of Christ. Paul, likewise, was called a "chosen instrument" to carry Christ's name before Gentiles, kings, and the children of Israel (9:15). In Peter's discourse with Cornelius, he spoke of himself being chosen by God as a witness (10:41). From these verses alone, we see that God chooses persons individually and calls them to join him in his mission to exalt the Son, who is ruler over a new and glorious kingdom.

What is more, this election of servants is not limited to historic Bible characters, nor to members of the clergy, for that matter (though it certainly includes them, as Eph. 4:11–13 shows). Scripture teaches us that every person God elects to salvation is also elected to service. Let us not miss the magnitude of this truth. The sovereign God of the universe has ordained from all eternity past not only to elect certain people for the glories of salvation, but to call and empower each and every one of them to join him in his mission to redeem the world through his only begotten Son, Jesus. Paul brought this marvelous truth out well in 1 Corinthians 12 through an analogy of the church as a body. Each elected person is filled with the Holy Spirit and gifted with a supernatural gift to be employed in Christian service. Like a unique part of a human body, so each elect and redeemed believer is put into Christ's body, the

1. The office of apostleship was a temporary office that ended with the deaths of the original apostles whose job it was to build a foundation for the church, which continues to this day (Eph. 2:20).

church, just as God chose (1 Cor. 12:18). It is not that service to our Savior is limited to only a few people or to so-called professionals. It is not that some people are called and gifted to strengthen the body and advance the Great Commission while others are not. Rather, each member of Christ's body is given a space and a spiritual gift that is absolutely essential for the health and well-being of the church (1 Cor. 12:7).[2]

Unconditional Election of Servants

Another commonality between election to salvation and election to service is its unconditional nature. Clarifications are in order here, for we do not want to say that God elects pastors or other leaders to shepherd his church who are not converts or fail to live holy lives (1 Tim. 3:1–13). Rather, much like election to salvation, God chooses people to service not because of their innate goodness or abilities but because of his good pleasure.

While we could look at Moses, who was not naturally gifted at speaking (and at times unfaithful) yet chosen for the task of leading the exodus; David, who was chosen to be king despite being the youngest and most unlikely to be chosen among his brothers; or the disciples, of whom many were uneducated fishermen, for the sake of focus we will look at these words of Paul to the church in Corinth:

> When one says, "I follow Paul," and another, "I follow Apollos," are you not being merely human?
>
> What then is Apollos? What is Paul? Servants through whom you believed, as the Lord assigned to each. I planted, Apollos watered, but God gave the growth. So neither he who plants nor he who waters is anything, but only God who gives the growth. (1 Cor. 3:4–7)

The divided Christians in Corinth needed to know that fruitfulness in Christian ministry does not come from the servant but from the one the servant serves, namely, God who gives the growth. Earlier, in 1 Corinthians 1 and 2, Paul made the case that their election to salvation and acceptance of the gospel was not rooted in anything the Corinthians or the apostles did. Solely because of God's good pleasure to bring them to faith did they believe. In a similar way, Paul was making the point that the messengers of God cannot take credit for the success of their ministry. While they co-labor with God and must faithfully sow and water the mission field, only God can bring about new life. Christian leaders are nothing more than appointed servants,

2. See Carl R. Trueman, *Grace Alone: Salvation as a Gift of God, What the Reformers Taught . . . and Why It Still Matters*, Five Solas (Grand Rapids: Zondervan Academic, 2017), 106–7.

not change agents. Thus, they have no ground for one-upmanship, superiority, or pride, for in themselves, the planter and waterer are nothing.[3]

There are often two dangers that ministers (be they pastors, evangelists, youth volunteers, or some other church leader) commonly fall into, which ultimately are sourced in the same error. One danger is to take the credit for seasons of spiritual health and growth in the church, leading to pride and self-glorification. They think that because of their great communication skills, fresh ideas, and extraordinary abilities, they built successful churches. Often, pride and self-glorification are veiled to the ministers and others because, after all, this work is a ministry for the church (and thus a worthy cause). However, we must guard ourselves from this wretched pride at all costs, for the acts of transforming children of darkness into children of God or bringing spiritual maturity from people who were spiritually depraved is nothing short of a miracle from God. We can, and must, be faithful servants who plant, water, and nurture the souls of those people entrusted to our care, but we can never take the glory for the sovereign, electing work of God.

The second danger related to the first is that of self-deprecation and despair. When church attendance declines, when they do not see their churches growing like others, when giving goes down or when they do not see the spiritual growth they want in their congregations, the first course of action by many ministers is to blame themselves. They think, "If only I was better. . . . If only I could be like that other pastor. . . . If only I were not like me, then our church would finally be better off." The sin of this danger is the same as the one before. It assumes that the power to effect change and bring about spiritual fruit is sourced in the servant. It believes that God has not specifically, individually, and sovereignly chosen that person to be at that church at that time for that purpose. It believes that what people need more than anything is this minister to be the savior of the church, a role that God has sovereignly elected for the Son alone to hold.

As ministers of the gospel, we should be comforted rather than discouraged when we hear that we, as appointed servants, are nothing. Paul did not mean our service is worthless or does not matter. There would be no harvest of souls unless the gospel seeds were sown and nurtured. Rather, ministers of all types (lay or clergy) can have great hope that the power to build the church, to bring the lost to salvation, and to see community transformation rests solely in the omnipotent hands of God almighty. Regularly, faithful ministers labor in the mission fields of their communities, sharing the gospel and trying to nurture people's hearts to believe in Christ. It is not their job to grow the biggest church. It is their job to be faithful in sharing the gospel, nurturing that gospel with the water of grace, and leading their people to do the same

3. D. A. Carson, *The Cross and Christian Ministry: Leadership Lessons from 1 Corinthians* (Grand Rapids: Baker, 2012), 76–77.

so that the Lord will build the church. God will give the growth in accordance with his own plans of election, so let us be free from the pressure and temptations that come along with feeling like we have to meet worldly standards for spiritual success. Because of divine election, God will certainly bring about the harvest he desires, and he will do so as ministers faithfully co-labor with him in gospel ministry.

Even more to the point, 1 Corinthians 3:4–7 shows that God unconditionally appoints servants as he sovereignly chooses. He does not look for the people who naturally possess all the right talents. In fact, we see God choosing the least likely candidates to accomplish his plans in service (Gideon the least of his father's house turned judge, Ruth the Moabite widow turned matriarch for the Davidic line that would bring forth Jesus, Esther the orphan turned queen who saved the Jews from annihilation, Matthew the tax collector turned apostle, and more). Extraordinary work is done through ordinary people by an extraordinary God. God chose us for service not because of what we bring to the table but because of what he brings.

Put simply, he chose us for ministry because he did, because he wanted to, because he found it to fit in his perfect will to say, "I want you to be my special servant through whom I work for my glory." God's choice of us is because of the goodness found in himself, not us. God individually and unconditionally chose us to such service, and by his might and grace we get to join the Lord in an extraordinary mission to reach the world for Jesus Christ.

Summary

God has sovereignly, individually, and unconditionally chosen the elect for service as well as to salvation. Here, we wanted to show how election frames our understanding of service. In whatever area of ministry God has given us, we are there by divine appointment. Election ensures God will get the outcome he desires, and we can rest assured that the power and outcomes are not rooted in ourselves. When we understand that God has placed us where he wants us to be, with the skills and abilities he has chosen to give us, we find extraordinary help in ministry as we labor faithfully in the fields of service that he has given us, to accomplish the purposes he has sovereignly ordained.

REFLECTION QUESTIONS

1. What similarities do you find between election to salvation and election to service?

2. What area of ministry has God individually chosen you to, and how has that calling been made evident to you?

3. How has God equipped you for ministry in the body of Christ, and how are you using it in your local church?

4. Do you struggle with believing God would choose you for service, and if so, what do you need to surrender to the Lord?

5. How else does the doctrine of election help frame our ministry?

QUESTION 40

How Does Divine Election Give Us Hope?

What hope does the church of the Lord Jesus have to offer the world when everything feels so hopeless at times? We hear of innocent people suffering as wars ravage whole countries. The news reports show politicians promising a brighter future, while at the same time reporting their corruption and abuse of power. Some churches flourish through the teaching of false prophets while faithful congregations fall deeper into decline. The world longs for something to give them hope but, inevitably, empty promises and fleeting pleasures often leave people with more disappointment than before, and soon the same rhetoric fails to convince them that there really is any reason to believe things will ever get better. The world is broken. Our churches are struggling. Life, at times, feels hopeless.

The apostle Paul found himself in a very similar context when he wrote a letter to a missionary companion of his, a man by the name of Titus who served on the Greek isle of Crete. By the time he wrote this pastoral epistle, Paul had already undergone unjust imprisonments for the sake of the gospel by the hands of corrupt political leaders. Heretics on the island, known as Judaizers, were tearing apart churches and families with their false teaching that someone must conform to the requirements of Jewish law in order to be accepted as God's people (Titus 1:5, 10–11). The moral climate of the first century was arguably just as depraved as culture today. Titus's people, much like Titus himself, needed hope. To encourage Titus and the church at Crete, Paul wrote them a letter which began in this way: "Paul, a servant of God and an apostle of Jesus Christ, for the sake of the faith of God's elect and their knowledge of the truth, which accords with godliness, in hope of eternal life, which God, who never lies, promised before the ages began" (Titus 1:1–2).

Imagine what these words meant for the Cretans. These people were God's elect, God's chosen people, and Paul was chosen as an apostle not only to bring about their faith and knowledge of the truth but to remind them of their hope of eternal life that God had destined for them before the ages began. For Paul, there is hope in this broken world because of election. This hope is not just some wishful thinking or idealistic dream that things may get better someday. Rather, in this context, hope is confident anticipation of what will certainly come true.[1] The elect have a lasting and abiding hope here and now that is certain to hold immeasurable blessings for eternal life, no matter what the future holds. While the Cretans (like us) had to wait to experience the fullness of this hope (as it lays in the future), they could be certain that such blessed eternal life would certainly come to pass because it was promised by God, who never lies, before the foundations of the earth. Thus, the Christian hope rests not in the fluctuations of a world chock-full of empty promises. Rather, it rests in the promises of God, who never lies.

It is our sincere hope that the doctrine of election will be known more for bringing Christians hope than division. As we close our study of the doctrine of election, we end with a message of hope. This hope is something God promises to us as individual Christians as we live out our lives in this broken world, but it is also a hope that God has given to his church corporately, assuring them that their best days are yet to come. We will explore Christian hope individually and corporately through this final question.

Hope Individually

We may be tempted to think that Christian hope merely means that believers must grin and bear the harsh realities of the world while holding to the thought that things will get better upon their deaths or the return of Christ, but such thinking is not the hope God has promised us in his Word. For Christians, hope is something we experience here and now. It is a new reality we are born into and a peace that assures us that, despite the cruelties of the world, Christ's victory over the world will be our victory as well. In his first letter, the apostle Peter wrote to who he called "elect exiles" (1 Peter 1:1). His audience was comprised of churches across Asia Minor (modern-day Turkey) who were experiencing persecution for their faith in Christ. Written around A.D. 65, shortly after the Great Fire of Rome in A.D. 64 that led to the persecution of many Christians under Emperor Nero, Peter wrote to believers who were rejected by the world (and thus "exiles") but chosen by God (thus "elect"). To God's chosen people, Peter wrote of the hope these elect exiles had in the here and now that could sustain them through their present suffering:

> Blessed be the God and Father of our Lord Jesus Christ! According to his great mercy, he has caused us to be born

1. William D. Mounce, *Pastoral Epistles*, Word Biblical Commentary (Nashville: Thomas Nelson, 2000), 46:380.

> again to a living hope through the resurrection of Jesus Christ from the dead, to an inheritance that is imperishable, undefiled, and unfading, kept in heaven for you, who by God's power are being guarded through faith for a salvation ready to be revealed in the last time. In this you rejoice, though now for a little while, if necessary, you have been grieved by various trials. (1 Peter 1:3–6)

As God's elect, they were born again into a living hope in the here and now. While this hope had a future dynamic (because the inheritance is a heavenly one that does not belong to this present world), it was nonetheless a "living" hope in the here and now by virtue of the resurrection of Christ from the dead.[2] As God's elect, they experienced a new life, and that new life gave new hope that God had not forsaken and would not forsake his people like the world had. Instead, there was an inheritance, one that they had to wait for, but when it did come, the good things the Father desires to give to his children would one day be theirs for all eternity.[3]

Being God's elect does not mean we will be without struggles; it means we will never be without hope. Our hope, grounded in the resurrected Lord Jesus, means that though the world can take away what belongs to the world, it can never take away what belongs to the world to come. The elect can endure life in the here and now because of their enduring living hope. As Jürgen Moltmann once said,

> Expectation makes life good, for in expectation man can accept his whole present and find joy not only in its joy but also in its sorrow, happiness not only in its happiness but also in its pain. Thus hope goes on its way through the midst of happiness and pain, because in the promises of God it can see a future also for the transient, the dying and the dead.[4]

That future for the dying and dead that Moltmann referred to is their absolute end. Christ will defeat suffering and death once and for all (1 Cor. 15:26). Hope (like suffering and death) is temporary, for it is limited to the sphere of this life. Soon hope (like faith; 1 Cor. 13:13) will be traded for sight,

---

2. See Richard Bauckham and Trevor Hart, *Hope Against Hope: Christian Eschatology at the Turn of the Millennium* (Grand Rapids: Eerdmans, 1999), 67–68, who rightly find that only through the God of resurrection, the God who brings life out of death, can everything work together for the good.
3. Thomas R. Schreiner, *1, 2 Peter, Jude*, New American Commentary (Nashville: Holman Reference, 2003), 37:62–64.
4. Jürgen Moltmann, *Theology of Hope: On the Ground and the Implications of a Christian Eschatology* (Minneapolis: Fortress, 1993), 32.

when we will receive the glorious inheritance we have long awaited. This inheritance is more than merely an end to our struggles. It is beholding the presence of Jesus Christ our Savior, and as the elect have Christ in the here and now, we can be confident that we will be with him forever.

Hope Corporately

While the hope that Christians have is ours personally, our hope is not in isolation. That is to say, the hope that Christians enjoy is a corporate hope, one that we share together as God's elect, the church. Divine election ensures that God has chosen the church to share in Christ's victory over the world. Despite every hardship thrown at the church, the world and the very gates of hell shall never prevail against it (Matt. 16:18). This hope is not based upon what the church can do in the world for God but on what God can do for the church in the world.[5]

As God's elect, churches should not think that their hope amounts to escaping from the world they are in, nor should we think hope means they do not suffer in the world. The church's suffering in the world is presented in Scripture as a given (Acts 14:22; 2 Tim. 3:12). Rather, the church's hope is that they will be with Christ in the new Jerusalem, as the very citizens of heaven, on this very earth. Just as Jesus was resurrected from the dead (and, by virtue of that resurrection, the elect are resurrected), so too the earth will be reborn anew with Christ setting the church as the new and glorious temple where he will dwell (Eph. 1:19–23; Rev. 21:2–3).[6]

The apostle Paul saw the resurrection of Jesus Christ as the very basis by which the dead in Christ will be resurrected, and when the Lord returns and the great trumpet sounds, the dead shall rise and the saints will forever be with the Lord (1 Thess. 4:14–17). Paul reminded the Thessalonian church to "encourage one another with these words" (v. 18).

It is to this last matter of encouragement that we should turn our attention. As believers going through the harsh realities of this broken world, we draw strength and encouragement from one another as we hold on to this present hope. The Christian life is never meant to be in isolation. The elect are chosen to belong to Christ's body, the church. In suffering together, we support each other. As sisters or brothers begin to fall into despair, seeing the world's darkness around them, the church comes alongside those people and draws their eyes to the glory of Christ and their eternal reward with him. To those suffering saints, the church offers on earth a foretaste of what all saints will enjoy forever, namely unconditional love flowing from the wellspring of

---

5. Allan J. Janssen, "Election and Hope: Van Ruler and Dort," in *The Calling of the Church in Times of Polarization*, eds. Heleen Zorgdrager and Pieter Vos (Leiden: Brill, 2022), 235.
6. N. T. Wright, *Surprised by Hope: Rethinking Heaven, the Resurrection, and the Mission of the Church* (New York: HarperOne, 2008), 100–01.

God. As Christians, we do not lose heart despite momentary afflictions, for the brokenness of this world is preparing the church for an eternal weight of glory beyond all comparison (2 Cor. 4:16–18). Therefore, let us encourage one another with these words.

Summary

There is a hope that this world can never have, for it does not come from the world. It is a sure and steady confidence that the promises given in the resurrected Son of God are sure and certain to entail glories too rich for words for the elect. Despite every hardship we face this side of eternity, there is a present and abiding hope we have for eternal life, a life with an imperishable, undefiled, and unfading inheritance kept by the power of God.

We have explored how election gives us hope individually by looking at the sure and certain confidence we have in the resurrected Christ. The elect can have a real and abiding hope that all suffering and death will one day cease. Any hardship we encounter will be overcome. These truths would give little comfort if the hope were only future-oriented; however, the hope that God gives the elect is living in the here and now. By virtue of the resurrected Christ, the elect can face any hardship with confidence, knowing that we will share in the final victory and that all enemies of the Lord (including suffering and death) will one day be destroyed forever. This hope, moreover, is for all the elect, and it is one we should stir up among each other. Here we have shown how the church, corporately, embodies the promises of God for future glorification. Our eternal prize is to dwell with the Lord forever in the new Jerusalem, the new creation, where we will trade our hopeful expectations for a certain new reality. As the church suffers together, we encourage one another by way of reminder that our future is as bright as the promises of God.

REFLECTION QUESTIONS

1. How is hope related to divine election?
2. How is a Christian's hope different from a non-Christian's hope?
3. How does the resurrection and second coming of Christ give Christians hope?
4. How does hope help you personally when you are going through something difficult?
5. How can your local church help foster hope among its body?

Scripture Index

Acts

Romans

1 Corinthians

2 Corinthians

Galatians

Ephesians

Philippians

Colossians

1 Thessalonians

2 Thessalonians

1 Timothy

2 Timothy

Titus

Philemon

Hebrews

James

1 Peter

2 Peter

1 John

2 John

Jude

Revelation

40 QUESTIONS SERIES

40 Questions About Angels, Demons, and Spiritual Warfare
John R. Gilhooly

40 Questions About the Apostle Paul
Miguel G. Echevarría and Benjamin P. Laird

40 Questions About Arminianism
J. Matthew Pinson

40 Questions About the Atonement
Channing L. Crisler

40 Questions About Baptism and the Lord's Supper
John S. Hammett

40 Questions About Bible Translation
Mark L. Strauss

40 Questions About Biblical Theology
Jason S. DeRouchie, Oren R. Martin, and Andrew David Naselli

40 Questions About Calvinism
Shawn D. Wright

40 Questions About Christians and Biblical Law
Thomas R. Schreiner

40 Questions About Church Membership and Discipline
Jeremy M. Kimble

40 Questions About Creation and Evolution
Kenneth D. Keathley and Mark F. Rooker

40 Questions About Divine Election
Daniel Kirkpatrick

40 Questions About Elders and Deacons
Benjamin L. Merkle

40 Questions About the End Times
Eckhard Schnabel

40 QUESTIONS SERIES

40 Questions About the Great Commission
Daniel L. Akin, Benjamin L. Merkle, and George G. Robinson

40 Questions About Heaven and Hell
Alan W. Gomes

40 Questions About the Historical Jesus
C. Marvin Pate

40 Questions About Interpreting the Bible, 2nd ed.
Robert L. Plummer

40 Questions About Islam
Matthew Aaron Bennett

40 Questions About Pastoral Ministry
Phil A. Newton

40 Questions About Pentecostalism
Jonathan Black

40 Questions About Prayer
Joseph C. Harrod

40 Questions About Roman Catholicism
Gregg R. Allison

40 Questions About Salvation
Matthew Barrett

40 Questions About Suffering and Evil
Greg Welty

40 Questions About the Text and Canon of the New Testament
Charles L. Quarles and L. Scott Kellum

40 Questions About Typology and Allegory
Mitchell L. Chase

40 Questions About Women in Ministry
Sue G. Edwards and Kelley M. Mathews